THE MUSICAL SYMBOL

* * * *A Study of the Philosophic Theory of Music*

* * * THE

Musical Symbol

A STUDY OF THE PHILOSOPHIC THEORY OF MUSIC

BY *Gordon Epperson*

IOWA STATE UNIVERSITY PRESS, AMES
* * *

* * * GORDON EPPERSON, professor of music at the University of Arizona, studied at the universities of Cincinnati and Rochester and at the Berkshire Music Center. His doctorate was completed in 1960 at Boston University, where his major fields were music and comparative literature. Mr. Epperson has taught at the University of Puget Sound, Louisiana State University, Phillips Andover Academy, Ohio State University, and has held summer appointments at the Eastman School of Music and the University of Texas. Concern for problems in the philosophy of music has been demonstrated by his articles in professonal journals. Affirming his view of music as a performing art, Mr. Epperson, one of the country's most active concert cellists, tours extensively throughout the United States and Canada.

Composed and printed by
The Iowa State University Press

Stock #1117

First edition, 1967

Library of Congress Catalog Card Number: 67-20152

* * * TO ANGELO P. BERTOCCI

* * *
INTRODUCTION

* * * WHAT IS MUSIC?

This is a philosophical question that sets the broad limits of musical theory. The question must be dealt with comprehensively by a theory concerned not merely with details of harmonic and structural analysis, acoustics, and the study of the musical learning process as an aspect of behavior but with the art of music in its totality. No such comprehensive theory exists at present.

Musicology might be expected to concern itself with the critical problems of musical meaning. But musicologists, in general, are historians rather than philosophers of music, and their scrutiny is in most instances turned upon the corpus of musical literature. Notwithstanding the careful examination accorded a great many pieces of music, one looks in vain for general yardsticks of critical judgment, particularly in regard to contemporary composition.

The twentieth century, thus far, has produced numerous works in the field of musical psychology, Carl Seashore and James Mursell being prominent investigators. There has also been significant study by acousticians and by scholars using techniques (appropriate to their own departments of research) which are relevant to music in some special way, as we see, for example, in the finding of musical therapists. And there are many works in which biographical or other extramusical considerations are the *raison d'être*. What is wanting is philosophical speculation.

Speculation has come mainly in recent years from such articulate composers as Schoenberg, Stravinsky, Hindemith, Copland, and Sessions. But they are not primarily theorists; and their insights, however penetrating some of them may be, are scattered and unsystematic. With the possible exception of Leonard Meyer's *Emotion and Meaning in Music*,[1] even tentative steps in the direction of comprehensive theory have yet to be made. The work of theorists such as René Wellek in literature and Susanne Langer in general aesthetics goes far beyond any comparable efforts by musical investigators. The last giants were Eduard Hanslick and Edmund Gurney in the late nineteenth century. Art theory, to be sure, carries important implications for music; and Langer, in particular, has written significant chapters on music in *Philosophy in a New Key* and in *Feeling and Form*.

[1] See bibliography for more recent writings by Meyer.

The semantic difficulties in writing about music are enormous. Music appears, on the surface, to defy any sort of verbal analysis. It is necessary, of course, to acknowledge the fundamental difficulty of dealing with music on the verbal level; but we are not thereby relieved of the responsibility for so dealing with it. If one keeps in mind the distinction between music and extramusical referents, it should be possible to remove some of the impediments which now interfere with a clear comprehension of music as an art.

It should be made clear from the outset, however, that I am not conducting an exercise in semantics. I have assumed that terms such as *meaning* and *value* have sufficiently fixed connotations in our common vocabulary to make them useful. They, and other potentially loaded terms (as what word is not?) have been invested with as much neutrality as I could muster. My aim has been to use these and other common words in the service of ideas, recognizing the fact that a concept may sometimes be expressed metaphorically with an amplification, rather than essential loss, of meaning.

Let me approach the problem of musical meaning obliquely.

The aura of a poem, a poem apprehended in its totality, is a fact of human experience; if the poem is good, the meaning reverberates without fixed boundaries: the individual words are transcended in the whole poem. Since the sensitiveness of human beings to poetry varies considerably, there can be no rigid setting of limits; the experience of a poem will not be identical even for two equally perceptive readers. And for the same reader, the poem may yield more meaning on one occasion than another.

There seem to be persons who are relatively immune to poetry as a mode of experience. All verbalizing, whether written or spoken, is for them a matter of literal statement. No matter how explicitly, then, words are defined, the real meaning in all its compass cannot be grasped. Here there is more meaning to be realized, and it is the "more"—and not meaning stripped bare—that corresponds most truly to that reality of human experience which the poem distils.

I took the example of a poem, instead of a piece of music, because words are its building blocks. Yet even in the examination of a poem, the appropriateness of linguistic analysis may be called in question. The poem, whatever its quality, is a unity of content and form: a symbol. "The mighty waters rolling evermore" is not at all the same thing as "The great waves breaking timelessly on shore," though one can take his choice of lines. Nor can we render "Thou still unravish'd bride of quietness" as "You yet unconquered, silent, still-new squaw" without doing a grave disservice to Keats.

If even a poem resists verbal clarification, should we not expect this to be much more true of music, employing as it does an altogether different modality from words? An acknowledgment of this distinct modality gives a new cogency to the old cliché, "music expresses what cannot be put into words." Just what that "what" can be is the concern of this essay. Human experience in all its complexity appears to require various modalities: interpenetrating, but each one retaining some essence that cannot be translated successfully, an essence that can only be hinted at, not rendered, in an alien modality. Is this so far-fetched an idea? Whitehead speaks of mathematical intuitions that flashed into his consciousness with their appropriate symbolism, so that rendering those concepts into language was for him an attempt at translation from one modality to another.

The curious notion has taken hold in our century that setting limits to the scope (or limits, at any rate, to the adequacy) of linguistic analysis is anti-intellectual. The notion seems to be based on the assumption that all communicable concepts are expressible in spoken or written symbols: expressible, that is to say, in language. Yet the mind obviously exercises prerogatives which go beyond verbal boundaries. The question of whether intellect extends to those areas or not is a problem in semantics.

Even if the operations of intellect were restricted to the verbal realm, however, the dimensions of artistic experience would then by definition be *non-*intellectual, not *anti*. In any event, the possible charge of anti-intellectualism need not deter us in the quest of a suitable instrument of analysis, since the accusation is a hackneyed weapon in positivistic circles for castigating the unorthodox. *Mysticism* similarly is now employed as an academic cliché to express a negative opinion of all excursions which depart from fashionable procedure in their investigations of the imperfectly known.

There is today a desiccation of theoretical speculation, accompanied by a growing preoccupation with ever more minute particulars. In their important search for accuracy of statement and careful definition of terms and in their concern for the meaning of meaning, semanticists have fixed attention, not surprisingly, upon the word, sometimes to the detriment of the idea.

But we cannot place blame, when blame is called for, at any single door. We are all fellow travelers in the migration from a world of generalities to a world of particulars. The preoccupation of electronic music experimentation and other contemporary movements with the uniquenesses of sound textures is testimony to this. And the explanations for what is going on are lengthy and articulate: ask, and you will be given enlightenment—by Stockhausen, for his idiom; by Babbitt, for his; by John Cage, for his. The verbal fluency, furthermore, of tone-row composers is a matter of record. Such explanations, such renderings of music into words, are often eloquent in the very modality of words. Even profound.

Nevertheless, we suffer from a terrible claustrophobia. We live in a world that is largely verbal. And for perhaps good reason, everybody distrusts it.

We cannot think or speak of music without conceptualizing. If we wish to experience music actively and directly, however, our primary aim must be to open ourselves to its peculiar modality—its wavelength, if you please—wherein its efficacy resides. In speaking or writing afterward of such experience, as we will and must if we are to do anything more than express simple approval or disapproval by appropriate grunts, a secondary aim should be to arrive at concepts which will reflect a disciplined insight, an at least partial understanding of just what processes have been at work. In postulating a secondary and derivative aim, I am assuming that the theory of music we are seeking is a matter of importance for understanding that human world which produced the music in the first place. I am carefully distinguishing the two aims, however, because it is apparent that there are many more persons who are capable of the actual experience of music and who actively desire it than there are theorists who wish to conceptualize its nature and purpose. The aims need not be mutually exclusive. The average listener exhibits an attitude of unthinking acceptance or rejection based upon his habitual likes and dislikes. His instincts and experience determine the range of idioms he will accept; within that compass, he will welcome any congenial extramusical associations. He is always eager for a "story."

Most practicing musicians, including the majority of composers, have been—and are—immersed in the daily exigencies of their craft in which the fusion of aural, kinesthetic, and conceptual elements is intense. Conceptual power is highly developed in the composer; it is also a strong quality in the gifted interpreter. Practicing musicians are ordinarily too absorbed in their musical work to write or speak of it in a systematic, inclusive way. They bring to their work the reinforcement of temperament and talent, those partially unconscious predispositions upon which the success of their efforts largely depends.

The artist is under no obligation to theorize; a musician need not be a philosopher of music. Expertness in one modality is no guarantee of equal competence in another. Men of unquestioned stature as artists have said outrageous and indefensible things. Wagner made extravagant and even false claims and created an amalgam of music and words in which genius and bathos intermingle in about equal measure. Mastery in one realm may lend a deceptive glamor or even the illusion of authenticity to less talented efforts in another expressive modality.

A great deal of nonsense has been written about music, and not by musicians only. Much recondite verbiage has been contributed by philosophic giants, towering figures who despite their attainments were not philosophers of music. Their failure to recognize the distinct and relatively autonomous modality of the art is more abysmal and carries more serious consequences for music than the verbal ineptitudes of master musicians.

This book develops the concept of music as a nonverbal symbolism. The always critical definition of terms is nowhere more difficult than in a study of this kind. My major task, especially in the last chapters of the book, has been to make clear what is meant by *symbol*. I have attempted an investigation of the art of music that will, I hope, falsify it as little as possible; yet I know that my formulations, at best, can be only approximate. So far as moving in the direction of comprehensive theory is concerned, I feel a little like the amoeba extending a tentative pseudopodium.

I have examined music as a human production, an art that is in dialogic relation to life, its universe one of human discourse without which it would be meaningless. I grant music the relative autonomy, the relative objectivity, that art achieves. But I avoid the extremes of Hanslick, on the one hand, who holds that music is completely autonomous and "means itself" and of those literary romanticists, on the other hand, who—in Stravinsky's words—are interested in music only "in so far as it touches on elements outside it while evoking sensations with which they are familiar."[2]

I acknowledge many debts, particularly to the writings of Cassirer, Whitehead, and Langer which first suggested certain avenues of thought to me. But my conclusions are my own. My hypotheses are intended as testable in the only possible laboratory, that of the unique human listener. Obviously, such laboratory conditions are exceedingly complex and very wanting in uniformity; but I do not believe that an arbitrary simplification and narrowing would serve my purposes.

Musical meaning is nonverbal. Although the attempt to elucidate that meaning through the written word is destined to be partially unsuccessful, as such efforts have always been, it should be possible to indicate verbally what music is *not;* to acknowledge its import without explaining it away; to form new concepts that can be an aid to liberated perception; and to make necessary distinctions between one expressive modality and another.

[2] Igor Stravinsky, *An Autobiography* (New York: M. & J. Steur, 1958), p. 163.

If our concepts fail to do justice to the reality, we can strive for more adequate ones. And the difference this conceptual struggle will make is crucial for the understanding.

ACKNOWLEDGMENTS

* * * FOR PERMISSION TO QUOTE COPYRIGHT material, I make grateful acknowledgment to Bailliere, Tindall and Cassell; The Bollingen Foundation; Dover Publications; E. P. Dutton and Company; Harcourt, Brace and World; Harper and Row; Harvard University Press; Horizon Press; Humanities Press; The Macmillan Company; W. W. Norton and Company; The Philosophical Library; G. P. Putnam's Sons; Random House; Charles Scribner's Sons; Simon and Schuster.

I wish particularly to thank Douglas N. Morgan for his careful reading of the manuscript and valuable criticism.

G. E.

* * *
TABLE OF CONTENTS

THE MUSICAL SYMBOL

*** A Study of the Philosophic Theory of Music*

CHAPTER ONE

TOWARD A PHILOSOPHY OF MUSIC

* * * THAT MUSIC IS A NONVERBAL ART WOULD appear to be self-evident. Even the long history of song does not bring this into question; for the alliance of words and music, no matter how successful it may be, is an association of disparate elements. There is no difficulty in distinguishing one from the other, though the union artistically may be a happy one. A work of art may, of course, combine still more components, as in ballet or music drama. Yet the Wagnerian *leitmotiv*, apart from any assigned (or signal) meaning, must exhibit a distinctly musical value: a value, that is to say, which is inherent in the music itself, a value that resides there. This musical meaning, if we arrive at it by eliminating verbal labels, may appear residual; yet it is the essential musical value.

The foregoing may be theoretically obvious; but in general discourse, even among professional mu-

sicians and philosophically disciplined scholars, it is not
obvious at all. The greatest confusion reigns, and the
vast majority of writings on music (scholarly and otherwise) have done nothing to alleviate this confusion.
One can read, for example, that the programmatic associations of a Strauss tone poem make up its content,
what the music is "about"—as though the tintinnabula-
tions of *Don Quixote* served up actual windmills that
any fool could recognize, or the murmurings of Debussy,
a real distillation of moonlight.

Music has acquired so many extraneous associations that it is easy to be distracted from the central
quest of musical meaning through the fascination of
these associations. Certain elementary distinctions must
be made before an approach to a philosophy of music
can be attempted: we must avoid at least the obvious
sources of confusion. It is entirely possible and perhaps desirable to enjoy *Don Quixote* for the complex
amalgam that it is. But if one is to be intellectually hon-
est, he must admit that if he were hearing the piece for
the first time and had not been coached it is highly
unlikely that imagery appropriate to its story would
flash into his mind, although if he were open-minded
and perceptive he might well appreciate its intrinsic
musical qualities, the brilliance of its sonorities, and
so on.

Similarly, a first hearing of *Clair de lune*—a hypothetical hearing hard to imagine nowadays—might
yield an image of a rosebush as readily as a vision of
moonlight, or the recollections of Mount Rainier on a
clear day, or a camel in the Sahara. Or no image at all.
There need be no objection, in principle, to a musical

program. But unless the succession of sounds has independent value, *qua* music, the program will not improve matters. It is important always to remember in such a combination that two different expressive modalities are being brought into juxtaposition.

It is pertinent as an illustration of this dichotomy to remark that Debussy appended descriptive titles to his piano preludes after he had written them. Consequently, we are at liberty to listen to the piece called "Goldfish" without being deluded by the idea that the label is integral to it. In speaking of the Berg violin concerto, a violinist recently informed me that the music took on added interest if you knew its story. That story does have considerable appeal and may have influenced the quality of the concerto profoundly, but a preoccupation with it is more likely to impede than to aid a musical apprehension. The music itself, moreover, cannot give us a sequence of events in human history; nor have we a right to expect that it do so. Words, on the other hand, can do this quickly and coherently. *Musical meaning is nonverbal.*

What is music? is a philosophical question, but most of the answers we have access to are not philosophical answers. How the very term *philosophy* is abused is everywhere apparent. It is surely ironic that a discipline intended to give clarity and precision to thought should lend its prestige, if only in name, to all sorts of questionable and sloppy verbalizing. Even in academic circles, "philosophy" is very commonly used as a synonym for "attitude."

"Philosophy of music" may conjure up all kinds of fixed associations, all verbal in character. Why, then, "philosophy" of music? Why not "aesthetics?" Here I admit the possibility of choice. Aesthetics of music, properly defined, would do very well, for aesthetics is a branch of philosophic inquiry. But in common use, aesthetics has even more unfortunate connotations than philosophy, for the aesthete typifies to a great many people the dilettante enamored of sensations which the arts afford him and narcissistically preoccupied with his own responses.

Apel, in his article on aesthetics in the *Harvard Dictionary of Music,* complains, and rightly, of the definition of aesthetics as the "philosophy or study of the *beautiful.*" He points out what is increasingly being realized, that canons of beauty are not the only criteria of value. He suggests this definition instead: "Musical aesthetics is the study of the relationship of music to the human senses and intellect."

Although "aesthetics of music" and "philosophy of music" will be regarded as synonymous throughout this book, I ask the reader's indulgence in the use of the (to me) stronger and leaner word *philosophy.* And I would like to suggest this definition: "The philosophy of music is the comprehensive study of the nature of music in whatever aspects are relevant to an inclusive and coherent explanation of its meaning and to an understanding of its relationship to the world of human discourse." If the word were not already in use with numerous established associations, I might be tempted to coin a term, *musicology.* But musicology, as we know—though it does not necessarily exclude philosophic inquiry into musical meaning—has become associated primarily with scholarly research of an historical nature.

Despite persistent misunderstanding of the art, important work has been done in the twentieth century that will reinforce genuine philosophical speculation regarding the nature of music. *Toward* a philosophy of music seems a necessary qualification, for even a pointing toward avenues of investigation—continuing ones, not cul-de-sacs—is an ambitious project, subject to many dangers.

In discovering a basis for evaluation and criticism, there must be, on one hand, no claim of accounting for everything, since this would be manifestly absurd; on the other hand, in dealing with that which is of relatively small compass, it is important to avoid the temptation of reducing the dimensions of the art just because we can manage it more conveniently, as in the concept of *Gebrauchsmusik* wherein Bach is a craftsman—a super craftsman, of course—but nothing more. It is all very well (in fact, essential) to investigate systematically what can be known; this may lead to a theory which can be tested, corrected, refined: it should then, properly, indicate the dependence of human investigation upon a matrix which makes such investigation—and all definition—possible. This is a metaphysical consideration. But examples are ready at hand, and they need not be dignified by the term *metaphysical* to indicate how one's frame of reference determines his response to experience.

Therefore, in attempting to bring analysis to bear on music, I am not trying to find some lowest common denominator after which everything else can be discarded; I am not trying to reduce music to some hypothetical "nothing but." My definition of the philosophy of music makes clear the need for synthesis as well as analysis; and in seeking a wide view, a view which cannot be exactly tested in the laboratory, we are not necessarily arriving at something less true than we might otherwise obtain, nor are we abandoning the philosophic method of inquiry, unless that method is arbitrarily and narrowly defined.

Hanslick's book *The Beautiful in Music,* in arguing for the autonomy of musical art, holds that music should be weighed on its intrinsic merits and not merely by the mood of the listener. Here he is fundamentally on the right track. But he goes too far when he rejects the idea that music can be an expression of human feeling. He oversimplifies, he leaves out aspects which we have a right to consider, but he does focus attention on the music itself; and this is a valuable service.

The relationship of music to emotion is not, indeed, of a one-to-one correspondence, but a relationship of a peculiar kind; to elucidate the nature of that kinship is one of the chief objectives of this study.

Julius Portnoy, in *The Philosopher and Music,* refers to Hanslick as an objectivist in aesthetics. What must be kept in mind, however, is the fact that no aesthetic pronouncement, whether it be labelled objective or subjective, can really ignore human participation without which no aesthetic experience can take place.

The human *given,* an indispensable element which is often ignored explicitly but which is a condition of all investigation, is inescapable. Consequently, the statement "music means itself" is nonsense.

The untutored or artistically unawakened person may say that he does not understand art but he knows what he likes. His failure to understand does not necessarily mean that the art work is incapable of evoking a response; his judgment may be looked upon as subjective but also as inadequate. It may be argued that all art with any degree of authenticity (and the yardsticks for authenticity will be discussed later) is inherently capable of calling forth an emotive response; this is its intrinsic quality which may be objectively assessed, though I am not sure that it can ever be totally assessed. Something is required of the percipient or of the hearer; he must have the requisite development, the necessary training, a sufficiently sensitive psychophysical organism. We do not expect a gorilla to respond to the *Eroica* except possibly in an unself-conscious way; he may be stimulated by the sounds but cannot (unless we are mistaken in our assumption of superiority) discern in them a musicoemotional Gestalt. Elements of artistic experience may indeed be present but not, for the gorilla, an understanding of Beethoven.

Assuming the capacity for such experience in the human being, we must assume also in the art work some measure of human universality. We may—hypothetically, for now—call this universality *symbolic.* It is the objective assessment of this universal element which is the concern of any philosophy of art and, more specifically, the concern of a philosophy of music. Obviously, a symbol so general must be potentially recognizable by any person who fulfills the necessary conditions; so that art, insofar as it expresses human feelings, must be a stylized representation of those feelings. This stylized representation is its form. And this stylized representation is also its content. Form and content are not mutually exclusive; they are inseparable, because the way something is said artistically is also, in that expressive modality, what it says.

Explanation is a term which is inappropriate in dealing with music, for that which paraphrases or attempts to render music into other terms does not make it comprehensible. All of us have, at one time or another, made this important discovery while reading program notes. Explanation tends, in fact, to be a serious impediment to apprehension of the art work, not because the mind cannot cope with the concepts being presented, but because it is distracted by them. This is the problem of all courses in "appreciation" and nowhere are the dangers greater than in the art of music. Students will ask what they are supposed to think about while listening to music. Is there a suitable descriptive title or, better still, a "story"? What prompted the composer to write the work? What was the relationship of the work to the composer's state of health and the conditions of his life at the time it was written? And so on.

Everyone can keep busy asking and answering such questions, and this is precisely what goes on at every level of musical study, graduate and undergraduate. Beyond the fertile biographical and historical explorations there are also, to be sure, numerous courses offered in musical anatomy: in structural, harmonic, and contrapuntal analysis and in acoustics. A few institutions offer instruction in the psychology of music; but courses bearing this title are generally less comprehensive than the name implies, since they usually seek to emulate those experimental techniques developed in laboratory sciences.

I grant all this its due. But is it too much to hope for a theory of music that will offer something more than bits and pieces—a theory that will cope, more adequately than heretofore, with the art of music *in toto?*

Within the developing concepts of a comprehensive theory we will find those aspects of symbolic presentation which are peculiar to music. These must be examined. I will try to make my use of the word *symbol* increasingly clear, as we come to deal with concrete examples of symbolism: examples which—it is not too early to say—are symbols in that they contain elements of what they stand for, so that they are not merely representative, and they are never to be regarded as substitutes for other things. The symbol—like Carlyle's iceberg, which he used for illustrating his own concept of the symbol as something partially hidden, partially revealed, but nevertheless a unity—may be large or small; if large, it may contain a number of more or less complete components in a gigantic cluster, as in Beethoven's Ninth Symphony. Chopin's A Major Prelude is a symbol of an altogether different magnitude.

Symbol refers to something very different, in

our lexicon, from *sign*. The lines and spaces of the
grand staff, for example, are not what is meant here by
musical symbolism; they are signs. Even such elaborate
techniques as "text-painting" in Baroque music must
qualify as signs. Bach's exercise on the letters of his
own name, therefore, is a "signal" practice very much
in keeping with the conventions of a style that culminated with him and is a mere detail in the mosaic of his
counterpoint, though performed with an artistry that
none could equal. The symbolic message is not in refinements of technical procedure that can be isolated,
like B–A–C–H, from the musical texture they embellish
(or which may be said, in a sense, to represent them),
but in the *Art of Fugue* itself.

The symbolic in music, as in all art, is that
quality which speaks—one sees at once the omnipresent
and pernicious influence of the verbal!—to the human
recipient (who is possibly a participant as well and to
the same degree) and awakens an echo, a recognition,
within him. Art can do this because it is, in Langer's
words, a "symbolic analogue of emotive life." Art
speaks to our common humanity. The response, like
the appeal, is general, though the individual feels the
dialogue in his own person and is himself integral to it.
He is able to recognize and respond to the invitation
precisely because of its generality. The process is emotional but on a plane other than that of his intense
personal feelings. He may, of course, superimpose those
strong feelings upon his experience of the art object, so
that an indissoluble association is set up for him; but
such associations, though fairly common, must be
looked upon as the fortuitous occurrences they are, and
therefore lacking in authenticity.

Because the emotions are called into play in any act of musical apprehension, it is easy—and usually dangerous—to move from a plane of listening in which something approximating the intended dialogue is occurring to a realm of languid fantasy and reminiscence where the composition, whatever its demands may potentially be, becomes music to daydream to. This passive listening is probably the rule rather than the exception, since active attention to music is a rigorous discipline. Naturally, the effort needed is in proportion to the complexity of the music, the psychophysical state of the hearer, and the familiarity of the idiom.

The relevance of music to emotional life is general. Thus, specific events, particular joys or tragedies, cannot be mirrored in it. What many listeners describe as "moods" do seem to inhere in certain idioms, so that impressions of "sadness," "playfulness," or "martial vigor" may be remarkably homogeneous for large numbers of people. Yet even here there can be the subtle influence of fixed association: the idea, perhaps implanted in childhood, that the major mode carries glad sonorities, the minor mode melancholy ones. The suggestive force of a descriptive title, such as "Funeral March," may also be considerable in conditioning a response, in determining a reaction which grows ever stronger in successive hearings of the work.

It is an easy step, then, to a more concrete application: one may imagine Chopin's *Marche funèbre* as commemorating, in essence, the death of one's own grandmother. This may seem a harmless, even if somewhat simple-minded, application of the *Gebrauchsmusik* concept. But the music, to its detriment, is serving only as a point of departure. Its function, then, is only to trigger a reflex. Its protean qualities count for nothing: the ambivalences of feeling it may have captured go unrecognized. The result for the bereaved listener is a serious diminution of meaning; Chopin's symbol has become opaque.

Verbal descriptions are always prejudicial to musical meaning because the mind eagerly seizes the labels in glad recognition and comes to rest in them; the journey may be over before it has begun. The descriptive approach will yield only superficialities, though it will yield these in abundance: this is the outside view that results from a preoccupation with verbal signposts. In contrast to this prevalent habit, it is necessary to get inside, following Bergson's injunction, to "enter into" the music so that it has some of the immediacy of carnal knowledge.

It will not help to protest that Bach wrote a "Capriccio on the Departure of a Beloved Brother," as though this settled the matter. We can, indeed, enjoy the title of this piece of occasional music, acknowledge the charming convention Bach was indulging, and then fix our attention where it belongs—on the music—realizing that the title has no connection whatsoever with the musical meaning of the piece. This is the essential, the all-important, distinction which the discriminating mind must make. One can do this perfectly well yet go along with many conventional juxtapositions, just for the joy of the dance. The release afforded may be even greater (thanks to the secret knowledge!) than it would be if the enterprise were conducted altogether in earnest—taken literally.

The general quality of the symbol, which may also be looked upon as its stylized aspect, is what engenders the possibility of an emotional catharsis in the listener. But catharsis need not be only of a noble or exalted character. Even a small sentimental song may capture some essence of common experience that makes it widely meaningful if not universal. But even a hackneyed symbol or a faded metaphor will be destroyed if the interpreter cannot achieve a certain objectivity. I remember a soprano, undertaking a rendition of "Danny Boy," who became racked by violent sobs, while tears streamed down her face. Her emotions, which she utterly failed to project, were too concretely engaged by that little piece and her embarrassed audience was moved to nothing more than suppressed laughter.

An objectivity must inhere in a musical composition as well as in its rendering. It is a source of much confusion to postulate, as Curt Sachs does, a dichotomy of *ethos* and *pathos,* with objectivity residing in one, subjectivity in the other. That art does move in cycles, that it may swing from one pole to another, from classical emphases to Romantic ones, is historically demonstrable; but the polarities are never mutually exclusive, and the relevance to emotional life is integral to every kind of art. Even the most characteristic works of a ripe Romanticism are, *qua* music, objective; they are symbols. Sachs, a great musical historian, is foisting off on us in *The Commonwealth of Art* newly minted pathetic (and "ethetic") fallacies.

E. F. Carritt, in his article "Aesthetics" in the *Encyclopaedia Britannica,* makes no reference to Sachs. But these lines directed against no one in particular are clearly applicable to him; for Carritt's choice of "sublime" and "romantic" let us simply substitute *ethos* and *pathos:* "Sublime and romantic are aesthetically irrelevant and the rules derived from them harmful—so shifty as to be no help for criticism, creation, or enjoyment of art." The reason lies in the fact that the terms are merely descriptive; they are labels to be attached. Sachs derives endless dualities from ethos and pathos, vitiating the unity he presupposes and failing to comprehend the aesthetic distance essential to the apprehension of all art, classical or Romantic: a real polarity set up by the percipient and the objective symbol.

If we look at musical criticism over a long period, in a work such as Slonimsky's *Lexicon of Musical Invective,* we will see that subjective judgments have been the rule; and they have been judgments which the verdict of history has reversed in a significant number of instances. A philosophy of music, if it can really throw light on the nature of musical symbolism, may provide a basis for musical criticism that will actually be something more than the personal reaction of the critic. I am thinking particularly of the examination of new scores, for which few of our critics, even by present standards, are equipped.

The reaction in the late nineteenth century against all forms of Romantic excess led to an attempt to impose the rigorous scientific objectivity of the laboratory upon all human experience, not excluding the artistic. This has led to very good as well as very bad results: good, in the demand for evidence; bad, in the application of inappropriate techniques. The whole trend of testing and measuring, which has culminated in such instruments as the Seashore tests and its derivatives, is the result of an extension of laboratory technique. Measurements of the kind developed by Carl Seashore can be very helpful in examining certain components of musical ability; but ironically, the far-flung psychological ramifications of musical experience are, in the main, outside the purview of his *Psychology of Music*.

The pioneer work upon which a philosophy of music may be based has been done largely in the twentieth century, though its roots, like those of all modernism, go back to the nineteenth. There is one notable exception which is so extraordinary that, although I give considerable space to it in Chapter 6, it must be mentioned here: *The Power of Sound* by Edmund Gurney. This remarkable and almost forgotten book, published in 1880, not only is far in advance of its own time but is superior to anything I have read in the published works of our own era. The author, a professor of psychology at Cambridge, had a mind of marvelous discrimination reflected in a literary style of elegance and precision. Hanslick can scarcely bear comparison with him. The astonishing fact about his work, as we shall see, is the way he anticipated the most cogent midtwentieth-century art theory in a technical vocabulary remarkably akin to ours, distinguished from present-day usage more by the absence of some of our recent barbarisms than by any difficulty in finding suitable terminology: his prose, like that of Gilbert Murray and Jane Harrison, is free of jargon. What could be more timely (or timeless!) than these lines concerning

conversation about music in his day?: "In general society musical talk almost always sinks into that most
barren and wearisome region, the discussion of the
merits or demerits of different executants and *virtuosi*."

One of the very few present-day references
to Gurney is in Donald Ferguson's *Music as Metaphor*—
a recently published work with a most promising title—
which unfortunately perpetuates the confusion of
expressive modalities and conceives of music as a kind
of catalyst: a triggering agency for consolidating various
associations, somewhat in the manner of Proust with his
Vinteuil theme. Ferguson in his brief mention of Gurney mistakenly credits him with consolidating Hanslick's views. Leonard Meyer in his more significant
study, *Emotion and Meaning in Music,* makes no mention of Gurney; nor does Langer, with whose thought
Gurney's has a strong affinity.

In 1877 William Pole gave a series of lectures,
an explication of musical acoustical theory based upon
Helmholtz, as a springboard for inquiry into principles
of art. These lectures were published in Boston under
the title *The Philosophy of Music.* Helmholtz and, of
course, William Pole, beyond their concern with laws
and phenomena of sound, sought a physiological basis
for a theory of music and dealt with questions of consonance and dissonance and with general philosophical
analysis, raising the question: To what extent does law
operate in every sphere?

This search for demonstrable law is precisely
the aim of philosophy, and it must therefore never
be forgotten that science (including the science of
acoustics) is itself a department of philosophy.

A work by H. H. Britan, also called *The Phi-*

losophy of Music, appeared in 1911 and marked a distinct advance over Pole's study. It was described as a pioneer investigation into musical aesthetics. Britan, a professor of philosophy at Bates College, saw the problem as "the nature of the psychological processes involved in the musical experience." He was concerned with principles of emotional as well as intellectual expression. He sought an explanation in "simplest possible terms." Though he went far, he did not face squarely the question of musical meaning. Like Plato, he was concerned primarily with the effects of music upon human beings. But in this quotation he shows significant insight which has found confirmation in later studies: "The secret of the versatile power of music over the emotions lies in the fact that the symbolism of music conforms so closely to the dynamics of the emotional unconscious." Writing at the very time that Jung's first important studies were appearing, Britan's lines themselves are testimony to what that psychologist was to call *synchronicity.*

The literature on the philosophy of music is meager, but a beginning has been made. It is apparent that all claims must be carefully scrutinized, all presuppositions questioned. We cannot assume, to begin with, that music is a universal language; it may be possible to defend this concept if agreement can be reached on a definition of language which will not falsify the art. *Language* may prove to be an unsuitable term.

In the chapters that follow, I give the historical background for the development of my theory, beginning with a panoramic survey of what philosophers and

others have said concerning the nature of music. I go
on to a detailed consideration of twentieth-century developments and finally to the delineation of principles
I am postulating as a viable basis for a philosophy of
music. I have already given strong indications of the
direction of my thought. Let me chart that course still
more explicitly.

I believe that we may expect to find a common
factor characteristic of all music to some degree, all
styles, all periods of history, East and West: this common factor is its *symbolic character.* The role of the
symbol in life and art is only beginning to be understood by the discursive intellect; as understanding
grows, the symbol is accorded more and more importance in the fields of psychology, philosophy, and art.

Far from being abstract, musical experience is
as empirical as anything can possibly be; yet there seems
to be an almost universal intuition that the art yields
constants which, for all their ineffability in performance, are there for further explorations, so that repetitions evoke new meanings or extensions of old ones.
Music is ephemeral, but it offers an apprehension of
what can only be described as transcendent. Richness
and ambiguity are characteristic of the art symbol. A
symbol may sometimes fade for the percipient; its
penumbra may dim. But the fully realized (one hesi-
tates to say "successful") symbol appears inexhaustible.
This is not a matter of measurable dimensions. In this
universe of discourse a Bach fugue may take precedence
over a Bruckner symphony: the determinable size of
the work is an irrelevancy.

The symbol in music is found in the autonomous realm, the ideal realm which is the world of art.
But this world and the world of life interpenetrate;
hence it is clear that in musical apprehension there must
always be recourse to the act of listening: a dialogue
between the living person and the work of art.

CHAPTER TWO

PHILOSOPHIC MUSICAL THOUGHT
THROUGH THE EIGHTEENTH CENTURY

* * * MUSICAL EXPERIENCE, I HAVE SUGGESTED, IS essentially an empirical affair; and, it follows, the process is admirably suited to personal testing. One has only to hear. The "only" may be gratuitous in current usage, for the listening can be of the most rigorous nature. But whether the music be hard or easy to comprehend, the hearing of it is the musical experience. There is every reason to believe that qualitative differences among musical compositions are crucial. It is the essence of discriminating listening to discern these, and as in any art the degree of preparation and attention brought to the enterprise strongly determines the result: not only, then, what is being played but who is listening—and not only who but when. For the human participant at best is a highly unpredictable, unstable entity.

But human participation there must be. The history of that participation is well documented in certain respects. The effectiveness of music has been acknowledged by many articulate observers, and its peculiar power has engaged the interest of philosophic giants. A few have attempted to explain its nature, to delineate its role in human society, and to warn, in some instances, of potential peril. Feeling, from Plato to Bergson, runs high. We will see in the following chapters that music has not been treated with indifference.

The fervent reaction is related somehow to that mysterious link which music provides with the emotional unconscious, that as yet incomprehensible analogue to the human psyche which acts in some instances as a catalyst, particularly when the music is reinforced with words. Music in the service of slogans (and now in the singing commercials) has been one effective instrument for manipulating men. In the absence of words the hearing of music has no doubt given rise many times to a species of contemplation that is unique in human experience. This kind of realization need not be limited to any historical period, though a happy conjunction of factors would be a necessary condition at any point of time and space. The concept of disinterested hearing appears, however, to be a relatively new one. The notion of listening to music for the sake of that listening alone seems never to have been articulated as an idea before the nineteenth century, though this would not preclude its having occurred, even habitually, in actual practice. But since there is an observable connection between the elucidation of concepts and the modes of experience to which large numbers of people are thereby given access, we may be witnesses to an evolutionary phenomenon: one of those openings which although they depend entirely on what has preceded them nevertheless point toward an extension of awareness and an enlargement of consciousness. The gradual rise of instrumental music as a distinct genre may well be testimony to such a development. If any attempt, then, to *explain* Brahms's use of the passacaglia—beyond describing its formal structure—is unsuccessful, this is no failure of the human mind, no failure even of words per se; we need only refer to the music itself, checking off the variations, if we are so disposed, as we listen. The modality of the Fourth Symphony is musical, and Brahms's work, the completed symbol, unique. Like the Hindu rejecting all descriptions of Reality as inadequate or misleading, we can only protest, in meeting verbal accounts, "Neti, neti." (Not this. Not that.)

Lest it be thought that such an idea is in any way restricted to special circumstances or to a particular culture, let us hear Mark Twain, who was addicted neither to the high-flown nor the highfalutin: "An ecstasy is a thing that will not go into words; it feels like music, and one cannot tell about music so that another person can get the feeling of it."[1] And Erich Fromm: "The understanding of the operation of unconscious elements has taught us to be skeptical towards words and not to take them at face value."[2] And Susanne Langer: "The limitations inherent in verbal con-

---

[1] Mark Twain, *Wit and Wisecracks* (Mount Vernon, N.Y.: Peter Pauper Press, 1961), p. 39.

[2] Erich Fromm, *Escape From Freedom* (New York: Rinehart & Co., 1941), p. 67.

ception and discursive forms of thought are the very *raison d'être* of artistic expression."[3]

The ecstatic possibilities of music have been recognized in all cultures and have usually been admitted in practice under particular conditions, sometimes stringent ones. In the civilization of India music was put into the service of religion from earliest times: the Vedic hymns stand at the beginning of our record. As the art developed over many centuries into a music of profound melodic and rhythmic intricacy, the discipline of a religious text or the guideline of a story determined the structure. Even today the narrator is central in most performances of Indian music, and the virtuosity of a skillful singer rivals that of the instrumentalists. There is very little concept of vocal or instrumental idiom in the Western sense. The vertical dimension of chord structure has never been developed in Far Eastern music; not surprisingly, contrapuntal complexity in Oriental music goes far beyond ours— retaining, what is more, an element of improvisation that is vital to the success of a performance. The spontaneous imitation carried on between a sarangist and narrator, against the insistent rhythmic subtleties of the tabla, can be a source of the greatest excitement, in large measure because a faithful adherence to the rigid rules governing the rendition of ragas is a condition of the game. The lack of accommodation to vocal or instrumental requirements—or the absence of clear distinction between them—suggests the counterpoint of a Bach or, indeed, the uncompromising character of any music in

[3] Susanne Langer, "Abstraction in Art," *JAAC*, XXII, No. 4 (Summer, 1964), 380.

which idea is paramount and the means of execution secondary.

Indian music is very emotional. Its microtonalism goes beyond Western chromaticism in expressive possibilities of a particular kind: the almost unbearable intensifications of pathos. Yet the tonal idiom, an exotic one to Western ears, may be an impediment, sometimes an insuperable one. A deep knowledge of a particular body of musical literature will not help the situation. It can be observed at any time that young children are more open to unfamiliar sounds than highly cultivated professionals; prejudice is acquired along with knowledge. I remarked that training and capacity for concentration will affect what the listener hears; but if he is to get sense out of a particular kind of music, his training must have some relevance to it. An Indian initially will encounter as much difficulty with Western musical idioms as the Occidental suffers when their roles are reversed. Aldous Huxley puts it nicely:

> An Indian, for example, finds European orchestral music intolerably noisy, complicated, over-intellectual, inhuman. It seems incredible to him that any one should be able to perceive beauty and meaning, to recognize an expression of the deepest and subtlest emotions in this elaborate cacophony. And yet, if he has patience and listens to enough of it, he will come at last to realize, not only theoretically but also by direct, immediate intuition, that this music possesses all the qualities which Europeans claim for it.[4]

[4] Aldous Huxley, "Beliefs," Collected Essays (New York: Harper & Brothers, 1958), p. 371.

Tagore, recalling his first encounter with Western music, corroborates Huxley's account of the dilemma: "As I went on hearing and learning more and more of European music, I began to get into the spirit of it; but up to now I am convinced that our music and theirs abide in altogether different apartments, and do not gain entry to the heart by the self-same door."[5]

Although he acknowledges the habitual combining of text and music in his civilization, Tagore deprecates the relative importance of words:

> The art of vocal music has its own special functions and features. And when it happens to be set to words the latter must not presume too much on their opportunity and seek to supersede the melody of which they are but the vehicle. The song being great in its own wealth, why should it wait upon the words? *Rather does it begin where mere words fail.* Its power lies in the region of the inexpressible; it tells us what the words cannot. . . . In the classic style of Hindustan the words are of no account, and leave the melody to make its appeal in its own way. . . . In Bengal, however, the words have always asserted themselves so, that our provincial song has failed to develop her full musical capabilities, and has remained content as the handmaiden of her sister art of poetry.[6]

If we acknowledge that our own readily accessible and frequently played musical literature is drawn from a period from about 1700 to the outer limits of the present, traditional Indian music—referred

---

[5] Rabindranath Tagore, *Reminiscences* (London: Macmillan & Co., 1945), p. 190.
[6] *Ibid.,* "An Essay on Music," p. 205. (Italics mine.)

to as "classical" by Tagore—is a patrimony that ante-
dates its Western European counterpart by a very considerable period. It took its definitive form early and
is conservative to an extent that is hard for us to imagine. "Classical" in our own lexicon, whether we refer
to the late eighteenth century as musicians commonly
do or to all serious music as the uninstructed do, has
become an almost meaningless epithet that we would
do well to drop altogether. But in Indian usage the
term makes sense because it refers to an art that has
crystallized, that is in a certain sense "finished." That
this music, with its carefully regulated freedom, can be
reanimated as occasion demands is proof of its authenticity: homogeneous, yet timelessly admitting elements
of the new through improvisation, this music is
classical.

"As occasion demands": Indian music is fundamentally a music of ritual. The dozens of modes
available, the plentiful ragas—prescribed for seasonal
use, for festive occasions, for morning, for evening—this
is music for use, a veritable *Gebrauchsmusik,* far exceed-
ing in scope any functional music Hindemith has envisioned. Its practitioners spend many years acquiring
proficiency in this highly developed, complex art, mas-
tering not only the aural difficulties but learning the
numerous rules that govern performance, so that the
right music (sans forbidden tones) will be available on
demand at the appropriate hour.

But aside from the random speculations of a
Tagore, there is no Indian theory to explicate musical
meaning nor to point in the direction of such meaning.
Manuals on Indian music, like their Western counter-

parts, describe the techniques, the melodic and rhythmic structure, the texts, the instruments, the occasions for performance. And nothing more.

In the practical applications of music the ancients far outstripped us. Confucius found an important place for the art in the service of a well-ordered moral universe:

> Music rises from the human heart when the human heart is touched by the external world. When touched by the external world, the heart is moved, and therefore finds its expression in sounds. These sounds echo, or combine with, one another and produce a rich variety, and when the various sounds become regular, then we have rhythm. The arrangement of tones for our enjoyment in combination with the military dance, with shields and hatchets, and the civil dance, with long feathers and pennants of ox-tails, is called music.[7]

He saw music and government reflecting one another: "The music of a peaceful and prosperous country is quiet and joyous, and the government is orderly; the music of a country in turmoil shows dissatisfaction and anger, and the government is chaotic."[8] Confucius believed that only the superior man who can understand music is equipped to govern.

Music reveals character through the six emotions it can portray: sorrow, satisfaction, joy, anger,

[7] Lin Yutang, (ed.), *The Wisdom of Confucius* (London: Michael Joseph, 1958), p. 208.
[8] *Ibid.*, p. 209.

piety, love. According to Confucius great music is in harmony with the universe, restoring order to the physical world through that harmony. He distinguished between music and ritual, ascribing an inner significance of harmony to the first, an outer preoccupation with order to the second. Simplicity was essential to both. Music was of heaven, ritual of earth. Music, as a true mirror of character, made pretense or deception impossible.

Confucius' view of music as a department of ethics was shared by Plato. Both philosophers were anxious to regulate the use of particular modes and their supposed effects on men. Confucius recognized these associations:

> The mode of C is the symbol of the king; the mode of D is the symbol of the minister; the mode of E is the symbol of the people; the mode of G is the symbol of the affairs of the country; and the mode of A is the symbol of the natural world. When the five keys are arranged in order, we do not have discordant sounds. When the key of C loses its tonality, then the music loses its fundamental and the king neglects his duties. When the key of D loses its tonality, then the music loses its gradation, and the ministers become unruly. When the key of E loses its tonality, then the music is sorrowful and the people feel distressed. When the key of G loses its tonality, then the music is mournful and the affairs of the country become complicated. When the key of A loses its tonality, then the music suggests danger, and the people suffer from poverty. When all five keys lose their tonality and upset one another, we have a general discord, and the nation will not have long to live.[9]

[9] *Ibid.*, pp. 209–10.

Confucius, in contrasting classical and modern music, poses a dichotomy which will later be discussed in another context as Apollonian versus Dionysian concepts of art. His description is enlightening both for the contrast it affords between two styles and as a clear statement of his own position:

> In ancient music the dancers move in formation forward and backward in an atmosphere of peace and order and a certain luxury of movement. . . . The music begins with the civil dance movements and ends with the military dance movements, and there is a continuity of movement from the beginning to the end, while the measure of the classical music prevents or checks the dancers who are inclined to go too fast. After listening to such music, the superior man will be in a proper atmosphere to discuss the music and the ways of the ancients, the cultivation of personal life and the ordering of national life. This is the main sentiment or character of ancient music.[10]

And in castigating modern music, Confucius clearly discerned dangers which were to make Plato such a stern musical disciplinarian:

> Now in this new music, people bend their bodies while they move back and forth, there is a deluge of immoral sounds without form or restraint, and the actors and dwarfs dressed like monkeys mix (or mix with) the company of men and women, behaving as if they didn't know who were their parents or children. At the end of such a performance it is impossible to discuss music or the ways of the ancients. This is the main sentiment or character of the new music.[11]

[10] *Ibid.,* pp. 216–17.　　　　　[11] *Ibid.,* p. 217.

Confucius made perfunctory acknowledgment of a higher origin: "Truly great music shares the principles of harmony with the universe."[12] But the great beyond troubled Confucius no more than it was to bother the eighteenth-century deist. Confucius recognized the necessary role of the human participant as well as some kind of connection between music and the emotions which it was necessary to codify. He also characterized the music of his time and recorded extramusical meanings ascribed to the modes, distinguishing between acceptable and unacceptable practice. But this was sufficient theory, if not more than enough. Confucius was a thoroughgoing pragmatist. He was concerned with music insofar as it had an instrumental function in society.

In Greek philosophy music was something to be reckoned with, but not for its autonomous merits; it was almost a department of mathematics for Pythagoras, who was the first musical numerologist. Music was good because it reflected numerical relationships and partook of the unity of numbers which were the realities underlying all manifestation. Pythagoras, who laid the foundations for acoustics, contributed a great deal to Greek musical theory, even prefiguring the doctrine of *ethos,* which holds that by virtue of its numerical basis music is a force of moral value. His idea of a numerical foundation for all things exhibits that extraordinary prescience so characteristic of Greek thought—insights gained, what is more, without the aid of mechanical

[12] *Ibid.,* p. 213.

devices. Busoni's claim that "music is a part of the vibrating universe" must be admitted. But the Greeks did not envision so dynamic a state of affairs. "The objective way was to trace only the constant, static relations. In acoustics the Greek scientists discovered the correspondence between the pitch of a note and the length of a chord. They did not, on the other hand, progress to a calculation of pitch on the basis of vibrations, even though an attempt was made to connect sounds with underlying motions."[13] Bruno Snell, the author of these lines, goes on to say: "In *Problemata* high pitch is explained as fast, low pitch as slow movement; but there Aristotle is concerned with single disconnected observations. He does not formulate a general exact law, nor does he associate a particular pitch with a particular speed of movement."[14]

Like Confucius, Plato saw a correspondence between the character of a man and the music that represented him; straightforward simplicity was best. The true musician, it is stated in the *Laches,* "has in his own life a harmony of words and deeds arranged—not in the Ionian, or in the Phrygian mode, nor yet in the Lydian, but in the true Hellenic mode, which is the Dorian, and no other."[15] In the *Laws* Plato declared that rhythmic and melodic complexities were to be eschewed as conducive to depression and disorder. A one-to-one (or note-for-note) correspondence between music and text (an early endorsement of first species

[13] Bruno Snell, *The Discovery of the Mind,* trans. by T. G. Rosenmeyer, (Cambridge: Harvard Univ. Press, 1953), p. 244.
[14] *Ibid.,* p. 320.
[15] Plato *Laches* 188D (Jowett trans.).

counterpoint!) was best. In this prescription Plato states
the truly classical objection to those recurring periods of
polyphonic excess following his own era.

Music for Plato partakes of divine harmony:
rhythm and melody imitate the movements of heavenly
bodies, thus delineating the music of the spheres and
reflecting the moral order of the universe. The expressive capabilities of earthly music, however, are suspect;
Plato distrusts its emotional power. Music must therefore be of the right sort; the sensuous qualities of certain
modes are dangerous, and a strong censorship must be
imposed. In the *Republic* he has Socrates say: "Musical
training is a more potent instrument than any other,
because rhythm and harmony find their way into the
inward places of the soul, on which they mightily fasten,
imparting grace, and making the soul of him who is
rightly educated graceful, or of him who is ill-educated
ungraceful."[16] But infection with wrong principles,
with passion, always threatens: "There complexity engendered license, and here disease; whereas simplicity
in music was the parent of temperance in the soul."[17]

Music and gymnastics in the correct balance
constitute a core curriculum: "He who mingles music
with gymnastics in the fairest proportions, and best at-
tempers them to the soul, may be rightly called the true
musician and harmonist in a far higher sense than the
tuner of the strings."[18] A lack of balance, however, is
pernicious:

---

[16] Plato *Republic* 401D (Jowett trans.).   [18] *Ibid.* 412.
[17] *Ibid.* 404E.

I am quite aware that the mere athlete becomes too much of a savage, and that the mere musician is melted and softened beyond what is good for him. . . . When a man allows music to play upon him and to pour into his soul through the funnel of his ears those sweet and soft and melancholy airs of which we were just now speaking, and his whole life is passed in warbling and the delights of song; in the first stage of the process the passion or spirit which is in him is tempered like iron, and made useful, instead of brittle and useless. But, if he carries on the softening and soothing process, in the next stage he begins to melt and waste, until he has wasted away his spirit and cut out the sinews of his soul; and he becomes a feeble warrior.[19]

Plato, then, admits music into the ideal society he envisions to the extent that it will be demonstrably desirable in an ethical sense; his concern is primarily with its effects and he defines it in terms of what it does. The ideal music he postulates in the realm of the eternal presents no clear and present danger. But actual music is intimately connected with human emotions, a fact that Plato clearly recognizes and fears; the emotions are easily aroused, subject to infection at all times; censorship is essential. Plato's prescriptions put one in mind, in many instances, of the strictures imposed upon Soviet composition in our own time: "that we may discover whether they are armed against all enchantments."[20]

The dichotomy that Plato emphasized between reason and the emotions has been of enormous influence in the aesthetics of Western music. With so powerful a

[19] *Ibid.* 410D; 411B.   [20] *Ibid.* 413E.

precedent, what course could there be other than that of exercising through the rational faculties a tireless control over the tumultuous feelings?

Yet Plato, regarding earthly music as a shadow of the Ideal, recognized a symbolic significance in the art. Aristotle carried forward the concept of art as imitation; but with Aristotle, musical symbolism was given added strength because it could express the universal. Mimesis was still the criterion. But the idea that actual works could contain a measure of truth in themselves was voiced by Aristotle and advanced more explicitly in the third century A.D. by Plotinus. This idea is of great importance in presaging later concepts of symbolic discourse and, in particular, in anticipation of my own thesis.

In quest of a happy mean, Aristotle—unlike the Socrates of the *Republic*—would admit all the modes. In defending the merits of such a rich musical diet, he applies the theory of catharsis, and recognizes happiness and pleasure as values to the individual and state:

> We accept the division of melodies, proposed by certain philosophers, into ethical melodies, melodies of action, and passionate or inspiring melodies, each having, as they say, a mode corresponding to it. But we maintain further that music should be studied, not for the sake of one, but of many benefits, that is to say, with a view to education and purgation. . . . Music may also serve for intellectual enjoyment, for relaxation, and for recreation after exertion. It is clear, therefore, that all the modes must be employed by us, but not all of them in the same manner. In education the most ethical modes are to be preferred, but in lis-

tening to the performances of others we may admit the modes of action and passion also. For feelings such as pity and fear, or, again, enthusiasm,
exist very strongly in some souls, and have more or
less influence over all. Some persons fall into a
religious frenzy, whom we see as a result of the
sacred melodies—when they have used the melodies
that excite the soul to mystic frenzy—restored as
though they had found healing and purgation.
Those who are influenced by pity or fear, and
every emotional nature, must have a like experience, and others in so far as each is susceptible to
such emotions, and all are in a manner purged
and their souls lightened and delighted. The pur-
gative melodies likewise give an innocent pleasure to mankind.[21]

"It is not easy to determine the nature of
music," said Aristotle, "or why anyone should have a
knowledge of it."[22] The nature of music can be inferred
only through its effects. With Aristotle, however, the
changes produced in the individual through his experience of music are crucial. Music, he states, has power to
mold the character: "Rhythm and melody supply imi-
tations of anger and gentleness, and also of courage and
temperance, and of all the qualities contrary to these,
and of the other qualities of character which hardly fall
short of the actual affections, as we know from our own
experience, for in listening to such strains our souls
undergo a change."[23] Here Aristotle, in acknowledging
the wide range of feelings music can "imitate," comes
very close to recognizing the possibilities of ambivalence, as well as other subtleties, nuances, and ambigui-

[21] Aristotle *Politics* 1341b33; 1342a (Jowett trans.).
[22] *Ibid.* 1339a14.
[23] *Ibid.* 1340a19.

ties of that protean emotional realm that finds expression in art. His attribution of predictable powers to particular modes is pertinent:

> Even in mere melodies there is an imitation of character, for the musical modes differ essentially from one another, and those who hear them are differently affected by each. Some of them make men sad and grave, like the so-called Mixolydian; others enfeeble the mind, like the relaxed modes; another, again, produces a moderate and settled temper, which appears to be the peculiar effect of the Dorian; the Phrygian inspires enthusiasms. . . . The same principles apply to rhythms; some have a character of rest, others of motion, and of these latter again, some have a more vulgar, others a nobler movement. . . . There seems to be in us a sort of affinity to musical modes and rhythms, which makes some philosophers say that the soul is a tuning, others, that it possesses tuning.[24]

"The soul is a tuning; it possesses tuning." If the soul is "a tuning"—here I am speculating—then it has readiness for music: it recognizes music as a mirror; it is taut with expectancy, eager for representation. If it "possesses tuning," the soul contains music; that which is externalized is therefore not an altogether separate phenomenon. With either interpretation the thought comes close to Langer's description of art as a "symbolic analogue of emotive life."

Of course I am reading something into Aristotle. But if there is in us "a sort of affinity to musical modes and rhythms," then why? "It is not easy to determine the nature of music." Aristotle not only stimu-

[24] *Ibid.* 1340a39.

lates further inquiry but his insights transcend the limitations of his own experience and terminology; acknowledgment of such quality in the seminal thought of a master is a commonplace. And he exhibits not only profound insight but a degree of prescience as well: the long and fruitful influence of the *Poetics* is testimony to this. What is even more remarkable is the balance achieved between the general concept and the concrete prescription. One of his suggestions might well be heeded to the greater health of musical specialists in our own day, though the context of the passage is the musical education of children and especially the problem of whether or not they should have instruction in what we are now condemned to call "applied music": "They should be taught music in such a way as to become not only critics but performers."[25]

Aristotle makes a distinction between those whose knowledge of music is secondhand or only theoretical and those who have a hand in producing it: "Clearly there is a considerable difference made in the character by the actual practice of the art. It is difficult, if not impossible, for those who do not perform to be good judges of the performance of others."[26] Extraordinary prowess, however, is not the *desideratum*: "The right measure will be attained if students of music stop short of the arts which are practiced in professional contests, and do not seek to acquire those fantastic marvels of execution which are now the fashion in such contests, and from these have passed into education."[27] He then goes on to distinguish between music intended

---

[25] *Ibid.* 1340b31.   [26] *Ibid.* 1340b22.   [27] *Ibid.* 1341a10.

for instruction and music designed for relieving the passions; he associates the flute and harp with the latter and finds them unsuitable for use in education, since they are conducive to excitement and not to the strengthening of moral character. He speaks of the popularity the flute once enjoyed in Athens.

> Later experience enabled men to judge what was or was not really conducive to virtue, and they rejected both the flute and several other old-fashioned instruments, such as the Lydian harp, and many-stringed lyre, the "heptagon," "triangle," "sambuca," and the like—which are intended only to give pleasure to the hearer, and require extraordinary skill of hand.[28]

The emotions, though Aristotle permits them more latitude than does Plato, must be kept in check. Pleasure is admitted, but it must be the right kind of pleasure. Moral improvement is the end sought and music remains merely a means. Plato objects to the use of music for which there is no text and also to innovations, since these lead to anarchy. Yet there is frank and admiring recognition of musical power by both Plato and Aristotle, whatever interpretations of its meaning they were impelled to offer. In contrast to their claims the skeptic Empiricus, who was in some respects a third-century Hanslick, was to say that music was an art of tones and rhythms which meant nothing outside itself. The sensuous pleasure invoked by its sounds is the listener's yardstick. "It means itself."

The historical purview yields valid insights. It also provides evidence of recurring practices. Both

[28] *Ibid.* 1341a36.

induce in the observer a sense of timelessness as well as a consciousness of limitation. Aristotle, in posing a question still valid for the musical education of our own day (when Paul Henry Láng can denigrate the "mere practitioner"), strives to unite theorizing with doing. Like perceptive thinkers of other eras—Langer of our own century among them—he realizes that the vitality of art and experience of art are somehow inextricably bound up with doing, though it is not "merely" that. But we can never come to the end of necessary distinctions. There are artists who are practitioners (this is surely a redundancy) and there are also, indeed, "mere" practitioners. I have given Edmund Gurney's scathing comment on the virtuoso-mongering of the nineteenth century. Aristotle pronounces an even more devastating indictment upon the music-making of his day. It requires little gift for analogy and even less imagination to direct these same lines against the musical fare now being offered under the guise of serious music in such quantities to organized audiences—to whom artists may be sold like cattle—throughout the United States:

> The performer practices the art, not for the sake of his own improvement, but in order to give pleasure, and that of a vulgar sort, to his hearers. For this reason the execution of such music is not the part of a freeman but of a paid performer, and the result is that the performers are vulgarized, for the end at which they aim is bad. The vulgarity of the spectator tends to lower the character of the music and therefore of the performers; they look to him—he makes them what they are, and fashions even their bodies by the movements which he expects them to exhibit.[20]

[20] *Ibid.* 1341b11.

Despite the plethora of pronouncements about music by the ancient Greeks, we have little idea how their music actually sounded. They were given to theoretical speculation; they had a system of notation; music was an art the practice of which enjoyed a good bit of their attention. But only a few notated fragments of Greek music have survived, and we lack the means—probably the situation is irreparable because of the loss of oral tradition—of restoring these to the authentic vocal and instrumental context.

The Platonic influence in musical thought was to be dominant for at least a millenium. Following that period of unquestioned philosophic allegiance there were times of rededication to Greek concepts, accompanied—as with the Florentine Camerata—by considerable drumbeating. The absence of an extant Greek music as illustration has perhaps given to its alleged spokesmen an immunity they might otherwise not enjoy and has lent to their prescriptions a general luster that no actual sounds of their own music can affect adversely. At any rate, such returns to simplicity, directness, and the primacy of the word have periodically been made out of loyalty to Platonic concepts, however much these neopractices may have differed from those of the Greeks themselves.

In the twentieth century the effects of Greek thought are still strongly evident in the belief that music influences the ethical life; in the idea that music can be explained in terms of some component such as number (which may itself be but a reflection of another, higher source); in the view that music has specific effects and functions which can be appropriately labelled; and in the recurrent observation that music is connected with human emotion. In every period of history there have been defectors from one or more of these views. And among the followers of this aesthetic, as with Plato and Aristotle themselves, there are differences of emphasis.

Aristoxenus, pupil of Aristotle, gave considerable credit to the human listener, his importance and his powers of perception; he denigrated the dominance of mathematical and acoustical considerations and the atomism of hypotheses then current. For Aristoxenus music had a functional significance: both the hearing and the intellect of the listener were essential to the enterprise, and individual tones were to be apprehended in their relations to one another and in the context of larger formal units. The effect of all this, moreover, was emotional. Aristoxenus, like Aristotle, was a Gestaltist.

The Epicureans and Stoics adopted a more naturalistic view of music and its function, which they accepted as an adjunct to the good life. In cosmologies which gave more primacy to sensation than Plato's, they nevertheless placed music in the service of moderation and virtue.

At this juncture, now that we have noted the moral, ritual, and cathartic roles of music and, particularly in the case of the Epicureans, its utility in a life of refined pleasures, we may remark the curious fact that nowhere—despite tributes to its inevitable presence—do we read any acknowledgment of its necessity in human discourse. Democritus (c. 420 B.C.), indeed, explicitly denied any fundamental need for music, which he described as the youngest of the arts: "For it was not necessity that separated it off, but it arose from the existing superfluity."[30]

The role of music as accessory to words is nowhere more clearly illustrated than in the long history of Christianity, where the primacy of the text has always been emphasized and sometimes—as in Roman doctrine—made an article of faith. The fact that glorious music has been produced in that tradition is not the point at issue. The point is that the definition of music in terms of extramusical factors has falsified its image in the rational consciousness and has made the art, by the canons of the highest authorities, subordinate to the word. The church has sponsored and even promoted what were looked upon as acceptable expressions of faith through music. But the misunderstanding of the real nature of music has been perpetuated and strengthened by this means: so that an art which was of political utility for Plato and Aristotle becomes, in the early church and throughout its history, of religious significance only, even in those instances—or perhaps especially in those—when its passionate character was thought to constitute a threat to the established order and was therefore attributable to Satan, along with every other threat to that order.

It is important to note that in the context of this book what is generally regarded as religious symbol-

---

[30] Kathleen Freeman, *Ancilla to the Pre-Socratic Philosophers* (Cambridge: Harvard Univ. Press, 1957), p. 105.

ism is of *signal* significance only. This is a matter of definition of terms and not disparagement. Thus the text-painting of a Bach or a Handel is the observance of conventions of technique as practiced during their lifetimes. The use of a descending motive for "Et incarnatus est" in the B Minor Mass, or the juxtaposition of string sound with the voice of Jesus in the *St. Matthew Passion,* or even the convolutions by which the melody imitates the text in Handel's aria "Every Valley" (the "crooked" tune becomes "straight")—these are signal techniques, immediately understood once they are pointed out. But they are neither self-suggesting (except to the extent that they represent the common craft of a period and are hence recognizable as typical devices by those who are contemporary with its practice) nor are they integral as "content," and being technical devices only, they have little bearing on the essential quality of a work.[31] The symbol, in contrast, is that essential quality.

What we are accustomed to hearing described as religious symbolism is, then, signal technique of an

[31] This distinction must be made no matter what the idiom and regardless of whether the devices have verbal referents, as in "text-painting," or follow some other scheme or formula, such as composing in "tone-rows." The tone-row, like major-minor tonality, is a technical substratum and must no more be explicit in the finished work than the chemical makeup of pigments in the Mona Lisa; the creator in either instance is aware of his devices, of his materials. But it is a serious error, and one to which modern musical criticism is all too prone, to suppose that the unmasking of the composer's procedures will be the crucial factor in the artistic apprehension of his completed work. The devices selected may affect the general comprehensibility or accessibility of the work, but they are not, per se, the determinants of its worth or quality.

obvious and superficial kind. W. T. Stace, in *Time and Eternity,* posits a religious symbolism, as expressed in the sacraments of the church, which is genuine in that the symbol has content and autonomy: it does not merely represent something else. The doctrine that the bread and wine become the body and blood of Christ, especially if accepted metaphorically and not believed literally, is such a symbol. Adherence to the metaphor as an article of faith, though shocking to the logical intellect, is rich in dramatic effectiveness. Bergson, never acknowledging the literal impossibility of doing so, states that one must "enter into" the object one apprehends intuitively. In religious symbolism the words—and the icons—provide the appropriate modality for the symbolic content. It is doubtful that music can ever be religious in that way—that is, be specifically religious in its own tonal modality. But in alliance with another mode—such as words or visual images—it may afford a strong enhancement, set up an effective association. It is the power of such reinforcement that has been exploited for political and institutional purposes.

Much of the Platonic-Aristotelian aesthetic, as restated by Boethius, was well suited to the needs of the church; the conservative aspects of that philosophy, with its fear of innovation, were conducive to the maintenance of order. St. Augustine, who was attracted by music and valued its utility to religion, was fearful of its sensuous element and anxious that the melody never take precedence over the words; these had been Plato's concerns also. Augustine (and his beliefs were reinforced by St. Thomas Aquinas centuries later) held the basis of music to be mathematical: music reflects—yet again!—celestial movement and order.

In the varieties of plainsong, melody was used for textual illumination: the undulations of sound took their cue from the words. The results of this pairing, particularly as we know them in Gregorian Chant, are very closely welded, intimate: the mutuality is almost productive of a *tertium quid,* as it can be in the *lieder* of Schubert or Brahms. This possibility remains one of the glories of art and is in no way to be denigrated by any canons of musical meaning set forth in this book; but the necessity for recognizing the component elements in such a union is no less obligatory for the discursive reason. The immediate experience of an artistic totality, however, carries no such obligations. As a creative process symbol building may draw on many components: the result may be a peculiar, or unique, Bayreuth; or it may be a miniature edifice by Webern. There are no rules. But the way materials are put together—what Aristotle calls the handling of plot materials or the fable—will determine the range and accessibility of the symbol: not forgetting, in addition, what materials (or modalities) are employed.

Luther was a musical liberal and reformer. The uses he envisioned for music were, however, despite his innovations, in the mainstream of tradition: music must be simple, direct, accessible, an aid to piety. His assignment of particular qualities to a given mode is reminiscent of the Platonic tradition, of course, but bears a special resemblance to Confucius. Calvin characteristically took a more cautious and fearful view than

Luther, warning against the inculcation through the
wrong use of music of voluptuousness, effeminacy, and
disorder. And the meaning of the words was not to be
jeopardized by the music.

        The Pythagoreans are reborn from age to age.
Kepler perpetuated, in effect, the idea of the harmony
of the spheres, attempting to relate music to planetary
movement. Descartes, too, saw the basis of music as
mathematical. He was a faithful Platonist in his prescription of temperate rhythms and simple melodies so
that music would not produce imaginative, exciting—
and hence immoral—effects. And for Leibniz, music
reflected a universal rhythm and mirrored a reality
which was fundamentally mathematical, experienced in
the human mind as a kind of subconscious apprehension
of numerical relationships.
        Kant ranked music as lowest in his hierarchy
of the arts, giving poetry, sculpture, and painting—in
that order—precedence. What he distrusted most about
music, its wordlessness, is its essential modality, which
he described as "sheer fantasy"—useful for enjoyment
but negligible in the service of culture. Allied with
poetry, however, it acquires conceptual value. Yet Kant,
in his *Critique of Judgment,* says that beauty, not
knowledge, gives awareness of the nature of mental
activity. We see that he is confining such activity to the
functions of the discursive faculties: "In the judgment
of Reason it [music] has less worth than any other of the
beautiful arts."
        Hegel, too, made reason the arbiter, saying that
art, though it expresses the Divine, must yield to phi-

losophy. He acknowledged the peculiar power of music to express many nuances of the emotions. Hegel, like Kant, preferred vocal music to instrumental, deprecating the wordless music as subjective and indefinite. The essence of music, he held, is rhythm. This rhythm finds its counterpart in our innermost selves. What is particularly important in Hegel's view is his claim that music, unlike the other arts, has no independent existence in space, is not objective in that sense. The fundamental rhythm of music—this aspect of number—is experienced within the hearer, is not separated from him. In his implicit acknowledgment of virtual time Hegel is anticipating certain features of Bergson's thought which are important in their implications for music.

It seems very curious that a faculty as productive as the human fantasy should be described by Kant as "sheer"; or that unconceptualized feelings, for Hegel, should be looked upon as "only" vague and indefinite. "Only" a universe of discourse that fatally overvalued discursive reason could so undervalue whole worlds of human experience. But we have seen repeatedly that any activity in which reason seems not to predominate is described by the wholly gratuitous epithet "mere." Thus Julius Portnoy, in his brief reference to Bergson, somehow deprecates a view of music that is vast in its implications, though the quotation he offers from Bergson's *Laughter* is accurate:

> Of the philosophers who have written about music in the 20th century, the Frenchman, Henri Bergson (1859–1941), included music as *just another member of the art family which gives man a more direct vision of reality.* Music, in the aesthetics of Bergson, "has no other object than to

brush aside the utilitarian symbols, the conventional and socially accepted generalities, in short, everything that veils reality from us, in order to bring us face to face with reality itself."[32]

The catalog of philosophers, not intended to be exhaustive, ends here. The three nineteenth-century giants who are next considered—Schopenhauer, Nietzsche, Bergson—stand in special and significant relation to the theory I am developing.

In viewing the long period that separates the eighteenth century from Plato, I think it is clear from the examples quoted that these great philosophers, often much concerned with music, were not speaking as philosophers of music. Music interested them in terms of something outside itself; in its observable effects; in its connections with dance, religious ritual, or festive rites; because of its alliance with words; or for some other extramusical consideration. The only common denominator, aside from the recognition of different types of music, is the acknowledgment of its connection—somehow—with the emotional life. This "somehow," this emotional modality whereby music is related to the emotions but also has an autonomous existence—not indeed as something unrelated to man, but related in a universal way, hence its accessibility—is the problem of a philosophy of music.

The reliance upon (or insistence upon) words for the explication of musical meaning was the principal impediment—and it remains so today—to viable concepts: the chief obstacle to the discovery of defensible ideas, capable of being rendered in discursive terms,

---

[32] Julius Portnoy, *The Philosopher and Music* (New York: Humanities Press, 1954), p. 223. (Italics mine.)

that would be relevant to the facts of musical experience. Writing of the efforts of poets to achieve musical effects, Wellek and Warren keep the modalities distinct:

> Poems have been, of course, written with the intention that music should be added, e.g., many Elizabethan airs and all librettos for opera. In rare instances, poets and composers have been one and the same; but it seems hard to prove that the composition of music and words was ever a simultaneous process. Even Wagner sometimes wrote his "dramas" years before they were set to music; and, no doubt, many lyrics were composed to fit ready melodies. But the relation between music and really great poetry seems rather tenuous when we think of the evidence afforded by even the most successful settings into musical terms. Poems of close-knit, highly integrated structure do not lend themselves to musical setting, while mediocre or poor poetry, like much of the early Heine or Wilhelm Müller, has provided the text for the finest songs of Schubert and Schumann. If the poetry is of high literary value, the setting frequently distorts or obscures its patterns completely, even when the music has value in its own right. One need not cite such examples as the lot of Shakespeare's *Othello* in Verdi's opera, for nearly all the settings of the Psalms or of the poems of Goethe offer adequate proof of the contention. Collaboration between poetry and music exists, to be sure; but the highest poetry does not tend towards music, and the greatest music stands in no need of words.[33]

If universals are expressible through music, there must be the possibility of a vision of reality—face to face; or, it would be more accurate to say, there must be an aural apprehension of at least some department

[33] René Wellek and Austin Warren, *Theory of Literature* (New York: Harcourt, Brace and Co., 1956), p. 116.

of "what is." But these universals, dimly sensed by the conceptualizing intellect, have gone begging for recognition. Portnoy, whom I took to task for his neglect of Bergson, states the facts succinctly:

> The philosopher has mainly evaluated music, up until the eighteenth century, in terms of metaphysics, ethics and mathematics. He has thwarted the creative musician at every turn by his defense of traditional values and by his zealous retention of the status quo. The philosopher has been quick to question musical change and he has taken it upon himself to evaluate new music in the light of the old. He has left behind a legacy of intellectual arguments which the theologian and statesman have used effectively to combat new musical ideas which might threaten the stability of the liturgy or the political status quo. The few philosophic voices which have cried out against such prevailing aesthetic views on music have insisted that music signified nothing beyond itself; that it was not a subject for metaphysics, a matter of ethics, a means of educational discipline, or a political expedient. . . . However much the philosophers have written about music, they have nevertheless had less to say about it than any of the other arts for the very reason that the emotion which music evokes in us does not lend itself to rationalization as easily as the conceptualized arts of poetry or the drama. . . . The philosopher has persistently believed throughout history, with few exceptions, that music without words is inferior to music with words.[34]

E. F. Carritt suggests that "the casual insights of artists are often more illuminating than the system-

---

[34] Portnoy, pp. xi–xii.

atic arguments of professional philosophers who have metaphysical axes to grind."[35] Langer, too, regards the insights of practitioners as important and makes frequent reference to what artists themselves have said.

Portnoy believes that a humanistic aesthetics of music can be realized

> by discarding the outmoded myths which have shrouded the creation and appreciation of music and by guiding ourselves by the principle that music is fundamentally the expression of feeling in a stylized art form of rhythm and tone. Music is born of feeling to appeal to feeling. It is created out of emotion to move the emotions. Music is rooted in the soil of reality. It is the product of human experience even if it transcends experience by crystallizing feeling. . . .[36]

It is the modality of this "crystallizing" that concerns us in the present work: the correspondence of real (or raw) emotion to the artistic analogue—that musical analogue which is its symbolic expression. What is music? What does it do—and how? What does it "mean"?

The modality of musical discourse, if this can somehow be isolated and examined, is the clue. The modality is tonal: music is sound—aurally, humanly apprehended. But sound that is random—what we may still be permitted to call noise—is not yet a modality, though it may give impetus to the musical imagination. An *artistic modality*, as I define it, may be any one of

[35] E. F. Carritt, "Aesthetics," *Encyclopaedia Britannica*, Vol. 1 (London: Encyclopaedia Britannica, Inc., 1956), p. 264.
[36] Portnoy, pp. xi–xii.

several distinct realms of human sensibility, wherein intelligible structures may be looked at, listened to, or enacted. Each modality has its particular possibilities and limitations—both dependent upon the human psychophysical organism.

Spoken language, like music, is sounded: but the heightened inflections of speech, which serve their own distinct purpose, are not music; nor is music language. They have much in common, especially music and poetry, hence the continual confusion between them. Both are heard—if not physically, then by the "inner" ear. The composer (I hope this is axiomatic) hears his work even in the absence of performance; but he wishes it to be heard in actuality by others. Like every artist, the composer, in giving form to his musical ideas, is living simultaneously on a plane of abstract concepts and in the empirical world; and the modality of his art is psychophysical: the modality of heard melodies.

By musical modality, then, I refer both to the peculiar materials and the characteristic processes that attend the realization of music in conception and performance: the inescapable conditions that attach themselves to the art of music. If these conditions limit, they also bestow *identity* and permit *repetition*. These are crucial points in a consideration of the musical symbol: for that symbol, according to my lexicon, must be recognizable; and it must have the capacity to recur again and again.

CHAPTER THREE

SCHOPENHAUER AND NIETZSCHE ON MUSIC

* * * SCHOPENHAUER AND NIETZSCHE BROUGHT TO
the theory of music a new concept, articulated by each
in different ways and in divergent terms but faithful to
the same principle: _dynamism_. Each one espoused a
world view in which the Newtonian framework appeared a fragile structure indeed, threatened on all
sides by the turbulent and destructive forces of the universe. Rebellion was in the air: something Dionysiac,
perhaps, certainly a facet of the Romantic spirit, conducive to movement and change and a melting-down of
crystallized modes of thought. Discursive reason itself
was a powerful ally in providing the rationale for new
cosmologies, as it is for the philosophic existentialists in
our own day.

From Heraclitus to Hegel, dynamism had been
in a bad way. Flux was that which took place between

fixed points, and the less said about it the better. One orthodoxy of thought succeeded another but the outlook, the overview—whether from the vantage point of Roman doctrine or of the Enlightenment—was dogmatic. Concepts produced a characteristic stasis, conservative, nearly invulnerable; and though tempestuous men danced and sang songs which are now in the hands of historians, they did not write intellectual history.

The force by which the reasonable and ordered world was torn apart is not something alien to the human being: it is known to him inwardly through that complex of dynamic feelings for which the discursive intellect has provided a pitifully inadequate vocabulary—an intellect by means of which those feelings seek in vain an apposite reflection. The search for order is intense, a human necessity, and the emotions themselves gravitate toward containment, toward ordered expression. Such expression, externalized, is art. Here is the symbolic analogue to the life of the emotions. The universe of conceptual discourse must provide the necessary stage or be destroyed.

But it must provide for everything. The range of experience—actual and mimetic—will have full play. The ugly, the chaotic, the frenzied, the inharmonious belong to this human universe no less than the well-ordered and beautiful; and art is accountable for everything. Art is not normative. Symbolic expression will occur whether we will or no, and the claims of Apollo and Dionysus will be honored out of necessity in one way or another. The terrible destruction that goes on, in contrast to the building of worlds, is acknowledged in the mythical traditions of every great culture—nowhere more dramatically than in the Hindu pantheon where Vishnu is the Preserver, Shiva the Destroyer; while Kali the Mother fulfills both functions, holding life on one side, universal dissolution on the other.

The belated recognition of *process* with its essential dynamism created as many problems as it solved. How is the changing related to the changeless, time to the eternal, manifestation to essence? Schopenhauer and Nietzsche presupposed a dualism—the former with the attributes of will and idea, the latter with his Dionysian dynamism versus the archetypes of the Apollonian dream world. Both were obliged to deal with the somewhat disparate demands of space and time, but both—and here Nietzsche acknowledged his strong debt to Schopenhauer—saw in music an art that is not spatialized in the way that other arts are by the necessities of their particular modalities; consequently music is not objective in the same way as the others. Music is closer to the inner dynamism of process; there are fewer technical (and no concrete) impediments to immediate apprehension, for an entire dimension of the empirical world has been, as it were, bypassed. Bergson, exercising the artist's prerogative, obliterates space altogether: all is process. In the Bergsonian world view, then, music, realized in a dimension of virtual time, is the complete metaphor for the dynamism he posits.

Schopenhauer does not burn his bridges: mimesis still prevails:

> The (Platonic) Ideas are the adequate objectification of will. To excite or suggest the knowledge of these by means of the representation of particular things (for works of art themselves are

always representative of particular things) is the end of all the other arts, which can only be attained by a corresponding change in the knowing subject. Thus all these arts objectify the will indirectly only by means of the Ideas; and since our world is nothing but the manifestation of the Ideas in multiplicity, though their entrance into the *principium individuationis* (the form of the knowledge possible for the individual as such), music also, since it passes over the Ideas, is entirely independent of the phenomenal world, ignores it altogether, could to a certain extent exist if there was no world at all, which cannot be said of the other arts. Music is as *direct* an objectification and copy of the whole *will* as the world itself, nay, even as the Ideas, whose multiplied manifestation constitutes the world of individual things. Music is thus by no means like the other arts, the copy of the Ideas, but the *copy of the will itself,* whose objectivity the Ideas are. This is why the effect of music is so much more powerful and penetrating than that of the other arts, for they speak only of shadows, but it speaks of the thing itself. Since, however, it is the same will which objectifies itself both in the Ideas and in music, though in quite different ways, there must be, not indeed a direct likeness, but yet a parallel, an analogy, between music and the Ideas whose manifestation in multiplicity and incompleteness is the visible world.[1]

"It is not easy," said Aristotle, "to determine the nature of music." Schopenhauer, pursuing the correspondence he discerns between music and ideas as related to the will, concurs: "The establishing of this analogy will facilitate . . . the understanding of this

[1] Arthur Schopenhauer, *The World as Will and Idea,* trans. by R. B. Haldane and J. Kemp (Garden City, N.Y.: [Dolphin] Doubleday & Co., 1961), pp. 268–69.

exposition, which is so difficult on account of the obscurity of the subject."[2] The independence of music from the phenomenal world which it ignores is a consequence of its spacelessness, a phenomenon Hegel observed: it has no objectivity in that sense. Objectivity (or "objectification") for Schopenhauer is the crystallization, in varying degrees, of the will. Matter, even the density of matter, is such an objectification: in its lowest grade, its crudest form, it makes up the mass of the planet. Schopenhauer pursues his analogy between music and the objectified will, with results which are fanciful in the extreme:

> Bass is thus, for us, in harmony what unorganised nature, the crudest mass, upon which all rests, and from which everything originates and develops, is in the world. Now, further, in the whole of the complemental parts which make up the harmony between the bass and the leading voice singing the melody, I recognize the whole gradation of the Ideas in which the will objectifies itself. Those nearer to the bass are the lower of these grades, the still unorganised, but yet manifold phenomenal things; the higher represent to me the world of plants and beasts. The definite intervals of the scale are parallel to the definite grades of the objectification of will, the definite species in nature. The departure from the arithmetical correctness of the intervals, through some temperament, or produced by the key selected, is analogous to the departure of the individual from the type of the species. Indeed, even the impure discords, which give no definite interval, may be compared to the monstrous abortions produced by beasts of two species, or by man and beast.[3]

[2] *Ibid.*, p. 269.   [3] *Ibid.*, pp. 269–70.

The deep bass, he goes on to say, must move slowly; this is physically essential: "A quick run or shake in the low notes cannot even be imagined." Apparently Schopenhauer had never heard a performance of the *Messiah;* he would not escape so easily today. Obviously, here Schopenhauer is grinding his metaphysical axe and applying its keen edge to an area where another kind of surgical skill is called for. Later in his essay, however, he makes an important qualification and restores the subject to that general realm where analogy can profitably be sought:

> But it must never be forgotten, in the investigation of all these analogies I have pointed out, that music has no direct, but merely an indirect relation to them, for it never expresses the phenomenon, but only the inner nature, the in-itself of all phenomena, the will itself. It does not therefore express this or that particular and definite joy, this or that sorrow, or pain, or horror, or delight, or merriment, or peace of mind; but joy, sorrow, pain, horror, delight, merriment, peace of mind *themselves,* to a certain extent in the abstract, their essential nature, without accessories, and therefore without their motives. Yet we completely understand them in this extracted quintessence.[4]

The "extracted quintessence," what we might call a distillation of feeling, is the universally accessible, hence symbolic, musical image. But this image, being general, gives no specific messages, as Schopenhauer has remarked. His use of "language" in relation to music therefore seems inappropriate: "The composer reveals

[4] *Ibid.,* pp. 272–73.

the inner nature of the world, and expresses the deepest wisdom in a language which his reason does not understand."[5] Or, again, "If music is too closely united to the words, and tries to form itself according to the events, it is striving to speak a language which is not its own."[6] But if we substitute "modality" for "language" we remove that particular difficulty. Others remain.

Taking his firm stand in the world of verbal discourse and conceptualization, Kant ranked music lowest in his artistic hierarchy. Sculpture took precedence with its greater visibility. Schopenhauer, granting each modality its due, has a predilection for the vital and organic:

> We may express the distinction between the Idea and the concept, by a comparison, thus: the *concept* is like a dead receptacle, in which, whatever has been put, actually lies side by side, but out of which no more can be taken (by analytical judgment) than was put in (by synthetical reflection); the (Platonic) *Idea*, on the other hand, develops, in him who has comprehended it, ideas which are new as regards the concept of the same name; it resembles a living organism, developing itself and possessed of the power of reproduction, which brings forth what was not put into it. . . . The concept, useful as it is in life, and serviceable, necessary and productive as it is in science, is yet always barren and unfruitful in art. The comprehended Idea, on the contrary, is the true and only source of every work of art. . . . Just because the Idea is and remains the object of perception, the artist is not conscious in the abstract of the intention and aim of his work; not a concept, but an Idea floats before his mind;

[5] *Ibid.*, p. 271. [6] *Ibid.*, p. 273.

therefore he can give no justification of what he
does. He works, as people say, from pure feeling,
and unconsciously, indeed instinctively. . . . The
man of genius alone resembles the organised, as-
similating, transforming and reproducing body.
For he is indeed educated and cultured by his
predecessors and their works; but he is really
fructified only by life and the world directly,
through the impression of what he perceives;
therefore the highest culture never interferes with
his originality. All imitators, all mannerists, apprehend in concepts the nature of representative
works of art; but concepts can never impart inner
life to a work.[7]

What Schopenhauer is describing in his own
terms is a *nondiscursive symbolism*. His references to
"language," of course, are analogical. In contrast to
Kant, he accords a special efficacy to music: "The effect
of music is stronger, quicker, more necessary and in-
fallible. . . . Men have practised music in all ages without being able to account for this; content to understand
it directly, they renounce all claim to an abstract conception of this direct understanding itself."[8] He grants
the Leibnizian premise of occult numerical relationships in music as being valid so far as it goes but sees in
it only an external and formal significance:

From our standpoint, therefore, at which the
aesthetic effect is the criterion, we must attribute
to music a far more serious and deep significance,
connected with the inmost nature of the world
and our own self, and in reference to which the
arithmetical proportions, to which it may be re-

---

[7] *Ibid.*, pp. 246–47.   [8] *Ibid.*, pp. 267–68.

duced, are related, not as the thing signified, but merely as the sign.[9]

The deep and serious significance is then seen to reside in musical meaning, and not in the relationships of structural components, numerical or whatever; the meaning, what is more, is a musical Gestalt, to superimpose a term not then current. Schopenhauer's romantic phraseology can be rendered into more matter-of-fact terms without destroying his clear intent. The analogue of the emotional life which music provides is not to be understood in the correspondence of externals such as may be observed, as a matter of fact, in the relationship of rhythm to number; the pointing out of such details, though it has its utility, is about as helpful to the understanding as the parsing of one of his soliloquies would be to a comprehension of Hamlet.

What I wish to offer, however, is not paraphrase of Schopenhauer, for his own words state his meaning, but interpretation in the light of thought current at his time and afterward. The importance of his contribution to musical theory has not in general been recognized, partly because of its being buried in the context of his larger work, partly because of the phraseology of extravagant and apparently unsupported claims, but mainly because the subject, as a theoretical problem, has not commanded the attention it deserves; men are content to understand it directly.

Schopenhauer has nevertheless attempted to deal in discursive language with the questions proper

[9] *Ibid.*, p. 267.

and peculiar to the philosophy of music: What is it? What makes it go and what does it express? How is it connected with humanity and the world; how does it reflect or represent them? His answers, and he has given answers to all of them, display extraordinary insight, and later theory has given reinforcement and corroboration on many points.

I have complained of his fanciful analogies between music and nature, and of his use of the term *language*. Schopenhauer also sows confusion in his discussion of *abstraction* in its relation to music and geometrical figures:

> Music . . . is related indeed to the universality of concepts, much as they are related to particular things. Its universality, however, is by no means that empty universality of abstraction, but quite of a different kind, and is united with thorough and distinct definiteness. In this respect it resembles geometrical figures and numbers, which are the universal forms of all possible objects of experience and applicable to them all *a priori,* and yet are not abstract but perceptible and thoroughly determined.[10]

How so? The concept of "triangle" is abstract until it is given form; the concept has then, consciously or unconsciously, been embodied; and if attention is centered on its triangularity, that element is again abstracted. Similarly, a piece of music depends upon the frequency of vibrations for its pitch, upon the regulation of recurring beats for its meter, and so on; these components can be abstracted for acoustical or rhythmic

[10] *Ibid.,* p. 273.

analysis, just as an architect will geometrize when he examines an actual building or visualizes one yet to be. The Gestalt to be realized in all these examples is a concrete universal, a symbol. An actual piece of music being played is "there"; it is ephemeral, it is invisibly passing, but it is not "abstract"; its meanings are to be apprehended musically. And if they cannot be rendered verbally, it is not necessarily because the meanings are too vague, too diffused; the meanings may be, as Mendelssohn suggested, too definite for verbal explication.

Most of this, indeed, is well understood by Schopenhauer. We cannot place the blame for all the tortured semantics of abstraction in art at his door. He has provided a range for the proliferation of musical symbols that these "concrete universals" may well be challenged to justify:

> All possible efforts, excitements, and manifestations of will, all that goes on in the heart of man and that reason includes in the wide, negative concept of feeling, may be expressed by the infinite number of possible melodies, but always in the universal, in the mere form, without the material, always according to the thing-in-itself, not the phenomenon, the inmost soul, as it were, of the phenomenon, without the body.[11]

The "mere form," translated from Schopenhauer's lexicon, is the symbol which *is* its content; it does not possess a separate content or material. Such material, however, may be associated with it by virtue of artistic and temperamental affinities or by mere accident. The analogue which it provides, *qua* symbol, is

[11] *Ibid.*

general: it has no specific referents in the external
world and hence no contents in that sense. Precisely
because of this generality, music lends itself to all sorts
of juxtapositions:

> This deep relation which music has to the true
> nature of all things also explains the fact that
> suitable music played to any scene, action, event,
> or surrounding, seems to disclose to us its most
> secret meaning, and appears as the most accurate
> and distinct commentary upon it. This is so
> truly the case, that whoever gives himself up
> entirely to the impression of a symphony, seems
> to see all the possible events of life and the world
> take place in himself, yet if he reflects, he can
> find no likeness between the music and the things
> that passed before his mind.[12]

This protean character of music, this accom-
modating capacity to intensify fantasy, is attested to by
universal human experience and by the present-day
commercial exploitation to which music—or some rough
approximation of it—is subjected. When listening is
passive, the mind supplies fantasy images on its own, as
an accompaniment to the sounds; if the music follows
a text, the words will provide the images. Schopenhauer
does suggest that a relationship may be possible between
a composition and its "perceptible representation" because both may be considered as emanating from the
same inner source; when a composer has written a particularly expressive song or opera, he has discerned that
correspondence by direct inner knowledge. But conscious imitation of external phenomena Schopenhauer

[12] *Ibid.,* pp. 273–74.

deprecates, as he does battle pieces. "Such music is entirely to be rejected."

But what of listening actively to music for its own symbolism, without words and without the accompaniment of food, action, or other distractions: what is one listening for?

> The unutterable depth of all music by virtue of which it floats through our consciousness as the vision of a paradise firmly believed in yet ever distant from us, and by which also it is so fully understood and yet so inexplicable, rests on the fact that it restores to us all the emotions of our inmost nature, but entirely without reality and far removed from their pain.[13]

Schopenhauer is here presenting music as an analogue of the emotional life; and by recognizing the distance from actuality, he is assigning it to that virtual realm of the art symbol which is also the world of the mythical archetypes He hints of enchantment, of the Dionysian; he is, indeed, describing the reconciliation that opposite principles may attain in art. For the paradise Schopenhauer's hypothetical music evokes is the Apollonian ordering of enchantment. "That we may discover whether they are armed against all enchantments," said Plato. He was surely wrong in not admitting enchantments to that realm where they can be realized "entirely without reality and far removed from their pain." It was the actuality of enchantments, of the Dionysian, that Plato feared for his ideal republic. But he mistook musical symbolism for something it cannot

---

[13] *Ibid.,* p. 275.

be, assigned it an instrumental power which it does not possess in the world. Art contemplates action and produces images. Plato, great poet that he was, feared the symbolic shadows.

Despite the reiterated assertions of the long Platonic tradition, there is not the slightest evidence that music—or any other art—is a determinant in itself of character or action. Belief that art has such an instrumental function is the result of a mistaking of the ideal, or virtual, for the actual. It is ironic that Plato, supreme spokesman for the ideal, should have inaugurated and perpetuated such a confusion through his followers. All art seeks ideal expression: this is what is meant by stylized representation. The style of the art, however, is not the crux of the problem. Curt Sachs in our own day has made the mistake of supposing that ethos is closer to the ideal realm than pathos.

Failure to recognize the artistic realm of the virtual results in a hopeless confusion of that realm with the actual. When Sachs says, "The basic difference behind all these partial antitheses is that ethos aims at the thing in itself, and pathos, at its changing aspects: the first wants the thing as it ideally *is,* and pathos, as it *appears* to the senses,"[14] he fails to recognize that in an art work in which pathos, according to his canons, predominated, the "changing aspects" presented artistically *would be, as an art work, the thing in itself.* That a work in which ethos predominated would also fulfill this condition, Sachs is already willing to admit. (The

---

[14] Curt Sachs, *The Commonwealth of Art* (New York: W. W. Norton, 1946), p. 205.

distinction, incidentally, which Sachs makes between ethos-pathos and Apollonian-Dionysian is not clear.)

Schopenhauer provides the essential distance; ideally, listening to music becomes contemplation. Music, already free of space, is removed from the immediate exigencies of time. But music has an ideal time of its own, which consumes an equal portion of actual time whenever its image is projected. Time is a necessary condition but is only the field of the musical modality. The fact that a composition lasts ten minutes has no bearing on the worth of a piece, and the ten minutes can be used for its rendition during any hour of the day or night without its making the slightest musical difference. Actual time is used in music the way actual space is used in painting: and both become, as ingredients of the work of art, *virtual.*

Schopenhauer comes very close to the concept of virtual time:

> I might still have something to say about the way in which music is perceived, namely, in and through time alone, with absolute exclusion of space, and also apart from the influence of the knowledge of causality, thus without understanding; for the tones make the aesthetic impression as effect, and without obliging us to go back to their causes.[15]

It is the discursive intellect, faced with the musical image, that is "without understanding." The music constructs no syllogism, gives no lesson in history, makes no concessions to the here and now, yet it offers a kind

---

[15] Schopenhauer, p. 277.

of knowledge: immediate, presentational, and we *feel* how it is to feel: ". . . only with greater concentration, more perfectly, with intention and intelligence."[16] The music imparts—in ten minutes if need be—a meaning that is essentially independent of the passing hour.

Nietzsche delivers his pronouncements in the authoritative accents of the intoxicated poet turned lawgiver. Poets are the unacknowledged legislators of the world, said Shelley; but Nietzsche would rule openly. Suggesting the mysterious wisdom of the Delphic oracle, only absorbed and rephrased by modern man, Nietzsche speaks compellingly, poetically, and without humor. The tone of *The Birth of Tragedy From the Spirit of Music* is one of feverish exaltation. The high pitch of excitement is consonant with his theme: the glorification of the Dionysian. And music for Nietzsche is the Dionysian art *par excellence*.

Nietzsche, opposed to system though he is, displays strong ties to the Platonic tradition, including those areas in which he effects a reversal. Nietzsche is a dualist; he poses an Apollonian-Dionysian dichotomy— the dream representing Apollo and drunkenness Dionysus. But for Plato the eternal archetypes are the Reality and the empirical world a derivative one of appearance and shadow. For Nietzsche the Dionysian is primary: it encompasses and takes precedence over even the most ideal unions of the opposed forces, as he sees them in

[16] *Ibid.*, p. 278.

Attic tragedy. The primacy of process is a prefiguring of Bergson: of lived life over the dream essence, of present-day existentialism.

"That we may discover whether they are armed against all enchantments," Plato had said. But hear Nietzsche:

> This enchantment is the prerequisite for all dramatic art. Under its spell the Dionysian reveler sees himself as a satyr, *and as a satyr he in turn beholds the god,* that is, in his transformation he sees a new vision outside him as the Apollonian consummation of his own state. With this new vision the drama completes itself. . . . As the objectification of a Dionysian state, it represents not the Apollonian redemption in appearance, but, conversely, the dissolution of the individual and his unification with primordial existence. *And so the drama becomes the Apollonian embodiment of Dionysian perceptions and influences.*[17]

Here is what happens to pathos in artistic form, and here is the clarification of Sachs's ethos-pathos difficulty, stated classically.

Nietzsche is speaking of aesthetic relationships and polarities and their *rapprochement* in Greek tragedy. The quotation just given is one of the best explanations of *aesthetic distance* I have encountered. The Apollonian treatment is an indispensable element in the work of art:

[17] Friedrich Nietzsche, "The Birth of Tragedy from the Spirit of Music," in *The Philosophy of Nietzsche,* trans. by Clifton P. Fadiman, (New York: The Modern Library, 1954), pp. 989–90. (Second italics mine.)

> This joyful necessity of the dream-experience has been embodied by the Greeks in their Apollo: for Apollo, the god of all plastic energies, is at the same time the soothsaying god. He, who (as the etymology of the name indicates) is the "shining one," the deity of light, is also ruler over the fair appearance of the inner world of fantasy. The higher truth, the perfection of these states in contrast to the incompletely intelligible, everyday world, this deep consciousness of nature, healing and helping in sleep and dreams, is at the same time *the symbolical analogue* of the soothsaying faculty and of the arts generally, which makes life possible and worth living.[18]

It is by now apparent that preoccupation with *dynamism* is characteristic of Nietzsche's thought: the dream matrix itself, which he values so highly, is derivative of life. But note the rich suggestibility and prescience of his insights: his concept of the "symbolic analogue"; the artistic function of ordering and heightening the ingredients of the actual world; the archetypal ("higher truth") world Jung was to shine a searchlight upon; and of course the very Apollonian-Dionysian conflict itself which we will meet again explicitly in Stravinsky, but which is in itself a personification of polarities of artistic experience which are generally recognized. The use of mythical names is peculiarly necessary to the purposes of Nietzsche's essay but is less appropriate in a treatment of symbolic modes of human expression and experience.

The inner world of fantasy, to be sure, does not have only a fair appearance:

---

[18] *Ibid.*, pp. 953–54. (Italics mine.)

> The serious, the troubled, the sad, the gloomy, the sudden restraints, the tricks of fate, the uneasy presentiments, in short, the whole Divine Comedy of life, and the Inferno, also pass before him, not like mere shadows on the wall—for in these scenes he lives and suffers—and yet not without that fleeting sensation of appearance.[19]

Not only Jung, therefore, is presaged but Freud as well. No dream content is without significance:

> All forms speak to us; none are unimportant, none are superfluous. . . . And perhaps many will, like myself, recall that amid the dangers and terrors of dream-life they would at times, cry out in self-encouragement, and not without success, "It is only a dream! I will dream on!" I have likewise heard of persons capable of continuing one and the same dream for three and even more successive nights: facts which indicate clearly that our innermost beings, our common subconscious experiences, express themselves in dreams because they must do so and because they take profound delight in so doing.[20]

Nietzsche anticipates, here, the twentieth-century revelation that symbol making—whether in dreams, myth, or art—is a necessary and to some extent even automatic human activity, and that nature is as generous in the proliferation of images as she is in the manufacture of spermatozoa.

The fascinations of this seminal thought are endless, and we must resist the temptation to explore further. Thus far, everything said has a bearing on the

[19] *Ibid.*, p. 953.   [20] *Ibid.*, pp. 952–53.

musical symbol, though some of the ramifications have been secondary or tertiary. What of music, the Dionysian art itself? For the most part, Nietzsche speaks in very general terms, of its "spirit," its influence, its union with drama. Nietzsche is interested in the power of music to stimulate and enhance words. But without making a great point of it, he does distinguish their modalities, as in these lines which serve further to put the whole problem of program music in a nice perspective, subordinating the extramusical components (as Schopenhauer does in very different phraseology) to the inner meaning:

> Even when the tone-poet expresses his composition in pictures, when for instance he designates a certain symphony as the "pastoral" symphony, or a passage in it as the "scene by the brook," or another as the "merry gathering of rustics," these too are only symbolical representations born of music—and not perhaps the imitated objects of music—representations which can teach us nothing whatsover concerning the *Dionysian* content of music, and which indeed have no distinctive value of their own beside other pictorial expressions.[21]

In this instance Nietzsche is using "symbolical" in the sense of "signal," though he does not always do so. His *"Dionysian* content" would be the true symbol in our lexicon. Nietzsche takes the position that language attempts to imitate music. Yet "language can never adequately render the cosmic symbolism of music, because music stands in symbolic relation to the primordial

[21] *Ibid.*, p. 977.

contradiction and primordial pain in the heart of the Primal Unity, and therefore symbolizes a sphere which is beyond and before all phenomena."[22]

Am I a Philistine if I smile as I read this passage, or is the reader if he shares my reaction? As a child of the more matter-of-fact twentieth century I attempt a paraphrase and a paring down of what seems unhelpful to a sober scrutiny, and I get this: "Language can never adequately render the 'meaning' of music, because music stands in a symbolic relation to the fundamental contradictions and ambivalences at the core of life and therefore refers to experiences which are inaccessible to discursive thought." Is this too drastic a surgery? I think not. And I compare these lines with a statement by Susanne Langer:

> The real power of music lies in the fact that it can be "true" to the life of feeling in a way that language cannot; for its significant forms have that *ambivalence* of content which words cannot have. This is, I think, what Hans Mersmann meant, when he wrote: "The possibility of expressing opposites simultaneously gives the most intricate reaches of expressiveness to music as such, and carries it, in this respect, far beyond the limits of the other arts."[23]

This insight, to which a remarkable unanimity of widely separated reporters bears witness, is essentially the same as Nietzsche's.

[22] *Ibid.*, p. 979.
[23] Susanne K. Langer, *Philosophy in a New Key* (New York: Mentor Press, 1954), pp. 197–98.

Concerning the essential nature of music, Nietzsche has more to say in lines that reveal his view of music, like Schopenhauer's, to be dynamic:

> If, therefore, we may regard lyric poetry as the fulguration of music in images and concepts, we should now ask: "In what form does music *appear* in the mirror of symbolism and conception?" *It appears as will,* taking the term in Schopenhauer's sense, i.e., as the antithesis of the esthetic, purely contemplative, and passive frame of mind.[24]

Nietzsche then makes an important departure from Schopenhauer's doctrine:

> We must make as sharp a distinction as possible between the concept of essence and the concept of phenomenon; for music, according to its essence, cannot possibly be will. To be will it would have to be wholly banished from the realm of art—for the will is the unesthetic-in-itself. Yet though *essentially* it is not will, *phenomenally* it *appears* as will.[25]

If we take Schopenhauer's "will" as a figure for the whole complex of emotional life, as I think in fairness we may, then Nietzsche clearly looks upon music, not as identical with the will as Schopenhauer maintains, but as mirroring the will: reflecting, giving a picture of the emotional complex. Here is the symbolic analogue. And "distance" inheres in it: "This is the phenomenon of the lyrist: as Apollonian genius he interprets music through the image of the will, while

[24] *Nietzsche,* pp. 977–78.　　　　　　　[25] *Ibid.,* p. 978.

he himself, completely released from the desire of the will, is the pure, undimmed eye of day."[26]

"Not the phenomenon," Schopenhauer had said, "but the inmost soul." Yet music restores our emotions to us, but entirely removed from reality and far removed from their pain. Schopenhauer's "distance" is given, but formulated less explicitly than Nietzsche's. If we pursue the mirror figure, then the phenomenon of music in Nietzsche's view is the unique reflector of the will or emotional complex; not only is its function that of a mirror but it is in itself a dynamic analogue of what it reflects.[27] There is mimesis, true, but with a difference: an imitation that follows the sinuosities of the will but is "completely released from the desire of the will." "Without the material," Schopenhauer would say, "without the body." Music is the expression *ne plus ultra* of the will, or as we would prefer to say, of the emotions: an aural image of how feelings feel, how they operate.[28] "Impelled to speak of music in Apol-

---

[26] *Ibid.*

[27] "Mirror" is too static a concept to justify carrying the analogy further. What a symbol can achieve—and a mirror cannot—is an actual embodiment, in some measure, of what it "stands for."

[28] The listener hears and responds; there is an inner recognition, a correspondence between music and the self; but sometimes there are new combinations, "picturings" that are strange or difficult, that tax the hearer's resources, reflections that may not stir or delight him; the "emotional complex" reflected can be thin, exotic, repellent, or incomprehensible. The patterns must then be made familiar through repeated hearings and what occurs is a learning process in which the hearer, through his powers of discrimination, will exercise choice: rejecting as much as he retains, and influenced always by experience and desire for the known.

lonian symbols," Nietzsche says of the lyrist, "he conceives of all nature, and himself therein, only as eternal Will, Desire, Longing."[29] But music has the ascendancy: "Our whole discussion insists that lyric poetry is dependent on the spirit of music just as music itself in its absolute sovereignty does not need the picture and the concept, but merely *endures* them as accompaniments."[30] Then, himself prefiguring Tagore in words of oriental splendor: "The poems of the lyrist can express nothing which did not already lie hidden in the vast universality and absoluteness of the music which compelled him to figurative speech."[31] And further: "I must not appeal to those who make use of the pictures of the scenic processes, the words and the emotions of the performers, to approximate musical perception; for *none of these speak music as their mother-tongue, and despite these aids get no farther than the outer precincts of musical perception.*"[32]

It must be acknowledged that neither Schopenhauer or Nietzsche was propounding systematic musical theory. They were artistically sensitive and responsive men; what they reveal is insight. Nietzsche, at any rate, must himself be accorded the rank of artist. Schopenhauer's attempt to construct a comprehensive metaphysics did not give him the superiority over Nietzsche as an expositor that might be expected; yet he exerted a profound influence over the younger man, as this comparison of their writings on music alone demonstrates. In view of their respective preoccupations and the importance accorded to music in the context of their

[29] Nietzsche, p. 978.

[30] *Ibid.*

[31] *Ibid.*, pp. 978–79.

[32] *Ibid.*, p. 1066. (Italics mine.)

works, it seems futile to explore further their differences concerning music and its connection with will, particularly since Nietzsche gives no systematic support to his semantic distinction. The general rapport of their views is remarkable.

Nietzsche's distinction, however, brings him closer than Schopenhauer to the concept of the symbol we are developing, though his actual use of the term is loose. The Dionysian transcendence of self which Nietzsche so loved to speak of does emphasize the human participant and his role in symbolic experience, even though his own boundaries are enlarged and blurred. In contrasting with this fervent music the earlier Doric genre which Plato extolled, Nietzsche says:

> The very element which forms the essence of Dionysian music (and hence of music in general) is carefully excluded as un-Apollonian: namely, the emotional power of the tone, the uniform flow of the melos, and the utterly incomparable world of harmony. In the Dionysian dithyramb man is incited to the greatest exaltation of all his symbolic faculties; something never before experienced struggles for utterance—the annihilation of the veil of Maya, Oneness as the soul of the race, and of nature itself. The essence of nature is now to be expressed symbolically; we need a new world of symbols.[33]

Nietzsche does not articulate a theory of the musical symbol—what it is, what it does. But virtually all the ingredients are present: its aural autonomy and intensity, its nonverbal intelligibility and reverberation,

[33] *Ibid.*, pp. 959–60.

the element of distance in the contemplation of it (which in musical discourse is an active hearing), and its relevance as a symbolic analogue to the life of "willing, longing, moaning, rejoicing." There is something more—another ingredient—that Nietzsche includes: the cathartic power of art: "When the will is most imperiled, *art* approaches, as a redeeming and healing enchantress; she alone may transform these horrible reflections on the terror and absurdity of existence into representations with which man may live."[34]

Given this much explicit acknowledgment of the facets of music, it is but a short step to the concept of the musical symbol. This concept synthesizes all these elements and recognizes in the phenomenon of music that indissoluble body of its formal expression, its integrity of meaning contained only in that unique structure which is an actual embodiment, in some measure, of what it stands for: an assertion, tonally, that goes beyond the scope of mirroring the emotions. This step Nietzsche does not take. But we have come a long way from Plato!

> For to me the *Doric* state and Doric art are explicable only as a permanent citadel of the Apollonian. For an art so defiantly prim, and so encompassed with bulwarks, a training so warlike and rigorous, a political structure so cruel and relentless, could endure for any length of time only by incessant opposition to the titanic-barbaric nature of the Dionysian.[35]

So far as the union of Dionysian and Apollonian elements in Attic drama is concerned, this ap-

---

[34] *Ibid.*, p. 985.   [35] *Ibid.*, p. 968.

pears to be in Nietzsche's terms a precarious balance of tensions: an ordering of the dynamism at the core of life. Nietzsche seems to stretch these tensions to the breaking point; the artistic (and in our narrower purview, musical) picturing may nevertheless be whole. It is outside the scope of this book to consider all the qualitative components of the musical symbol in their dynamic interrelationships, yet these are profoundly pertinent to further work in comprehensive theory. It is enough for now to suggest that Nietzsche remains, finally, a dualist, notwithstanding his awareness of process and its all-encompassing demands. The kind of armed truce he postulates between Apollo and Dionysus is not reconciliation on a deep level; the balance is superficial, unsteady. Lancelot Law Whyte holds that a fundamentally dualistic mode of thought has been characteristic of European man for two thousand years; he sees Nietzsche as an extreme type and as a genius who signals, in certain respects, the outer limits of these dualistic possibilities. "That we may discover whether they are armed against all enchantments," was Plato's concern. "This enchantment is the prerequisite for all dramatic art," said Nietzsche. "The genius of man lies in his growing faculty for enchantment without illusion," says Whyte. But let us not make the mistake of equating vision—even the vision of Apollo and Dionysus locked in never-ending conflict!—with illusion.

Nietzsche is careful to distinguish between what is given by nature and the worlds created by artists, recognizing as natural the "pictorial world of dreams"— that archetypal world of symbols Jung was to explore— "whose completeness is not dependent upon the intel-

lectual attitude or the artistic culture of any single being." There is also the natural reality of the Dionysian.

> With reference to these immediate art-states of
> nature, every artist is an "imitator," that is to
> say, either an Apollonian artist in dreams, or a
> Dionysian artist in ecstasies, or finally—as for
> example in Greek tragedy—at once artist in both
> dreams and ecstasies: so we may perhaps picture
> him sinking down in his Dionysian drunkenness
> and mystical self-abnegation, alone, and apart
> from the singing revelers, and we may imagine
> how now, through Apollonian dream-inspiration,
> his own state, i.e., his oneness with the primal
> nature of the universe, is revealed to him in a
> *symbolical dream-picture.*[36]

Nietzsche does, nevertheless, point toward a rapprochement, or at the very least, containment of contraries on
another level: the level of symbolic expression with its
capacity to render paradox, to synthesize opposites by
means of formalized articulations. The articulations,
when they work, yield insight.

The examination of Nietzsche's contributions
is not yet ended, though it might be thought that the
constituents of his musical thought, insofar as they can
be had from a single source, have now been assembled.
But his rich insights are scattered throughout *The Birth
of Tragedy;* and he is no more compounding a neat
formula for musical theory than he is constructing a
systematic philosophical argument. I think it is the
absence of ordered presentation (and the hyperbole of
his poetic diction) that must explain the insufficient at-

[36] *Ibid.,* p. 957.

tention his ideas on music have received—insufficient, certainly, in view of their cogency. It is also probable that Nietzsche has appeared to musical theorists in general as an unlikely source of valuable insights.

I want particularly to note Nietzsche's repeated references to a process of symbol building in which the components are given objectivity: "The Apollonian appearances, in which Dionysus objectifies himself." And the transforming power of the symbol, whereby actuality is made virtual, is a recurrent theme: "The world of day is veiled, and a new world, clearer, more intelligible, more vivid and yet more shadowy than the old, is, by a perpetual transformation, born and reborn before our eyes."[37]

Another aspect of the symbol which is prominent in Nietzsche's thought, to which we will be returning in other contexts, is its capacity to transcend the limits of language and thus to defy explication within those limits. Transcendence, as used here, need carry no supernatural connotations whatsoever. Nietzsche, in pointing to Socrates as the exemplar of the "theoretical" man, opposes him with all the force of his own temperament: "Whenever the truth is unveiled, the artist will always cling with rapt gaze to whatever still remains veiled after the unveiling; but the theoretical man gets his enjoyment and satisfaction out of the cast-off veil."[38] Nietzsche regards as illusion the "belief that, with the clue of logic, thinking can reach to the nethermost depths of being, and that thinking can not only perceive being but even modify it."[39] Socrates, how-

[37] *Ibid.,* p. 992.   [38] *Ibid.,* p. 1028.   [39] *Ibid.,* p. 1029.

ever, haunted by a dream apparition which admonished him to "practice music," was not invulnerable.

> The voice of the Socratic dream-vision is the only sign of doubt as to the limits of logic. "Perhaps"—thus he must have asked himself—"what is not intelligible to me is not therefore unintelligible? Perhaps there is a realm of wisdom from which the logician is shut out? Perhaps art is even a necessary correlative of, and supplement to, science?"[40]

Here we should recall the comment of Susanne Langer, herself the author of a work on symbolic logic: "The limitations inherent in verbal conception and discursive forms of thought are the very *raison d'être* of artistic expression."[41]

Nietzsche sees in the development of the new Attic dithyramb a degenerate music, influenced by the conceptual, "scientific" spirit of Socrates, and leading to involved programs characterized by "effective tricks and mannerisms":

> Music is outrageously manipulated so as to be the imitative portrait of a phenomenon, for instance, of a battle or a storm at sea; and thus, of course, it has been utterly robbed of its mythopoeic power . . . a musically imitated battle of this sort exhausts itself in marches, signal-sounds, etc., and *our imagination is arrested precisely by these superficialities.* Tone-painting is thus in every respect the antithesis of true music with its mythopoeic power.[42]

[40] *Ibid.*, p. 1026.
[41] Langer, "Abstraction in Art," *JAAC*, XXII, No. 4 (Summer, 1964), 380.
[42] Nietzsche, pp. 1042–43. (Italics mine.).

Nietzsche goes on to castigate the "word-and-tone-rhetoric of the passions" in the *stilo rappresentativo* of the seventeenth century, that "rapidly changing endeavor to affect now the conceptual and representative faculty of the hearer, now his musical sense."[43] It is ironic that Nietzsche should compain of this *mélange de genres* in a work dedicated to Wagner.

Musical numerology receives short shrift from Nietzsche. Speaking of the demon of German music, he holds that it will be understood "neither by means of the zig-zag and arabesque work of operatic melody, nor with the aid of the counting-board of fugue and contrapuntal dialectic."[44] Optimistic and facile depictions of "beauty," he likewise deplores: "It is precisely the function of tragic myth to convince us that even the ugly and unharmonious is an artistic game which the will plays with itself in the eternal fullness of its joy."[45] He speaks of the "wonderful significance of *musical dissonance*," suggesting that here is the essential key for expressing the tragic. It is pertinent to observe that the use of chromaticism to achieve an effect of pathos is characteristic of what might be termed the "common practice" period in Western music: a period of well over three hundred years, beginning with the establishment of secure major-minor tonality in the seventeenth century and proceeding to the disintegration of that system in the hands of many composers in the twentieth. No doubt the phenomenon can be observed earlier, as in the madrigals of Gesualdo. But with Bach and Mozart, for example, and certainly for numerous nine-

[43] *Ibid.*, p. 1052.　　[44] *Ibid.*, p. 1058.　　[45] *Ibid.*, pp. 1084–85.

teenth-century composers—Wagner particularly—a concentrated chromaticism was a deliberate expressive device which, being primarily musical, went considerably beyond text-painting, though it was sometimes put to the service of words.

The strongly chromatic style of Schoenberg's composition lends itself to musical expressions of pathos, regardless of whether the context is still tonal, as in *Pierrot Lunaire,* or without a key "center." From this point of view it is no accident that the themes of musical Expressionism are characteristically lugubrious. Although attempts have been made to look upon twelve-tone writing as a technique only, the history of the movement belies this. The very effort to transcend fixed tonal boundaries was Romantic in impulse, and Schoenberg was hailed as a prophet of the "inner self" by his early disciples. The extramusical associations of Schoenberg's compositions, when they carry such labels, attest to a Romantic temperament, as do his utterances. Adherents of that idiom find great intensity in it, and Schoenberg himself looked upon the course of his musical evolution as organic and inevitable. Despite the facile pronouncements of Sachs and others who hold that the preoccupations of Schoenberg are technical and external—though of course these can be the preoccupations of composers in any idiom—it seems more plausible to believe that the motivating forces of the Viennese Expressionists were—to be redundant—*expressive* ones. Expressive power will make itself felt in whatever idiom is employed, though an exotic or very difficult musical vocabulary may render certain compositions inaccessible to all but a few initiates.

The aims and preoccupations as well as the spirit of Viennese Expressionism seems to me to have been marvelously presaged by Nietzsche in the passage that follows:

> Is it not possible that by calling to our aid the musical relation of dissonance, we may meanwhile have essentially facilitated the difficult problem of the tragic effect? For we now understand what it means to wish to view tragedy and at the same time to have a longing beyond that viewing: a frame of mind, which, referring to the artistically employed dissonance, we should have to characterize simply by saying that we desire to hear and at the same time have a longing beyond the hearing. That striving for the infinite, the beating wings of longing accompanying the highest delight in the clearly perceived reality, remind us that in both states we must recognize a Dionysian phenomenon.[46]

I have said that Nietzsche's concerns, in *The Birth of Tragedy*, are aesthetic. He explicitly raises this question: *How is music related to image and concept?*

> Image and concept, under the influence of a truly corresponding music, acquire a higher significance. Dionysian art therefore is wont to exercise two kinds of influences on the Apollonian art-faculty: music incites to the *symbolic-intuition* of Dionysian universality, and music allows the symbolic image to emerge *in its highest significance*. . . . I infer the capacity of music to give birth to *myth* (the most significant exemplar), and particularly the *tragic* myth: the myth which expresses Dionysian knowledge in symbols.

[46] *Ibid.*, p. 1085.

. . . Music at its greatest intensity must seek to
attain also to its highest symbolization.[47]

This, too, is Expressionism. Or, at the very least,
expression!

Bergson, the relevance of whose thought to
music is considered in Chapter 4, speaks of "entering
into" an object of contemplation, by an intellectual "act
of intuition." *One gets inside;* this is metaphor. "For
the true poet," says Nietzsche, "a metaphor is not a figure of speech, but a vicarious image which actually
hovers before him in place of a concept."[48] Bergson,
philosopher-artist, allows the metaphor to remain implied. Nietzsche comes close to this; he looks upon art
as being not "out there," not separate from the world,
but as "the unvarnished expression of truth"[49]—a phrase
Bergson might have used—and in its contemplation "we
actually have the individual surrendering himself by
the fact of his entrance into an alien nature."[50]

The Bergsonian world of process is Dionysian
in spirit, though he does not say so. Where the dynamism of Schopenhauer and Nietzsche is balanced by
repose—the Idea, the Primal Unity, the Apollonian
dream state—for Bergson all is dynamism, all process:
there is only movement. And in holding a mirror up to
that world, music performs a role that is apposite to a
degree Bergson himself scarcely realized.

[47] *Ibid.,* pp. 1037–38.
[48] *Ibid.,* p. 988.
[49] *Ibid.,* p. 986.
[50] *Ibid.,* p. 989.

CHAPTER FOUR

BERGSONIAN DYNAMISM AND MUSIC

* * * THE RECOGNITION OF REALITY AS MOBILE appears to be the central organizing principle in Bergson's thought. Under his dynamic aegis ideas similar to his, but endowed with a different quality by other minds (for example, the "force" of Spencer, postulated because of evidences of changes observed *ex post facto* rather than experienced), are subtly transmuted: so that instead of the commonplaces of "change" or "movement" we are given *élan vital,* key words pregnant with meaning. "A great current of creative energy is precipitated into matter, to wrest from it what it can."[1]

Bergson, in contrast to Schopenhauer and Nietzsche, breaks completely with Platonic idealism:

---

[1] Henri Bergson, *The Two Sources of Morality and Religion,* trans. by R. Ashley Audra and Cloudesley Brereton (New York: [Anchor] Doubleday & Co., 1956), p. 209.

> The whole of philosophy which begins with Plato and culminates in Plotinus is the development of a principle which may be formulated thus: "There is more in the immutable than in the moving, and we pass from the stable to the unstable by a mere diminution." *Now it is the contrary which is true.*[2]

Mobility is the concept by means of which we may gain entrance to Bergson's thought; and in its relation to time mobility is of central importance to a consideration of music, once we have ruled out Keats's "ditties of no tone" and other petrified or frozen counterparts. For Bergson—as for the musical performer who transforms written indications into actual sound—it is the expression of mobility which is primary, "given," "the reality which flows."[3] With points in space, ab-

---

[2] Bergson, *An Introduction to Metaphysics,* trans. by T. E. Hulme (New York: Liberal Arts Press, 1949), p. 54. (Italics mine.)

[3] The clearest explanation of what Bergson intends mobility to convey is given in his reference to Zeno's arrow, an illustration of which he was fond. For his explicit discussion of this problem we turn to *Creative Evolution,* pp. 335–36. (See bibliography.)

"Take the flying arrow. At every moment, says Zeno, it is motionless, for it cannot have time to move, that is, to occupy at least two successive positions, unless at least two moments are allowed it. At a given moment, therefore, it is at rest at a given point. Motionless in each point of its course, it is motionless during all the time that it is moving.

"Yes, if we suppose that the arrow can ever be in a point of its course. Yes again, if the arrow, which is moving, ever coincides with a position, which is motionless. But the arrow never *is* in any point of its course. The most we can say is that it might be there, in this sense, that it passes there and might stop there. It is true that if it did stop there, it would be at rest there, and at this point it is no longer movement that we should have to do with. . . . A single movement is entirely, by the hypothesis, a movement between two stops; if there are intermediate stops, it is no

stracted from the mobility of Zeno's arrow by the conceptualizing intellect, we will never arrive at movement (which is single), not even with an infinite number of such points which are merely so many "snapshots":

> With stoppages, however numerous they may be, we shall never make mobility; whereas, if mobility is given, we can, by means of diminution, obtain from it by thought as many stoppages as we desire. In other words, *it is clear that fixed concepts may be extracted by our thought from mobile reality; but there are no means of reconstructing the mobility of the real with fixed concepts.*[4]

And, as he observes in the last section of *The Two Sources of Morality and Religion,* "It is always the stop which requires explanation, and not the movement."[5]

How then is reality in its essential mobility to be apprehended and experienced? By intuition. Berg-

----

longer a single movement. At bottom, the illusion arises from this, that the movement, once effected, has laid along its course a motionless trajectory on which we can count as many immobilities as we will. From this we conclude that the movement, *whilst being effected,* lays at each instant beneath it a position with which it coincides. We do not see that the trajectory is created in one stroke, although a certain time is required for it; and that though we can divide at will the trajectory once created, we cannot divide its creation, which is an act in progress and not a thing. To suppose that the moving body *is* at a point of its course is to cut the course in two by a snip of the scissors at this point, and to substitute two trajectories for the single trajectory which we were first considering. It is to distinguish two successive acts where, by the hypothesis, there is only one. In short, it is to attribute to the course itself of the arrow everything that can be said of the interval that the arrow has traversed, that is to say, to admit *a priori* the absurdity that movement coincides with immobility."

[4] *Ibid.,* p. 51.
[5] *Two Sources,* p. 312.

son distinguishes three ways of knowing an object: the way of analysis by the discursive *intellect* which examines the object from the outside and which will never obtain more than relative knowledge; the way of *instinct;* and the way of instinctive-intellect or intellectual-instinct he calls *intuition.* Intuition is the way of entering into the object directly without mediating symbols; this Bergson describes as *intellectual sympathy.* "I insert myself . . . by an effort of imagination. . . . I am inside the object itself. . . . I have rejected all translations in order to possess the original . . . in its entirety . . . without, however, exhausting it or impoverishing its essence."[6]

Intuition, says Bergson, is simple. "There is nothing mysterious in this faculty."[7] He refers repeatedly to its use in terms of *effort:* an emphasis which sets him apart from many other observers of the characteristic manifestations of that faculty. This aspect of intuitive apprehension will be examined later in its relevance to music. Other facets of his world view must be rapidly summarized before we can investigate music in proper Bergsonian perspective.

The imaginative projection of the self into an object, in order to experience its primal unity (Nietzsche!), its absolute quality, seems a kind of inversion of Whitehead's "ingress" into actuality, an ingress of that which, from the world of possibilities, is in process of being realized. But Whitehead's world of actuality in space-time is presumably, for Bergson, the jumping-off place on which one gets set for the act of intuition. In

---

[6] *Introduction to Metaphysics,* p. 22.
[7] *Ibid.,* p. 60.

other words, there is another mode of ingress into another actuality.[8]

If Bergson recognizes this imaginative projection as metaphorical, he never says so. Suppose we accept such projection as a fact and ask how it is to be effected—and this request for direction could be asked without profaning a philosopher who is truly gifted in being explicit about other matters—and receive this answer: "We at once place ourselves in it by an effort of intuition."[9] The answer, to be sure, is explicit: and so stated, very effective artistically. Yet one cannot help wondering if philosophically it is not begging the question.

Almost in the manner of a Zen monk Bergson uses, whether he intends it or not, what proves to be a kind of shock technique to break up habitual patterns of thought. He is requiring a reversal of the characteristic function of the mind, and he makes this a definition: "*To philosophize, therefore, is to invert the habitual direction of the work of thought . . . to adopt the mobile continuity of the outlines of things.*"[10] Change is postulated as being itself the reality, and not, as in the Platonic tradition, a mere shifting semblance of an unchanging, permanent—and static—reality that

---

[8] Bergson was a strong influence on Whitehead, who found virtually everything acceptable in the Bergsonian metaphysics except the rejection of *space*. "Whitehead found himself unable to understand how the use of spatial concepts in scientific procedure could enable the scientists to predict with the precision they achieve, were spatialization the falsification of fact which Bergson maintained." (F. S. C. Northrop, "Whitehead's Philosophy of Science," in *The Philosophy of Alfred North Whitehead*, P. A. Schilpp, ed., p. 169. See bibliography.)
[9] *Introduction to Metaphysics*, p. 47.
[10] *Ibid.*, p. 52.

lies behind all change. Reality is dynamic and accessible only to intuition which grasps it whole; while the intellect can know only the broken-up fragments, the stoppages of flow symbolized by verbal concepts. The intellect, in Bergson's view, is an instrumental means of dealing with objects in the world; it has great practical utility, but it does not have the capacity to transcend measurement or to synthesize disparate particulars in a perception of absolute knowledge. Its function is analytical. Bergson maintains one cannot pass from analysis to intuition, but it is possible to move from intuition to analysis.

Bergson's refusal to employ intellectual concepts to describe experience which for the discursive mind is inaccessible and incomprehensible is characteristic of the mystical consciousness: or perhaps it would be truer to say that it is simply further evidence—as mystics have claimed with impressive unanimity—of the impossibility of such translation. If this is the case, Bergson's use of language (as in the dictum *to place oneself within an object*) must be regarded as symbolical.[11] All of Bergson's acts of intuition are, indeed, examples of symbolic apprehension, or what Jaspers

[11] As W. T. Stace in his interesting and highly conjectural book, *Time and Eternity*, would hold (see bibliography). Two mutually exclusive orders of time and eternity, permitting only a symbolic reference in the former to the religious infinite, seem to avoid some of the difficulties in Bergson's thought, though the *interpenetration* at every point of time and space which Stace postulates appears to raise the whole question anew. Stace's "negative divine," of which Bergson, if my juxtaposition is correct, has an intuition, is characterized by Bergson (not, of course, in Stace's terms) as the *eternal,* but empty of the *concrete duration* which distinguishes reality.

calls "cypher-reading." Bergson himself rejected the term *symbol* altogether because it denoted for him the "literal symbol," or "sign."

Bergson makes passing references to music throughout his works, but the art is not central to his awareness and he does not readily turn to it for illustration. Much less then than Nietzsche is he an expositor of musical theory. Yet the close correspondence between his ideas and their objectification in music may, in the absence of explicit statements by Bergson himself, be inferred: and then repeatedly observed. Though it may seem bold to point to such connections, I believe the thesis will recommend itself. That Bergson was musically unsophisticated is suggested in these lines:

> Thus, in music, the rhythm and measure suspend the normal flow of our sensations and ideas by causing our attention to swing to and fro between fixed points, and they take hold of us with such force that even the faintest imitation of a groan will suffice to fill us with the utmost sadness.[12]

But let us ignore the groan and give attention to the "fixed points," as these determine the duration of the piece. "If musical sounds affect us more powerfully than the sounds of nature, the reason is that nature confines itself to *expressing* feelings, whereas music *suggests* them to us."[13] Here we must clarify terms, as

[12] Bergson, *Time and Free Will*, trans. by F. L. Pogson (New York: [Torchbook] Harper & Brothers, 1960), pp. 14–15.
[13] *Ibid.*, p. 15.

with Bergson's "symbol." If "suggests" is rendered as "reminds," we will see that there is a recovery of experience of the kind that occurs in artistic apprehension: a remembering in the present—and hence a contemplation, a sensation of aesthetic distance:

> How will the expressive or rather suggestive power of music be explained, if not by admitting that we repeat to ourselves the sounds heard, so as to carry ourselves back into the psychic state out of which they emerged, an original state, which nothing will express, but which something may suggest, viz., the very motion and attitude which the sounds impart to our body?[14]

This brings us to a significant aspect of Bergson's thought, not yet touched upon, which is integral to his mode of intuition and to further discussion of music in his terms: it is the apprehension of *durée*—duration or real time. This is an intriguing but difficult concept. Bergson is careful to make many qualifications and distinctions in order to save *durée* from abstraction, which seems to be its fate if we postulate it as something transcending the immediacy of the flux. The concrete content of that flux is what Bergson is most anxious to maintain. If we recognize the ceaseless change that is mobility, we see that it takes place in time, it uses up time as its essential condition of being—not as a separate thing which it devours. This is real duration. Bergson means something more by *durée* than heterogeneous slices of experience, selected anywhere at random. He necessarily makes the individual consciousness his start-

[14] *Ibid.*, p. 44. Roger Sessions, in *The Musical Experience*, explores this idea. (See bibliography.)

ing point, and he acknowledges, as characteristic of mind, the existence both of a *"multiplicity* of successive states of consciousness, and . . . a *unity* which binds them together. *Duration will be the 'synthesis' of this unity and this multiplicity."*[15]

Duration, thus expounded, seems to be something in the nature of a *tertium quid,* born of the unity and multiplicity of the intuiting consciousness. Fortunately Bergson gives us a musical illustration:

> There are, indeed . . . two possible conceptions of time, the one free from all alloy, the other surreptitiously bringing in the idea of space. *Pure duration* is the form which the succession of our conscious states assumes when our ego lets itself *live,* when it refrains from separating its present state from its former states. For this purpose it need not be entirely absorbed in the passing sensation or idea; for then, on the contrary, it would no longer *endure.* Nor need it forget its former states: it is enough that, in recalling these states, it does not set them alongside its actual state as one point alongside another, but *forms both the past and the present states into an organic whole,* as happens when we recall the notes of a tune, melting, so to speak, into one another. Might it not be said that, even if these notes succeed one another, yet we perceive them in one another, and that their totality may be compared to a living being whose parts, although distinct, permeate one another just because they are so closely connected? The proof is that, if we interrupt the rhythm by dwelling longer than is right on one note of the tune, it is not its exaggerated length, as length, which will warn us of our mistake, but the qualitative change thereby caused in the

[15] *Introduction to Metaphysics,* p. 46. (Italics for the final sentence are mine.)

whole of the musical phrase. We can thus conceive of succession without distinction, and think of it as a mutual penetration, an interconnexion and organization of elements, each one of which represents the whole, and cannot be distinguished or isolated from it except by abstract thought.[16]

This is very close to the theory of "involuntary memory" developed by Marcel Proust—who was strongly influenced by Bergson's thought—in *Remembrance of Things Past:* certain sensations (inspired by the taste of a *madeleine* dipped in tea, the sound of a hammer striking a car wheel or similar sound suggesting it, the noise of a hot-water pipe, or the exquisite phrase of the Vinteuil Sonata) had the power to trigger a response in the narrator, making it possible for his being

> to seize, isolate, immobilise for the duration of a lightning flash what it never apprehends, namely, a fragment of time in its pure state. . . . I felt them as if they were occurring simultaneously in the present moment and in some distant past, which the sound of the spoon against the plate, or the unevenness of the flagstones, or the peculiar savour of the *madeleine* even went so far as to make coincide with the present, leaving me uncertain in which period I was . . . qualities independent of all considerations of time . . . the only environment in which he could live and enjoy the essence of things, that is to say, entirely outside of time.[17]

Bergson does not speak, to be sure, of getting outside of time; and the particular kind of ecstatic

---

[16] *Time and Free Will,* pp. 100–101. (Italics for "pure duration" and "forms both the past and the present states into an organic whole" are mine.)

[17] Marcel Proust, *The Past Recaptured,* trans. by Frederick A. Blossom (New York: Modern Library, 1932), pp. 196–98.

experience which the Proustian narrator describes falls
short of the "complete mysticism" that Bergson advocates; this ecstasy (and, indeed, Proust's literary style)
has a static quality. But the involuntary memory which
could not be forced by effort seems remarkably similar
to the exposition of *durée*. Both *durée* and Proust's
"real time" seem to belong to *virtual* time—as time in
music may be described as virtual—rather than actual
time.

Again, Bergson supplies a musical example of
durée:

> Let us listen to a melody, allowing ourselves to
> be lulled by it: do we not have the clear percep-
> tion of a movement which is not attached to a
> mobile, of a change without anything changing?
> *This change is enough, it is the thing itself. And
> even if it takes time, it is still indivisible; if the
> melody stopped sooner it would no longer be the
> same sonorous whole, it would be another, equally
> indivisible.*[18]

Bergson continues:

> We have, no doubt, a tendency to divide it and
> to picture, instead of the uninterrupted continu-
> ity of melody, a juxtaposition of distinct notes.
> But why? Because we are thinking of the discon-
> tinuous series of efforts we should be making to
> recompose approximately the sound heard if we
> were doing the singing, and also because our audi-
> tory perception has acquired the habit of absorb-
> ing visual images. *We therefore listen to the mel-
> ody through the vision which an orchestra-leader*

[18] Bergson, *The Creative Mind*, trans. by Mabelle L. Andison (New York: Philosophical Library, 1946), p. 174. (Italics
mine.)

would have of it as he watched its score. We picture notes placed next to one another upon an
imaginary piece of paper. We think of a key-
board upon which some one is playing, of the bow
going up and down, of the musicians, each one
playing his part along with the others. *If we do
not dwell on these spatial images, pure change remains, sufficient unto itself, in no way divided, in
no way attached to a "thing" which changes.*[19]

Pursuing his analogy with music, Bergson describes *durée* as the indivisible melody of the inner life,
which goes on from the beginning to the end of conscious existence. *Durée* is that which has been called
time— but it is indivisible time:

When we listen to a melody we have the purest
impression of succession we could possibly have
—an impression as far removed as possible from
that of simultaneity—and *yet it is the very continuity of the melody and the impossibility of breaking it up which make that impression upon us.*
If we cut it up into distinct notes, into so many
"befores" and "afters," we are bringing spatial
images into it and impregnating the succession
with simultaneity: in space, and only in space, is
there a clear-cut distinction of parts external to
one another. I recognize moreover that it is in
spatialized time that we ordinarily place ourselves. We have no interest in listening to the
uninterrupted humming of life's depths. And yet,
that is where real duration is. Thanks to it, the
more or less lengthy changes we witness within us
and in the external world, *take place in a single
identical time.* Thus, whether it is a question of
the internal or the external, of ourselves or of
things, *reality is mobility itself. . . .*

[19] *Ibid.,* p. 174. (Italics mine.)

> An attention to life, sufficiently powerful and
> sufficiently separated from all practical interest,
> would thus include in an undivided present *the
> entire past history of the conscious person. . . .
> What we have is a present which endures.*[20]

If *durée* is looked on in this light, it will not
be subject to the dismissal which Bertrand Russell accords it, when he speaks of "the confusion between
present remembering and the past event remembered,
which seems to be at the bottom of Bergson's theory of
time."[21] Both Bergson and Proust regard the past as
possessed with the present in some way that goes beyond
merely remembering. This is why I believe that the
time experienced is in some way ideal, or virtual, rather
than actual; "real duration," in short, is virtual and, as
such, it may be real enough. Again, if this is true,
logical analysis will be frustrated in every attempt to
deal with it, and references to the experience must be
looked upon as symbolic. Russell's account of "duration," before he launches into interpretation, is a
helpful clarification.[22]

Notwithstanding Bergson's scattered references
to the lulling or hypnotic effect of music—which might
be expected to trigger an involuntary memory—his intuition is realized through effort, or what he referred to
above as "attention to life." Music, as a symbolic analogue to life, requires equal attention if it is not to be
dismissed as a soporific. It seems unlikely that Bergson

[20] *Ibid.*, pp. 176–77, pp. 179–80. (Italics mine.)
[21] Bertrand Russell, *A History of Western Philosophy* (New
York: Simon and Schuster, 1945), p. 807.
[22] *Ibid.*, p. 806.

was fully aware of the implicit support of his doctrines that music affords.

Its effectuality for this purpose is at once apparent when we read that the experience of duration, according to Bergson, cannot be "translated" into terms of the conceptualizing intellect, cannot be frozen into the "immobility of a point of view." Again, "It is quite otherwise if we place ourselves from the first, by an effort of intuition, *in the concrete flow of duration.* Certainly, we shall then find no logical reason for positing multiple and diverse durations.[23] These lines, aside from reiterating his thesis, contain a tribute (perhaps unintended) by Bergson to the role of reason.

Mobility, we have seen, is intuitively apprehended in time. Its necessity for space in which matter has objectified Bergson does not speak of; that this was a source of dissatisfaction to Whitehead has been observed. Matter, from Bergson's standpoint (a spatial concept!), appears to be an obstacle—a concentrated inertia, as it were—which the *élan vital* must struggle against. Yet it would seem that an object, by definition, would require a spatial mode. If space, as Bergson said, is a falsification in fact, then there might not be the difficulties in placing oneself inside an object that suggest themselves in such profusion to the intellect.

Music alone in its peculiar modality avoids this dilemma.

Schopenhauer emphasized the nonspatial character of music. We see that Bergson, more than Schopenhauer, more than Nietzsche, has removed music

[23] *Introduction to Metaphysics,* p. 48. (Italics mine.)

from the world of objectivity so that it can be apprehended by the liberated perception—perceived whole,
entered into (like all experience of *durée*, through attention to life)—freed for the act of contemplation. The
experience is its own objectivity: the subject of contemplation, from which the hearer is not separate, being in
this instance an aural symbol. Here, it appears, is
aesthetic contemplation raised to a higher power, in
which the beholder—or the listener—is not separated
from what he intuits. Bergson attempts to retain the
content which Schopenhauer writes out when he says
that music "restores to us all the emotions of our inmost
nature but entirely without reality and far removed
from their pain.[24] But for Bergson *durée* is lived: it is
its own objectivity; we are not leaving out anything.
Yet the experience of *real duration* that he describes,
in transcending the immediate, does inevitably impart
to the consciousness a measure of detachment; there
may be ecstasy, but the experience is structured: there
is the intuition of a Gestalt; there is order. There is *art*

A crucial distinction must be made here. In
the passages quoted, Schopenhauer and Nietzsche are
both, though to an unequal degree, making aesthetic
pronouncements upon music; their self-consciousness as
expositors implies an awareness of their somewhat theoretical role. That is to say, they assume distance consciously or unconsciously. Bergson does nothing of the
sort. He is speaking not of art, except when it serves for
illustration, but of lived life; and he expects, it would
seem, the most literal carrying-out of his injunctions.

[24] Arthur Schopenhauer, *The World as Will and Idea*, trans.
by **R. B. Haldane** and **J. Kemp** (Garden City, N.Y.: [Dol-
phin] Doubleday & Co., 1961), p. 275.

But when carried out in the empirical world, his directions are productive of art: they impose the virtual upon the actual. Bergson is temperamentally an artist; he is fervently committed to the demands of his temperament, and the world must yield.

His expectations of experience can probably be fulfilled only in art, where the attention swings "to and fro between fixed points"; but Bergson will no more acknowledge such a distinct realm than he will admit our inability to enter, Houdini-like, into an object. He requires active participation as the necessary test of truth, but through the introspective mode of intuition and only through that mode. How appropriate that means of participation would be outside the realm of art is not the immediate concern here; but the appropriateness of that means to musical apprehension is a problem we are prepared to consider.

Let us limit ourselves therefore to what is relevant to music. I have stated that musical experience is as empirical as anything can possibly be. Another person may tell you about his musical reactions, but he cannot have your experience for you; he does not hear with your ears nor intuit meanings with your intelligence. The experience, in essence, is therefore private. The only possible verification of what music is, what it does, takes place in the listener; all other considerations, even though they may be important, are tangential to this. Without falsifying his intent, we may paraphrase Bergson's "attention to life" as "attention to music." "We cannot understand music," said Tagore, "unless we wish to hear it."

Whether our experience of space is real or

illusory will not greatly matter for the Bergsonian test: the experience of music will—given the indispensable effort and attention—be nonspatial in feeling. The listener's apprehension is not directed outward; he experiences the sounds within himself. The modality of music is indeed mobile and it uses up time. Nothwithstanding the efforts of color organists or the whole crew of "synesthetists," we do not see music; it does not require a spatial mode. Music, to be precise, provides an analogue of Bergson's *durée*. It is difficult to imagine any way other than through one of the modalities of art that *durée* can be realized in human consciousness. But through such a modality—of ideal hearing, for example—*durée* can move from conjecture to demonstration. Music is a particular content of virtual time; and even an articulation as evanescent as Chopin's "Minute Waltz" moves in a realm coextensive with the world of the grandfather clock and in no way integral to the actuality of that clock or any other, although the swinging pendulum of the machine may measure a particular playing of the waltz—its duration in actual (and hence not real, not ideal) time. However, *durée*—the Bergsonian mobility—is in the music itself.

Bergson's annihilation of space is of course symbolic; he reaffirms the simplicity of a complete action, a whole encompassment, while Zeno mistakenly identifies himself now with one point, now with another:

> But you can do away with the whole, at a stroke, if you deny its existence. That is what the philosopher did who proved movement by walking: his act was the negation pure and simple of

the effort, perpetually to be renewed, and therefore fruitless, which Zeno judged indispensable
to cover, one by one, the stages of the intervening
space.[25]

Susanne Langer states (what she says Bergson
never clearly saw) that "his 'concrete duration,' 'lived
time,' is the prototype of 'musical time,' namely *passage*
in its characteristic forms."[26] If we think of musical time
as an example of concrete duration, of characteristic
"passage" (of which the flight of the arrow is an illustration too), it will be interesting to see if this disciple of
Whitehead's can offer convincing explication. She says
that metaphysically Bergson deals with matters that go
to the core of all the arts and especially music:

> His all-important insight is, briefly, that every
> conceptual form which is supposed to portray
> time oversimplifies it to the point of leaving out
> the most interesting aspects of it, namely the char-
> acteristic appearances of passage, so that we have
> a scientific equivalent rather than a conceptual
> symbol of duration. This criticism throws out a
> new challenge to the philosopher's powers of logi-
> cal construction: find us a symbolism whereby we
> can conceive and express our firsthand knowledge
> of time![27]

Since Professor Langer's support of Bergson
takes a different form from that ordinarily encountered,
particularly among professional philosophers, it will be
worthwhile to quote a few more lines to indicate the
direction of her arguments:

[25] *Two Sources,* pp. 53–54.
[26] Susanne K. Langer, *Feeling and Form* (New York: Charles
Scribner's Sons, 1953), p. 115.
[27] *Ibid.,* p. 114.

The demand Bergson makes upon philosophy —to set forth the dynamic forms of subjective experience—only art can fulfill. Perhaps this explains why he is the artists' philosopher *par excellence*. Croce and Santayana make demands on art that are essentially philosophical; philosophers, therefore, find them interesting, but artists tend to ignore them. Bergson, on the other hand, sets up a task that is impossible to accomplish in the realm of discursive expression, i.e., is beyond the philosopher's pale (and cannot force entrance there by resort to instinct, either), but is exactly the artist's business. Nothing could seem more reasonable to a poet or a musician than Bergson's metaphysical aim; without asking whether it is feasible in philosophy, the artist accepts this aim and subscribes to a philosophy that lays claim to it.[28]

It appears to me that in suggesting such procedures as "doing away with the whole in one stroke," Bergson is referring to something in experience analogous perhaps in some way to Stace's "religious infinite," experientially verified in its own realm and not susceptible of literal rendering in space-time conceptual terms. Bergson is thus speaking symbolically (though not by his own definition) and is satisfying Stace's definition of the religious symbol as possessing that to which it refers and being possessed by it. We can see, if the analogy is valid, why Bergson would disdain the use of "symbol" *qua* "sign." I have suggested that Bergson's *durée* is an actuality of a virtual, transcendent realm. Whether this belongs to eternity I am not able to say. Though the term *virtual* is hers, Langer surely does not suggest it; and I find no indication that she is assuming any kind of superstructure nor any dynamic organism with whom

[28] *Ibid.*, pp. 114–15.

we might establish rapport. She impresses me as unmystical.

Bergson, in contrast, is mystical by anybody's definition, though he postulates no eternity beyond process, no unchanging essence supporting his universe of mobility and dynamic forms. His argument that only the active, positive mysticism is complete seems to me a rationalization. Or a guess.

But let him reject a matrix: it is no more necessary for the understanding of musical dynamism than as a cornerstone for his cosmology. And yet if the timeless were divisible, I would be prone to grant to Bergson's "real duration"—and to the musical art that exemplifies it—the status, at least, of a department in eternity.

CHAPTER FIVE

EDUARD HANSLICK

* * * *THE BEAUTIFUL IN MUSIC* WAS FIRST published in 1854. That it has exerted a strong influence on aesthetic thought for so long a time is testimony not only to its undeniable merits but also to the paucity of philosophical works in the field of music. The notoriety Hanslick gained through prolonged controversy with the Wagnerites of his day, his championing of Brahms, and his prominent position as critic and later as a professor of music in Vienna all had the effect of reinforcing his pronouncements. I have spoken earlier of his *reductio ad absurdum:* music means itself. "The beautiful, strictly speaking, aims at nothing, since it is nothing but a form which, though available for many purposes according to its nature, has, as such, no aim beyond itself."[1] We understand, of course, that Hans-

---

[1] Eduard Hanslick, *The Beautiful in Music,* trans. by Gustav Cohen (New York: Liberal Arts Press, 1957), p. 9.

lick is reacting passionately against the excesses of musicians and writers of his time, their hopeless confusion
of artistic modalities, their sentimentality, their generally fuzzy thinking. He advocated an aesthetics that
would be more scientific than the musical thought then
current. His book was of great importance for making
certain fundamental distinctions that needed to be
made then, as they need to be made now.

     Yet Hanslick is not altogether consistent in ad-
vancing the theory that music is quite independent of
extramusical elements. He speaks of "the one immutable factor in music, *purely musical beauty.*"[2] Morris
Weitz points out that Hanslick "rejects the view that
emotion is central," but classifies his views as a "modified heteronomous theory."[3] Hanslick, indeed, betrays
a certain ambivalence; in his preface to the seventh
edition he speaks of his essay as "mainly and primarily
*directed against the widely accepted doctrine that the
office of music is 'to represent feelings.'* It is difficult to
see why this should be thought equivalent to 'affirming
that music is absolutely destitute of feeling.'"[4] Of
course one grants this point. Hanslick is troubled, however, by the prevalence of feelings: "The mere fact that
this particular art is so closely bound up with our feelings by no means justifies the assumption that its aesthetic principles depend on this union."[5] Why does
he say *"mere* fact," in this instance? Or, in the
preceding quotation, *"nothing but* a form"?

     In his supposed refutation of two ideas: first,
that music is intended to arouse the emotions and,
second, that emotions are the subject matter of music,

[2] *Ibid.,* p. 6.   [4] *Ibid.,* p. 4. (Italics mine.)
[3] *Ibid.,* pp. x, xii.   [5] *Ibid.,* p. 10.

Hanslick begs the question. He is amazed by the re-current idea that music has to do with feelings:

> But what the nature of the link is that con-nects music with the emotions, or certain pieces with certain emotions; by what laws of nature it is governed; what the canons of art are that determine its form—all these questions are left in complete darkness by the very people who have "to do" with them.[6]

Precisely. Or, as Aristotle said, "It is not easy to determine the nature of music"!

Yet Hanslick states, in Chapter 3 of his book, that "a musical composition, as the creation of a thinking and feeling mind, may, therefore, itself possess intellectuality and pathos in a high degree."[7] And in implicit acknowledgment of the difficulty of arriving at that classification whose absence he complains of: "The object of every art is to clothe in some material form an idea which has originated in the artist's imagination. In music this idea is an acoustic one; it cannot be ex-pressed in words and subsequently translated into sounds."[8] Lest it be thought, however, that Hanslick is giving any special importance to the "acoustic" per se, here is his disclaimer:

> Creations of inventive genius are not arith-metical sums. Experiments with the monochord, the figures producible by sonorous vibrations, the mathematical ratios of musical intervals, etc., all lie outside the domain of aesthetics, which begins only where those elementary relations cease to be of importance.[9]

[6] *Ibid.*, p. 9.
[7] *Ibid.*, p. 52.
[8] *Ibid.*
[9] *Ibid.*, p. 66.

While recognizing the human architect of an art object, Hanslick accords the object an independent, indeed, objective existence. Most aestheticians would, I believe, go this far, seeing in the object that active capacity to stimulate contemplation that characterizes art. But Hanslick goes farther: "The beautiful is and remains beautiful though it arouse no emotion whatever, and though there be no one to look at it."[10] Later, however, he concedes that metaphors may fade:

> There is no art which, like music, uses up so quickly such a variety of forms. Modulations, cadences, intervals, and harmonious progressions become so hackneyed within fifty, nay, thirty years, that a truly original composer cannot well employ them any longer, and is thus compelled to think of a new musical phraseology. Of a great number of compositions which rose far above the trivialities of their day, it would be quite correct to say that there *was* a time when they were beautiful.[11]

How are we to reconcile these statements? Is not Hanslick admitting here that the independent art object must subsist in and draw nourishment from the human environment?

Though Hanslick does not make it explicit, he is assuming, throughout his book, an intellectual-emotional dichotomy; and he is giving his allegiance to the intellect with a fervor that widens the cleavage. His feelings are committed to intellect: the aesthetic scrutiny will be scientific; contemplation will be purer; listening will be thoughtful for the student "who, in

[10] *Ibid.*, p. 10.   [11] *Ibid.*, p. 58.

order to learn something about the real nature of music, will, above all, remain deaf to the fitful promptings of passion and not, as most manuals on music direct, turn to the emotions as a source of knowledge."[12] The predominant action of the feelings Hanslick calls *pathological*. His emphases are productive of valuable insights and, not surprisingly, of a real dilemma. He does not argue for an exclusively intellectual contemplation which would yield only logical relations, but his dilemma lies in the dichotomy he sets up. Had he imagined intellect-feeling in closer, indissoluble relationship, he might have avoided much confusion. He speaks of the irresistible power of art, of the individuality of a particular art, yet says that "no canon peculiar to musical aesthetics only can be deduced from the fact that there is a certain connection between music and the emotions."[13] He believes that we must not confuse emotional impressions and musical beauty; the application of scientific method will enable us to make the distinction. He apparently does not question the feasibility of applying that method to the object. But if we were to assume that Hanslick had somehow acquired a suitable instrument of analysis, we could not take issue with this statement: "The crux of the question is the specific mode in which music affects our feelings."

Hanslick did not imagine, however, a specific mode which might possibly involve intellect and emotion in equal measure; nor did he conceive of emotion so refined and detached as to correspond to what he called *imagination*—that "organ of pure contemplation." Feelings, for Hanslick, were "in the raw." It

[12] *Ibid.*, p. 7.   [13] *Ibid.*, p. 13.

will soon appear, nevertheless, that Hanslick was closer
to the idea of music as a symbolic analogue to emotional
life than his text suggests.

Much of his thought is nicely pertinent to the
theory I expound in the final chapters. Surely there is
nothing to quarrel with in his assertion that "instead of
enlarging on the vague and secondary effects of musical
phenomena, we ought to endeavor to penetrate deeply
into the spirit of the works themselves and to explain
their effects by the laws of their inherent nature."[14] And
in affirming in regard to music and feeling that "everything depends upon the specific *modus operandi* by
means of which music evokes such feelings,"[15] he is
voicing the *raison d'être* of the present work.

"The primary Imagination," said Coleridge, "I
hold to be the living Power and prime Agent of all
human Perception, and as a repetition in the finite mind
of the eternal act of creation in the infinite I AM."[16]
"The poet," said Wordsworth, "binds together by passion and knowledge the vast empire of human society,
as it is spread over the whole earth, and over all time."[17]

Hanslick would not go so far. But his concept
of "imagination" is not very different from Coleridge's.
Imagination provides Hanslick the aesthetic distance
he desires, holds up the mirror to nature: "For we have
already seen that the excitation of feelings by the beauti-

---

[14] *Ibid.*
[15] *Ibid.*, p. 15.
[16] Samuel Taylor Coleridge, "Biographia Literaria," *Selected Poetry and Prose*, ed. Elisabeth Schneider (New York:
Rinehart & Co., 1956), Chap. 13, p. 268.
[17] William Wordsworth, "Preface to Lyrical Ballads," *The
Prelude and Other Works*, ed. Carlos Baker (New York:
Rinehart & Co., 1957), p. 18.

ful in music is but one of its indirect effects, *our imagination only being directly affected*."[18] In suggesting that we eschew peripheral matters and "endeavor to penetrate deeply into the spirit of the works themselves," Hanslick is presumably issuing a clarion call to the imagination, with all the urgency of Bergson's command to "enter into" the object and possess it by an intellectual act of intuition or with (almost) the fervor of Wordsworth when he says that the truth of poetry is "carried alive into the heart by passion." Hanslick does not—again—go so far. Yet he holds that "our imagination, withal, is not an isolated faculty, for though the vital spark originates in the senses, it forthwith kindles the flame of the intellect and the emotions."[19] He then immediately takes umbrage at his own temerity: "A true conception of the beautiful is, nevertheless, independent of this aspect of the question."[20] Why, one wonders, must this necessarily follow?

Moreover one suspects that in his quest for a cogent theory Hanslick tends to minimize or even to eliminate from consideration those troublesome anomalies which nevertheless keep popping up to challenge the neatest formulas. His egotism and his temperamental zest for the enterprise of attacking recalcitrant elements would naturally add color and interest to the promulgation of his theory; and the warfare was raged concretely, as Hanslick's strong attachments and antipathies testify. Yet his driving force seems to have been a consuming desire for intellectual integrity. Egotism

---

[18] Hanslick, p. 13. (Italics mine.)
[19] *Ibid.*, p. 11.
[20] *Ibid.*

is an attribute of the critic; and Hanslick was a great
critic. Coleridge and Bernard Shaw spoke in tones no
less peremptory. Certain affinities with Coleridge,
which, in my opinion, Hanslick exhibits, will be looked
at presently.

The obvious distinctions (or the distinctions
that one would expect to be obvious, but which in
practice are seldom obvious at all) between music and
nonmusic Hanslick makes clearly and unequivocally.
"Definite feelings and emotions are unsusceptible of
being embodied in music."[21] This much is incontrovertible. Obligingly he also carries forward the dynamic
motif of the last two chapters in his recognition of the
mobile properties of music:

> A certain class of ideas, however, is quite sus-
> ceptible of being adequately expressed by means
> which unquestionably belong to the sphere of
> music proper. This class comprises all ideas
> which, consistently with the organ to which they
> appeal, are associated with audible changes of
> strength, motion, and ratio: the ideas of intensity
> waxing and diminishing; of motion hastening
> and lingering; of ingeniously complex and simple
> progression, etc. The aesthetic expression of
> music may be described by terms such as graceful,
> gentle, violent, vigorous, elegant, fresh—all these
> ideas being expressible by corresponding modi-
> fications of sound. We may, therefore, use those
> adjectives as directly describing musical phenom-
> ena without thinking of the ethical meanings
> attaching to them in a psychological sense, and
> which, from the habit of associating ideas, we
> readily ascribe to the effect of the music, or even
> mistake for purely musical properties.[22]

[21] *Ibid.*, p. 21.   [22] *Ibid.*, pp. 22–23.

This is admirably lucid. Hanslick states that music cannot have a subject in the sense that a poem or a painting or a statue may; in his use of "subject" he is predicating an idea that can be assigned more or less adequately to a verbal referent. There is some doubt that even representational art is susceptible to such rendering to a really significant degree; nevertheless, it is an outright impossibility in music, so for practical purposes the point may be yielded. But Hanslick grants "meaning" a linguistic frame of reference only, so that any import, or significance (what you will) that is not verbally accessible is by definition meaningless.

If the experience of an artistic modality is "meaningless" by the semantic canons of Hanslick, this does not mean that it is without importance or value in his world of discourse. My chief objection to his restricted use of "meaning" is that only those marginal, descriptive elements surrounding a composition, those extramusical associations Hanslick himself has found so inimical to the apprehension of *musical* import, can be "meaningful" in such a lexicon. Surely "meaning," in nonscholarly usage at any rate, carries emotional reverberations that exceed linguistic boundaries.

Hanslick is not using "subject" in the sense that a musician intends when he refers to a fugal theme or subject. (For that genuine musical "subject" substitute "musical idea" and the confusion disappears.) Hanslick is referring instead to any of those supposed extramusical referents for which a musical depiction is claimed, and he rightly denies the possibility of a musical subject in that sense. "What part of the feeling, then, can music represent, if not the subject involved in

them? Only their dynamic properties. . . . Whatever
else there is in music that apparently pictures states of
feeling is symbolical."[23]

The nature of the "beautiful in music" is,
Hanslick says, specifically *musical*. What is expressed
in music is musical idea. "The essence of music is
sound and motion." Hanslick maintains further that
not only music but every art "sets out from the sensuous
and operates within its limits."[24] We have, then, *idea;*
we have also the specific tonal modality—a sensuous
modality of sound and motion—which presents the idea
to human apprehension.

Hanslick has been called a formalist. But the
sense in which he is a "formalist" has been misunder-
stood and oversimplified. He wishes the uniqueness
of the composition to be recognized—a recognition
which would acknowledge the indissolubility of what is
characteristically referred to as "content" with its form.
The musical idea, the "thought," is expressed in this
way and in no other; musical contemplation is directed
at "a thing of beauty in just this particular form."[25]
The musical structure or form is the real substance of
the piece. Hanslick here satisfies two important constituents of the musical symbol as I define it: in any
given example he accords music the embodiment of
meaning and he maintains that the apprehension of
import realized through such a particular means cannot be had in any other way. The "concrete musical
image" is the thing itself. Hanslick complains that "the
habit of looking only for some abstract feeling instead

---

[23] *Ibid.*, pp. 24–25.   [24] *Ibid.*, pp. 48–49.   [25] *Ibid.*, p. 89.

of judging the concrete work of art is, in any great measure, practiced in music alone."[26]

He explicitly states that no distinction can be made between substance and form. He cites the incontrovertible fact that "we cannot acquaint anybody with the 'subject' of a theme except by playing it."[27] Those who claim a "subject" outside the music itself are in reality referring to "intellectual merit": "They conceive the act of composing as a translation into sound of a given subject, whereas the sounds themselves are the untranslatable and original tongue."[28] Hanslick grants that the individuality of a composer will find "symbolic expression" in his work,[29] but what he produces *qua* music is an objective image: an object for contemplation. He distinguishes nicely between the uses of sound in speech and music and at the same time provides the necessary distinction between signal and symbolic functions: "While sound in speech is but a sign, that is, a means for the purpose of expressing something which is quite distinct from its medium, sound in music is the end, that is, the ultimate and absolute object in view."[30]

But it is a misreading of Hanslick (though he himself failed to give systematic clarification) to construc his musical form—the objective image—as empty, merely because it is not referring to something else. On the contrary, by virtue of its autonomy the image yields more to the percipient than any "sign" could ever do:

> The term "form" in musical language is peculiarly significant. The forms created by sound are

[26] *Ibid.*, p. 90.
[27] *Ibid.*, p. 124.
[28] *Ibid.*, pp. 125–26.
[29] *Ibid.*, p. 74.
[30] *Ibid.*, p. 67.

not empty; not the envelope enclosing a vacuum, but a well, replete with the living creation of inventive genius. Music, then, as compared with the arabesque, is a picture, yet a picture the subject of which we cannot define in words, or include in any one category of thought. In music there is both meaning and logical sequence, but in a musical sense; it is a language we speak and understand, but which we are unable to translate.[31]

Contemplation is the function of the imagination, not the emotions. Hanslick concedes a close relationship between them but argues that the composer strives for perfection of the image in seeking to give objective form to his musical ideal. "It is not the feelings but a specifically musical and technically trained aptitude that enables us to compose."[32] Composition is constructive. Coleridge offers many instances of the contemplative imagination. Here is a presentation of visual imagery which corresponds in that modality to Hanslick's concept of pure contemplation:

And still I gaze—and with how blank an eye!
And those thin clouds above, in flakes and bars,
That give away their motion to the stars;
Those stars, that glide behind them or between,
Now sparkling, now bedimm'd, but always seen;
Yon crescent moon, that seems as if it grew
In its own starless, cloudless lake of blue—
I see them all, so excellently fair!
I see, not feel, how beautiful they are.[33]

[31] *Ibid.*, p. 50.
[32] *Ibid.*, pp. 72–73.
[33] Coleridge, "Principles of Genial Criticism," p. 381.

Hanslick admits the importance of feelings, both to the composer and the listener: "Nothing great or beautiful has ever been accomplished without warmth of feeling."[34] But the feelings are a human *given:* they nourish but do not constitute the imagination. The imagination as Hanslick describes it is the faculty through which the artist gives form to the virtual: the objective image transcends the here and now. Here again is the symbolic analogue—and of course I am rendering Hanslick into my own terms but nevertheless, I believe, faithfully. Distance from the immediacy of life inheres in art. The imagination is also the instrument of that contemplation Hanslick postulates as the necessary condition for understanding music. "Music, then . . . is a picture."

Throughout his book Hanslick is preoccupied with the thrust of the extraneous, the tyranny of the extramusical. Describing the Greeks' concern for the effects of their principal modes, Hanslick confirms the thesis of my second chapter:

> As a result of this one-sided culture, music had become an indispensable and docile accessory of all the arts, a means for the attainment of educational, political, and other ends; it was a maid-of-all work but not a self-subsistent art. If the strains of Phrygian music sufficed to incite warriors to acts of bravery, if the faithfulness of grass widows could be secured by Doric songs, let generals and husbands lament the extinction of the Greek system—students of aesthetics and composers will cast no regrets after it.[35]

[34] Hanslick, p. 73.   [35] Ibid., p. 97.

And in one succinct paragraph he summarizes the impediments to musical contemplation that have exerted their dominance of the art throughout the history of human culture:

> Now the most essential condition to the aesthetic enjoyment of music is that of listening to a composition for its own sake, no matter what it is or what construction it may bear. The moment music is used as a means to induce certain states of mind, as accessory or ornamental, it ceases to be an art in a purely musical sense. The elemental properties of music are very frequently confounded with its artistic beauty; in other words, a part is taken for the whole, and unutterable confusion ensues. Hundreds of sayings about "music" do not apply to the art as such, but to the sensuous action of its material only.[36]

Hanslick gives detailed attention to the problems which face the composer as he strives for the successful image: the rigorous demands of the medium, requiring unity in the completed work—the discarding of the trivial, obvious, and inappropriate and the subordination of parts to the whole. The composer's style, his "grasp of the technical side of music" is crucial:

> The architectonic side of beauty in music is brought into bold relief by the question of style. The laws of style being of a more subtle nature than the laws of mere proportion, one single bar, if out of keeping with the rest, though perfect in itself, will vitiate the style. Just as in architecture we might call a certain arabesque out of place, so we should condemn as bad style a ca-

[36] *Ibid.*, pp. 100–101.

dence or modulation which is opposed to the unity of the fundamental thought.[37]

Coleridge, in *Principles of Genial Criticism,* gives a similar account of the process of "symbol building" through which the idea is finally achieved—allowed, as it were, to "shine forth." The transparency he postulates would be realized through consummate technique: an art that disguises art. One may think of a sculptor as "liberating" a form which is—through his imagination—implicit in the marble. Through the ministrations of Michelangelo, David is brought forth. Idea and medium are one, and without them both we have neither:

> Something there must be to realize the form, something in and by which the *forma informans* reveals itself: and these, less than any that could be substituted, and in the least possible degree, distract the attention, in the least possible degree obscure the idea, of which they (composed into outline and surface) are the symbol. An illustrative hint may be taken from a pure crystal, as compared with an opaque, semi-opaque or clouded mass, on the one hand, and with a perfectly transparent body, such as the air, on the other. The crystal is lost in the light, which yet it contains, embodies, and gives a shape to; but which passes shapeless through the air, and, in the ruder body, is either quenched or dissipated.[38]

I have juxtaposed Hanslick and Coleridge, first, because of the strong affinity between them and, second, because Coleridge provides an opening for

[37] *Ibid.,* p. 75.   [38] Coleridge, p. 379.

"something more." There is in Coleridge's concept of the *objective image* an allowance for what may be called transcendence. This opening is what I find wanting in Hanslick, except to the extent that the objectivity which he predicates for music is in itself a transcendence of the immediate.

It is also a limitation in his thought that he rejects what may be construed as the "ugly"—according to what objective canons? one may well ask. Hanslick refers music to the criterion of sensual response; the means by which he might hope to keep the senses separate from the feelings would surely require careful investigation. But he evidently finds no problem here.

It is especially surprising, however, that in a book which invokes the support of science for its arguments, Hanslick appeals to the intuition alone in distinguishing beauty from ugliness. He is content, moreover, to justify this appeal by a quotation from Grillparzer to the effect that music is "perceived and assimilated directly by the senses, and the verdict of the intellect comes too late to correct the disturbing factor of ugliness. It is for this reason that Shakespeare was justified in making use of the horrible, while Mozart was obliged to remain within the limits of the beautiful."[39] In having recourse to the "experienced ear," Hanslick is calling as witness that very conditioning of reflexes (which may later be confused with instinct), those very associations, albeit they be musical ones, which can prejudice human reactions to the unfamiliar:

> All musical elements are in some occult manner connected with each other by certain natural af-

[39] Hanslick, p. 51.

finities, and since rhythm, melody, and harmony are under their invisible sway, the music created by man must conform to them—any combinations conflicting with them bearing the impress of caprice and ugliness. Though not demonstrable with scientific precision, these affinities are instinctively felt by every experienced ear, and the organic completeness and logic, or the absurdity and unnaturalness of a group of sounds, are intuitively known without the intervention of a definite conception as the standard of measure.[40]

Yet professional musicians, as Hanslick had reason to know, are often the first to challenge and deny examples of "new music" as incoherent and disorganized, absurd or unnatural, frivolous or offensive. That such judgments may appear correct in many instances is not in general the result of musical perspicacity in apprehending new idioms. An almost certain oblivion awaits the vast majority of musical compositions, whatever era they belong to. "Experienced ears" have a strongly vested interest in the established patterns, and they bring their expert knowledge to bear upon the "heard-before." An untutored child may on occasion be more open to a radically new departure in musical expressivity than a savant.

Hanslick would like to establish the "protean science" of musical aesthetics on a solid foundation. He is most successful in explaining what music is not. In his quest for firm ground, however, he does not succumb to the reductionism of a physiological view:

It is true, of course, that the cause of every emotion which music arouses is chiefly to be found in some specific mode of nerve activity induced by

[40] *Ibid.*

an auditory impression. But how the excitation of the auditory nerve (which we cannot even trace to its source) is transformed into a definite sentiment; how a physical impression can pass into a state of mind; how, in fine, a sensation can become an emotion—all this lies beyond the mysterious bridge which no philosopher has ever crossed.[41]

Hanslick saw no less clearly than Schopenhauer that music does not express "this or that particular and definite joy, this or that sorrow, or pain, or horror, or delight, or merriment, or peace of mind. . . . " To the extent that dynamic musical ideas might correspond to such emotional states, they would subsist in a symbolic analogue or what Hanslick calls the "objective image." As in Nietzsche's Apollonian objectification of a Dionysian state, however it "pictures" the life of feelings, the embodiment is "far removed from their pain." The modality is dynamic; content, a static concept, would be rendered in the Bergsonian dialect as process itself: and music, as an ideal—or virtual—unity of sound and motion mirrors the apprehension of dynamic process as no other modality can. (We are here concerned with modalities which are specifically artistic.) Hanslick's "objective image" is aural; but the figure is not intended to suggest the synesthesia that so intrigued the *symbolistes.* For his "objective image" let us substitute *musical symbol.* We have now achieved, in large measure, a provisional concordance of Schopenhauer, Nietzsche, Bergson, and Hanslick in what will

[41] *Ibid.,* p. 85.

increasingly appear as a progressive development of musical thought. The counterpoint is intricate, but the main strands are clearly discernible and point to an evolution in musical philosophy which is not yet at an end.

CHAPTER SIX

EDMUND GURNEY AND IDEAL MOTION

* * * WITH ONE THOUGHT, SAID EMERSON, WE can surpass whole populations. I suspect that such power is the prerogative of genius; and I would acknowledge it unhesitatingly in Edmund Gurney, as I do in Emerson. Gurney, psychologist and fellow of Trinity College, Cambridge, published *The Power of Sound* in 1880 when he was at the height of his productivity; he was to die in 1888 at the age of forty-one. He was, according to Ralph Barton Perry, the dearest of those close friends with whom William James became identified while living in England. The nucleus of James's philosophic society was the Scratch Eight, of which he became the ninth member. The first meeting which he attended is described in the following extract from a letter to his wife:

> Dec. 16, 1882
>
> Last night I dined at Gurney's with the "Scratch Eight," spoken of in the invitation I enclosed to

you. Gurney himself, whose *Power of Sound,*
which I have now half finished, proves him to be
one of the first-rate minds of the time, is a mag-
nificent Adonis, six feet four in height, with an
extremely handsome face, voice, and general air
of distinction about him, altogether the exact opposite of classical idea of a philosopher. The other
seven were Robertson, Hodgson, Sully, Carveth
Read, Frederick Pollock, Leslie Stephen, and a
certain Maitland, he being, so far as I know, the
only one not known to fame.[1]

James's *Varieties of Religious Experience* ends
with a *bon mot* from Gurney's *Tertium Quid:* "No fact
in human nature is more characteristic than its willing-
ness to live on a chance. The existence of the chance
makes the difference, as Edmund Gurney says, between
a life of which the keynote is resignation and a life of
which the keynote is hope."[2]

In view of the oblivion that Gurney—a fan-
tastically gifted man—has passed into, it is especially interesting to observe the extent of James's esteem for
him. Again I am indebted to Professor Perry:

> The first of the circle to be "gathered in" . . .
> was Edmund Gurney, he whom James loved the
> most . . . He saw in him the promise of an "in-
> tellectual synthesis" that should be "solider and
> completer than that of anyone . . . except per-
> haps Royce." Adding to Gurney's "rare metaphys-
> ical power," his "tenderest heart," it is not
> strange that in Gurney's death "the destroying
> angel had outdone even himself in heartlessness."[3]

[1] Ralph Barton Perry (ed.), *The Thought and Character of
William James* (New York: George Braziller, 1954), pp.
154–55.
[2] William James *The Varieties of Religious Experience*
(New York: Modern Library, 1929), p. 516.
[3] Perry, p. 157.

In a letter of 1888 James wrote:

> Poor Gurney! How I shall miss that man's pres-
> ence in the world. I think, to compare small
> things with great, that there was a very unusual
> sort of affinity between my mind and his. Our
> problems were the same, and for the most part
> our solutions. I eagerly devoured every word
> he wrote, and was always conscious of him as
> critic and judge. He had both quantity and qual-
> ity, and I hoped for some big philosophic achieve-
> ment from him ere he should get through. And
> now—*omnia ademit una dies infesta*—! The world
> is grown hollower.[4]

Earlier, when Gurney was very much alive, James had
written to his wife: "I had a delightful evening last
night at the Scratch Eight. Charming fellows all. Gurney strikes me as a big man with any amount of loose
power about him."[5]

So much for tribute. Unlike those eminent
figures we have thus far examined, Gurney has a name
that conjures up no associations for the general reader
nor even for the musician. His theory of music—for
this is what it should be called—appears not to have
been examined by those scholars who make occasional
references to it; they no doubt regard it as an obscure
and curious work, out of date, not worth reading.[6] In

[4] *Ibid.*
[5] *Ibid.*
[6] A notable exception is John Hospers' treatment of
Hanslick and Gurney in his *Meaning and Truth in the
Arts,* which quotes at length from these authors. Although
I believe that Hospers' interpretations oversimplify the
thought of both men, I am more troubled by his failure to
point out the differences between them, when the very
quotations he employs show their pronounced divergences.

point of fact, however, *The Power of Sound* is still in advance of present-day musical aesthetics.[7]

In establishing the framework for his musical ideas, Gurney examines the characteristics of art in general. His conclusions reveal an extraordinary prescience: the work of art is an "organism." As a product of the imagination art—though it may resemble a scientific treatise in its complex organization and interdependence of parts—possesses vitality; it has permanence; it is not utilitarian in any narrow sense. Gurney speaks of the special *differentia* of the imaginative work, which ordain that

> its life and growth is *from within;* that it does not appear as an external result, bearing to its author's activities the relation merely of a manufactured article to a machine; but as an actual picture of the activities themselves, of the author's living ideas and emotions, whose only result is to be reborn as part of others' lives.[8]

Have we not in this delineation of art the *symbolic analogue?* "In the imaginative work the ideas and emotions are embodied *as such,* to be again and again reawakened as such."[9]

---

[7] The dreadful condition of this neglected field is quite indefensible when we observe what has been produced in the twentieth century in theories of the plastic arts and literature. We have historians and journalists writing musical criticism. But there is no musical counterpart to Herbert Read.

[8] Edmund Gurney, *The Power of Sound* (London: Smith, Elder, & Co., 1880), p. 45.

[9] *Ibid.,* pp. 45–46.

My readings of the authors so far discussed have provided articulate and, I believe, soundly based reinforcement of my central concept in this work, namely, that music is a nonverbal symbolism which can be understood by means of its distinctive modality and can be apprehended only in that way. If this modality operates through a symbolism unrelated to verbal concepts, such a modality (such a symbolism) must inevitably be accorded its proper place. Meantime, the *word* holds as dominant a position in present-day human consciousness as ever the earth held in the pre-Copernican universe and with perhaps as little ultimate justification. Significantly, it is often among the very masters of discursive language that we find the most acute awareness of its limitations. The basic difficulty in apprehending symbolism today, according to Robert Graves, derives from the fact that scientific techniques are discursive; symbolic language is another modality of consciousness.

"The limitations inherent in verbal conception and discursive forms of thought are the very *raison d'être* of artistic expression," says Langer. Gurney, writing in 1880, puts it this way: "The grounds which preclude verbal interpretations and set verbal descriptions lie at the root of the art's wide comprehensibility and diffusion."[10] The lines which follow show as clearly as could be desired that Gurney did not, as Hospers has claimed, regard music as isolated from and irrelevant to "life-situations" and "life-emotions":

> The very fact that not one in a hundred of those who care for Music take the smallest interest in any external treatment of it is as good an

[10] *Ibid.*, p. 529.

indication as could be had of its exceptionally swift and easy channels to the comprehension and the heart. At the same time there is plenty for words to do.[11]

Gurney uses words to make the fundamental distinctions that can and must be made between music and the extramusical. But he acknowledges the fact that words can do no more than point toward the characteristics of a nonverbal modality. It is this recognition, and not the ascription of "meaninglessness" to music, that accounts for his emphasis upon the limitations of verbal descriptions of music. The addiction to externals which a preoccupation with verbal description necessitates is a disease from which Lessing suffered. Gurney observes:

> The very fact that the intellectual side of the imagination is so prominent, and reasoned criticism therefore so possible, in the case of the representative arts, involves a special danger of substituting ingenuity for intuition and of evolving reasonable "laws and rules" which bear no relation to the true *differentia* of beautiful works. There could not be a more effective means of realising this danger than a perusal of the *Laocoön*, where the *whole* merit of works of art is throughout found in things which a person without the slightest artistic genius could and would think of naturally as an artist. A great painter is differentiated not by *common sense* but by *vision*.[12]

"Vision" yields an image which in the modern vernacular might be termed the presentational symbol. Whitehead refers to "presentational immediacy":

[11] *Ibid.*   [12] *Ibid.*, p. 180.

> It expresses how contemporary events are rele-
> vant to each other, and yet preserve a mutual inde-
> pendence. This relevance amid independence is
> the peculiar character of contemporaneousness.
> This presentational immediacy is only of impor-
> tance in high-grade organisms, and is a physical
> fact which may, or may not, enter into conscious-
> ness. Such entry will depend on attention, and on
> the activity of conceptual functioning, whereby
> physical experience and conceptual imagination
> are fused into knowledge.[13]

There are a number of threads which must be
drawn together before we can proceed. Gurney looks
upon a work of art as an organism. The world view of
Whitehead has been called "the philosophy of organism." There are two concepts in the lines just quoted
from Whitehead which are especially pertinent to Gurney's thought and to my own theory: the "relevance
amid independence" as an attribute of presentational
immediacy and the process by which the stuff of life—
with the catalyst of the conceptual imagination—
becomes knowledge.

Such knowledge, *qua* art, is the symbol. The
imagination is conceptual: it holds the picture, gives it
permanent form. Not being subject to the exclusive
claims of the here and now, the symbol is not utilitarian.
The environment of the symbol is human; the symbol
contributes to a dialogue in which the ideas and emotions it fuses are "reborn as part of others' lives."
Moreover, the ideas and emotions are embodied as such.

Unity in diversity may be looked upon as an
example of relevance amid independence. A living or-

---

[13] Alfred North Whitehead, *Symbolism* (New York: [Capri-
corn] G. P. Putnam's Sons, 1959), p. 16.

ganism exhibits such unity in diversity: a man is a complex amalgam; no division of his components into "form" and "content" can possibly be imagined. As a living creature he exhibits that unity we are postulating for the symbol; and the strong central focus (or control) varies in intensity from man to man as it does from one art work to another. Gurney predicates vitality for the art work. By analogy to living organisms the symbol is a unity of form and content: it *is* what it is *about!* and in this sense even Hanslick's dictum that "it means itself" would not be a *reductio ad absurdum*.

Concerning the unity of artistic works, Gurney gives an overview (of the relation of parts to the whole) in which he is supported by the experiences which Mozart and Hindemith have spoken of: experiences of insight or illumination in which an entire composition was clearly envisaged, so that the "writing out" (particularly, one would imagine, in Mozart's case) was a derivative, secondary activity—a mere concession to the demands of calligraphy. Yet we can readily see that the radically different technique of Beethoven, in whom the music struggles laboriously, like a sculptor's marble, to be "liberated," leads no less surely to the salutary artistic results which Gurney here describes:

> In imaginative production, the rounding into completeness, the conception of the work as a whole, and the pervading influence of this conception in the development of the subject-matter, are as much matters of internal and individual activity as any of the separate ideal or emotional elements. A true organic unity, not conceived as just comprising the parts or conditioned by them, but as the natural form in which their vital quali-

ties find fullest realisation, is that towards which the whole process of development tends: and the artistic faculty must find the secret of such unity in itself. Slightness and fulness of detail are alike compatible with this perfect and independent completeness. The one condition which we attach to the scope of the imaginative work is one which, as it happens, we find to hold in the organisms of Nature, in spite of her very common indifference to our comprehension and pleasure; namely, that it shall not be too vast, nor the relations of its parts too complicated, for the sense and the mind to apprehend.[14]

We have now reached a point at which I think further attention must be given to the word *symbol*. We have seen how the term has been used by different writers to serve for experiences, particularly artistic ones, in which the ambiguities of the situation rendered the observer verbally incompetent. Despite the varieties of meanings imposed upon it, the word *symbol* has consistently recommended itself to those areas of life and imagination which linguistic thought cannot adequately render in its own terms. The symbols referring to these "departments" of human discourse are inevitably, to a degree, signs of something else; yet they have a penumbra, an extension of import that is felt within the modality, not stated by it. "Sign," however, remains the primary dictionary definition of *symbol*. But even in spoken or written language the symbolism exceeds any fixed limits. "The mere sound of a word," says Whitehead, "or its shape on paper, is indifferent. The word is a symbol, and its meaning is constituted by the ideas,

[14] Gurney, pp. 46–47.

images, and emotions, which it raises in the mind of the hearer."[15]

In his use of *meaning* here, as well as in his reference to that knowledge resulting from the fusion of physical experience and conceptual imagination, Whitehead is apparently not limiting himself to the "signal" information which spoken and written language transmit. That a more restricted definition of terms can be arrived at is obvious, but the gains that would accrue from this reduction are less apparent. Simplicity of terminology is desirable only to the extent that it adequately corresponds to its intended referents. In the effort to reduce terms to their minimal definitions, refusing all associations and accrued meanings and rejecting all emotional overtones as irrelevant, we can find ourselves with language that is impotent as an instrument of analysis, except for dealing with its own self-contained minutiae in a world of syntactical and structural preoccupations: a world of glorified anagrams where certain problems cannot even be permitted to arise—or if they do obtain a hearing, cannot be dealt with or even understood in the terms available.

What may seem, initially, a tempest in a semantic teapot may assume such proportions that it can become a serious impediment to what has always been looked upon as the acquisition of knowledge. Let me take, as an example, the case represented by John Hospers, who confines knowledge to that which is capable of being rendered in terms of the assertions—or "propositions"—of the discursive intellect. I choose

[15] Whitehead, p. 2.

Hospers because of his extreme position as set forth in
Meaning and Truth in the Arts and because he deals
in that book with two figures whose thought is germane
to this book: Edmund Gurney and Susanne Langer.
What I regard as Hospers' profound misunderstanding
and undervaluation of both thinkers is directly attributable to his semantic premises. He accepts the distinction which Moritz Schlick makes between knowledge and acquaintance; knowledge must be explanatory,
and immediate awareness is excluded from its province.
Thus Hospers is able to speak of "mere awareness."
What we are confronted with here is a remarkable inversion of Bergsonian thought—an example, indeed, of
what Bergson most feared from the conceptualizing
intellect.

If we accept Hospers' view that knowledge is
not knowledge unless it is capable of discursive statement, then "carnal knowledge" in the sense of the King
James rendering is mere acquaintance—an experience,
one would suppose, of a more trivial order altogether.
In the possible solution of such a problem in semantics,
it is fervently to be hoped that the ear (and perhaps a
healthful sense of the ridiculous as well) will play a
major role. Here is the impasse as Hospers gives it:

> If you want to know what a mango tastes like,
> the best thing to do is to let you taste one, to give
> you the experience, rather than describing it to
> you in propositions.
> But are tasting the mango, hearing the music,
> really cases of knowing? If so, they are surely
> quite different from knowing *that* something is
> the case.[16]

[16] John Hospers, *Meaning and Truth in the Arts* (Chapel
Hill: Univ. of N.C. Press, 1946), p. 233.

Yet even the dictionary meanings of *knowledge* go far beyond the connotations Hospers will accept. In a language which gives very heavy duty to a term such as *love,* we are to exercise an unwonted Puritanism in the possibilities of knowing:

> I do not deny that from hearing the music one may know *that* something is the case, e.g., that the piece is in sonata form, or that it is a piece for the piano. But what fact, outside the music and its effect on us, we can be said to know, I am at a loss to see.[17]

Aside from invoking the ghost of Quiller-Couch to exorcise all these cases, I can only point to the appositive in the last sentence, and refer the question of "music and its effect"—knowledge of which I would have expected to be the heart of the matter—to Gurney:

> The words *theoretic* and *speculative* which I have used . . . need not alarm any reader with a vision of remote hypotheses and recondite arguments. . . . Still less need the most ardent believer in the spiritual character of the art fear to find the domain of genius measured by mechanical rules, or the feelings whose indescribable and mysterious nature no one, I think, can have realised more deeply than myself, docketed off under cut-and-dry psychological formulas. . . . One of the first results of my analysis is to define the boundary of the vast region that lies beyond it; and one of the most direct conclusions from my general explanations is the hopelessness of penetrating Music in detail, and of obtaining, whether in objective facts of structure or in fancied analogies and interpretations, any standpoint external

to the actual inward impression, from which to judge it.[18]

But Gurney finds, to be sure, that there is "plenty that words can do" in illuminating a region which is "naturally a foggy one." It presumably is on the basis of Gurney's definitions and distinctions that Hospers concludes he is a formalist. *The Power of Sound,* however, is a comprehensive work; the parts—like those of the musical organism Gurney postulates—can be fully understood only in the context of the entire book; its thread of unity is then discernible through the author's complex counterpoint of ideas with their numerous shades of meaning. Early in the book Gurney gives considerable attention to preparing the stage for what follows: he removes obsolete and inappropriate furnishings and he builds a new set.

We have seen what a protean concept the *symbol* is, how it lends itself to all kinds of manipulation and shaping. It is a richly loaded term. For reasons which will presently be given, I think this deposit of meanings is an advantage; but the term, of course, is not the point. The point is to secure in discursive terms as coherent and faithful an account of the "orderings" of art as we can. Words must sometimes be coined and given currency in order to say what has not been said before; but in the present work this procedure would create more difficulties than the continued use of the ambiguous *symbol* with its wealth of associations.

I spoke earlier of the affinity between Gurney's and Langer's thought. Gurney does not develop his

[18] Gurney, p. viii.

concepts under the term *symbol,* though his Ideal Motion fulfills all the criteria for the symbol that we have discussed. "Symbol," which she carefully distinguishes from "signal," occupies a central place in Susanne Langer's terminology. She takes pains to clarify the terms and to use them in a consistent way. Notwithstanding this, Hospers cannot go along with her use of "symbol" and consequently finds her thought inaccessible. He quotes Ernest Nagel's review of *Philosophy in a New Key:* "The perplexed reader, remembering that symbols must have objects in order to be symbols, must conclude either that sensory forms are not symbols at all, or that they arc 'symbols' in a radically new and hitherto unspecified sense."[19]

But this is not so; the symbols need not be radically new—though they have been called by many names!—nor are they (certainly not in Professor Langer's lexicon) unspecified. We have seen that the use of "symbol" in a nonsignal sense has a long tradition, and the exploration still has a good way to go. Hospers' bibliography not surprisingly betrays his ignorance of this background. Thus he can say:

> I should have thought that the very essence of anything's being a symbol is that it is used to stand for (represent) something else. Is not a symbol that merely presents, not represents, a contradiction in terms? I can see no way out of this difficulty unless a presentational symbol is defined in a way which is quite at variance with the obvious implications of the term.[20]

[19] Ernest Nagel, *Journal of Philosophy,* XL, No. 12 (June 10, 1943), 325–26, as quoted in Hospers, p. 61.
[20] *Ibid.,* p. 60.

Again, we have the anomalous use of "mere" for what happens to be presented to the field of consciousness at a given time. Hospers is no existentialist! He will not, moreover, tolerate a bending of his definition. Yet in a discussion of "Artistic Truth" he is quite willing to consider the substitution of another term for "truth."

> I must remark once again that I am not particular about the use of the word "true"; if a more satisfactory term can be found, then so much the better. But whatever other term be devised, it must refer to the same sort of thing . . . and *the same facts must be recognized, no matter under what names they may appear.*[21]

Had Hospers replaced *symbol* with "semantic" or "significant form" in reading Langer, he would perhaps have been able to recognize the same facts she did or at the very least conceive their equivalents.

Melody, says Gurney, is "ideal motion": a fusion of rhythm and pitch. It gives us a form presenting the character of motion and a motion presenting the character of form. Both changes in pitch and in rhythmic structure exemplify movement, consume "time." In a remarkably Bergsonian explanation Gurney says:

> We must now turn to the actual *process* by which Music is followed, to the facts connected with the evolution of melodic form moment after

---

[21] *Ibid.,* p. 205. (Italics mine.)

moment in time. The translation which this will involve of the phraseology of *form* into the phraseology of *motion* will make clearer the essential difference of this experience when form and motion are blended—where form is perceived by continuous advance along it—from perceptions both of visible form and of physical motion. It is the *oneness of form and motion* which constitutes the great peculiarity of melody and of the faculty by which we appreciate it. . . . When a melody is familiar to us we realize it by a gradual process of advance along it, while yet the *whole* process is in some real manner present to us at each of the successive instants at which only a minute part of it is actually engaging our ears.[22]

How close this is to a recent pronouncement by E. M. Forster:

Music, more than the other arts, postulates a double existence. It exists in time, takes half an hour to play or whatever it is, and also exists outside time, instantaneously. . . . I can conceive myself hearing a piece as it goes by and also when it has finished. In the latter case I should hear it as an entity, as a piece of sound-architecture, not as a sound-sequence, not as something divisible into bars.[23]

Note the "unity" presupposed by both observers, and Gurney's emphasis on the "oneness" of form and motion. Elsewhere he states that in music "the subject-matter throughout is not *invested* in form, but *is* form."[24] The musical idea is found in its unique formal

[22] Gurney, pp. 164–65.
[23] Richard F. French, (ed.), *Music and Criticism: A Symposium* (Cambridge: Harvard Univ. Press, 1948), p. 29.
[24] Gurney, p. 526.

expression: "The common use of the term *idea,* in relation to Music, to express some special bit of striking
form is thus entirely accurate, in spite of the extraordinary bungling to which it often leads, as though the
idea were one thing and the music another."[25]

This "bungling," to which the twentieth century is no stranger, is demonstrated by Lessing, whose
Laocoön gives Gurney the impression that the "mere
mental survey of the subject-matter seems quite sufficient satisfaction"[26] for its author. His further remarks
on Lessing are equally applicable to recent works by
Ferguson, Hospers, and indeed, the majority of present-
day writings about music: "Almost every page of the
book gives the same impression of a man laboriously
striving from outside to discover reasons for admiring
approved works."[27] But beyond the wordplay stands
art, mirroring, according to Gurney, large tracts of the
inner world of feeling in an altogether "special sphere,"
sounding the depths of human experience. Art sets
forth "in all its myriad relations and aspects the image
of the world on the individual soul."[28] The altogether
special sphere is the virtual; that image of the world is
the objective image of art, the analogue to life.

The musical analogue is what Gurney calls
"Ideal Motion," and what I have called the musical
symbol. In explaining *ideal motion,* therefore, Gurney
is also defining the musical symbol. He points out, first
of all, that the characteristics of melodic forms cannot
be abstracted from the continuous process which enables
us to perceive them, and then states:

[25] *Ibid.,* p. 165.
[26] *Ibid.,* p. 181.

[27] *Ibid.,* p. 182.
[28] *Ibid.,* p. 183.

> I can think of no better term to express this unique musical process than *Ideal Motion;* ideal not just as giving a refined and idealised and glorified version of something already known, in the sense that a painter may often be said to glorify and idealise the objects he represents—not an idealised quintessence of any sort of *physical* motion—but ideal in the primary Greek sense . . . ideal as yielding a *form*, a unity to which all the parts are necessary in their respective places.[29]

It may have occurred to the reader that in postulating an aural image which we call a "symbol" we have been rather vague about its dimensions. Admittedly; this problem of "size" must be dealt with, and it receives a fair share of attention in ensuing chapters. We will not, however, arrive at a rule of thumb. The ideal of an organic unity is assumed as the principal yardstick of symbolic comprehensibility, and the symbol belongs to a world of human discourse: "it shall not be too vast, nor the relations of its parts too complicated, for the sense and the mind to apprehend."[30] *Mutatis mutandis*, it must not be too small.

Gurney offers a nice clarification in terms of musical intelligibility (which cannot be defined by size alone): "The point to notice is that the cardinal idea of organic form in any musical sentence or paragraph is not to be connected with this length or that length, but with *cogency of sequence* at each point: a long series of periods may exhibit it throughout, and the shortest fragment may lack it."[31] The constituents of a piece of music must therefore exhibit a dynamic unity. Gurney limits his use of the word "form" to "such single orga-

[29] *Ibid.*, p. 165.   [30] *Ibid.*, pp. 46–47.   [31] *Ibid.*, p. 204.

nisms as are palpably grasped as unities whose elements are entirely interdependent, and in the strictest sense necessitate one another."[32]

In Gurney's view music should give pleasure; and the pleasure itself is intensified by the quality of organic vitality in music: "Thus pleasure in the whole has no meaning except as expressing the sum of our enjoyments from moment to moment; a sum which will be increased in proportion as the organic principle pervades the whole."[33] Gurney suggests that rhythmic and melodic stimulation, joined in ideal motion, are the roots of musical pleasure. He proposes a unique faculty as the agency for human apprehension of music. This element of his theory, in my opinion, has least to recommend it. Gurney separates the musical faculty from other general intellectual ones, such as the imaginative or logical. In distinguishing the act of hearing music from the processes of the discursive reason, however, I think Gurney is correct. The subsuming of his hypothetical musical faculty under the department of *intuition,* while still acknowledging its distinctive function and modality would be more satisfactory from my point of view. Gurney himself affirms at one point that musical forms are "invented and appreciated by a wholly unique and intuitive faculty."[34]

A recurring concept, the reader will have observed, is the *objective image:* the autonomous art work. The contemplation of the image, the hearing of ideal motion, is an act in which the participant is involved; he is necessary to it; moreover, he "feels" some-

[32] *Ibid.,* pp. 205–6.   [33] *Ibid.,* p. 214.   [34] *Ibid.,* p. 217.

thing. Gurney says that music "is perpetually felt as strongly emotional while defying all attempts to analyze the experience or to define it even in the most general way in terms of definite emotions." We are, Schopenhauer said, "far removed from their pain." Nietzsche spoke of the Apollonian representation of the Dionysian. Langer refers to the symbolic analogue; the picturing of "how it is to feel."

In whatever terms we may choose to couch the phenomenon, we are encountering the fact of distance as a concomitant of artistic experience; the object mediates between the human percipient and the components of the object itself, fused therein into an "is-ness" of authentic symbolism, having the quality—in the Taoist vernacular—of "suchness." Coleridge's analogy to the crystal is particularly apt here. The crystalline symbol yields images of those things (and they may, as in the imagery of T. S. Eliot, be "radical juxtapositions") that go into it; and those things are focused and unified for the percipient through the symbol. The symbol, however, is not exactly analogous to a mirror; it does not merely reflect; it arranges a constellation. It resembles more nearly a diviner's crystal ball; its function always is part magical.

Gurney is something more than a "formalist" when he says that only through *forms* do the higher and more complex mental faculties come into close and habitual relation with sense impressions. Intelligibility itself is a correspondence of structural (formal) elements in experience to the human recognition and understanding. Gurney, though he lived too soon, would readily have comprehended the tenets of Gestalt psychology; indeed, he anticipated some of them. He speaks of two modes of apprehending the relation between parts and whole: namely, the specific and the general. Of the second mode he says:

> The sense of the whole is the primary and fundamental fact, and the only point of identity perceived in the parts is their common character of belonging to the whole, the exercise by each a function impossible to it in isolation: as in the profile of a face, or in some irregular natural object, or in a line of changing curvature.[35]

He is not wholly committed to either mode—apprehension through the whole or through the part—recognizing in polyphonic music, for example, a "complexity and unity . . . both so striking that the sense of ease and power with which we grasp them becomes an important element of our enjoyment. . . . Unity under variety is a characteristic, or rather is the definition, of all form, not specially of beautiful form."[36]

In apprehension of *aesthetic* form Gurney discerns the strong confluence of the intuition with other factors which make artistic "law and order" something more than a reasonable matter. "It is of course begging the question to call a form reasonable because we first found it beautiful: that is an argument drawn from our own sanity, not from the nature of the phenomenon."[37] Gurney holds that the "element of beauty and impressiveness" cannot be accounted for by the discursive reason. His argument in support of this reflects the

[35] *Ibid.,* p. 188.   [36] *Ibid.,* p. 189.   [37] *Ibid.,* p. 198.

mind of a comprehensive psychologist—one who sensed, what is more, the significance of unconscious factors in the human psyche. Intuitive perception of

> each special kind of presentation seems often con-
> nected with some special range or ranges of asso-
> ciation, dating back, perhaps, to the very dawn
> of emotional life. . . . This element [of beauty
> and impressiveness] is specially characteristic of
> the units, which, while entering as parts into some
> larger -composition, are themselves more com-
> pletely and essentially organic, inasmuch as fur-
> ther reduction or analysis of them would mean
> absolute mutilation and loss of all characteristic
> impressiveness; as, for instance, if we divide a face
> or figure into its separate features or limbs, or a
> theme from some musical piece into detached
> notes or bars. At the same time it is impossible
> to lay down hard and fast limits: we have already
> seen that different sorts of work differ greatly in
> the extent to which they concentrate the chief in-
> terest on any such complete or semi-complete
> units.[38]

Remembering Coleridge's use of the crystal image to shape his concept, the lines that follow take on additional relevance. Here, too, Gurney is concerned not only with the distinct "size" of a given image but with the relationships of the more or less autonomous parts to a larger whole—or what I might hypothesize as a composite symbol:

> We could not isolate a piece of delicately gra-
> dated light as a form; and yet the sense of free
> and sunny space, or of endless aerial perspective,
> which it might suggest, would come distinctly

[38] *Ibid.,* p. 185.

under the head we are considering. *Both in land-
scape and buildings shifting effects and general
effects are often more essential to the emotional
result than the more permanent characteristics of
particular forms.* . . . Even in the case of music,
which does, as we have seen, in a remarkable degree concentrate attention on each part in turn,
and where any melody or "subject" or phrase
which can be thought of and enjoyed in detachment has enough completeness to constitute a form
in the sense meant . . . it is useless to attempt to
draw any distinct line, dividing off what shall be
regarded as complete organisms from the clauses,
themselves organic, which combine into larger
forms.[39]

It is noteworthy that Gurney speaks of the
"emotional result" of contemplation: the apprehension,
in this instance, of a "picture" having—formally, stylis-
tically—a relevance to human experience. One can
think of the objective image as being crystalline or
prismatic in its functioning; it would be a mistake to
equate it, *qua* symbol, with the crystal or prism. But the
highly colored, intense connotations of a prismatic
rendering appear apt in terms of the concentration
which an art object gives to its elements:

And Music condenses a very large amount of
inner life, of the sort of experience which might
lend itself to such general associations, into a very
brief space of actual time. The successions of in-

[39] Gurney, pp. 185–86. (Italics mine.) Impressionism in
painting was just being born in 1880, and musical Impressionism was to follow sometime after; but Gurney's discern-
ment of the artistic image in *evanescence* is another example
of what I have called his extraordinary prescience. The
recognition of the reality in change, in process, is also
Bergsonian.

tensity and relaxation, the expectation perpetually bred and perpetually satisfied, the constant
direction of the motion to new points, and constant evolution of part from part, comprise an im-
mense amount of alternations of posture and of
active adjustment of the will. We may perhaps
even extend the suggestions . . . so far as to
imagine that this ever-changing adjustment of the
will, subtle and swift in Music beyond all sort of
parallel, may project on the mind faint intangible
images of extra-musical impulse and endeavor;
and that the ease and spontaneity of the motions,
the certainty with which a thing known or dimly
divined as about to happen *does* happen, creating
a half-illusion that the notes are obeying the con-
trolling force of one's own desire, may similarly
open up vague channels of association with other
moments of satisfaction and attainment. But these
affinities are at any rate of the most absolutely
general kind; and whatever their importance may
be, they seem to me to lie in a region where
thought and language struggle in vain to penetrate.[40]

Objectivity is a quality of the art work: or to
be redundant, of the objective image. The image condenses, concentrates its elements, in order to "present"
them for contemplation. Visual aids are perhaps over-
worked as a means of pointing to symbolic functions,
yet they suggest themselves readily to the imagination;
thus we speak of an "aural" image. The immediacy of
artistic import is implied in the term *presentational,* a
word that so disturbed Hospers. But Gurney used it in
1880, in the form of "presentative": "It is true, of
course, that the presentative or 'essential pictorial qualities' are the indispensable condition for the objects and

[40] *Ibid.,* p. 348.

ideas to be wrought into a transfigured and illuminated presentment, a unique and untranslatable work of art."[41] Gurney speaks also of "the difficulty of conceiving an art as *presentative,* as primarily bound, by presenting its *own* things, whether in harmony with other things or not, to stir up its own indescribable emotions."[42]

Gurney, it should be remarked here, seems to accord to music a presentative power denied to other arts, precisely because of those verbal and representational associations which they possess and which music essentially lacks. Thus he fails to ascribe to poetry that same unity of form and content that he claims for music. He does not go all the way with his support of the distinct modalities of other arts. Of painting, he asserts that

> however much form and matter in a picture may be described as "presenting, in their union and identity, one single effect to the imaginative reason" [he is quoting Pater's *The School of Giorgione*] that effect is a very complex one, and all the ideas and associations which the represented and recognized objects suggest are inevitably part of what the imaginative reason is occupied with.[43]

While Gurney cannot wholly support Pater's dictum that "all art constantly aspires toward the condition of music," he would agree with him that "it is the art of music which most completely realizes this artistic ideal, this perfect identification of matter and form."[44] His

[41] *Ibid.,* p. 396.
[42] *Ibid.,* p. 490.
[43] *Ibid.,* pp. 396–97.
[44] Walter Pater, *The Renaissance* (New York: Mentor Press, 1959), pp. 97–98.

agreement on this point takes the form of a denial of such form-content unity—to the same degree—in poetry:

> In a musical presentation the *whole substance* is apprehended through the sense, consisting as it does essentially of form; and owing to this entire dependence on a sense, the faculty of viewing as a whole the relations of affinity or contrast which different parts of a musical movement present, has a much shorter tether than the free intellectual faculty which is concerned with literary work. One may comprehend the unity of a poem which takes many hours to read; whereas the furthest limits to which it would be possible to extend the comprehension in the other case would be reckoned by minutes. And the mode of structure within these limits entails, as we have seen, organic forms very much less extended still, these last being the elements whose character is all-important.[45]

It seems, indeed, that the term *presentational* would have little relevance to an extended literary work in which discursive elements, however fused and transcended through symbolic transformation, were inevitably included. But the relevance of the presentational to modalities other than music is nevertheless apparent; more than that (Hospers to the contrary), it is apposite in a consideration of symbolism. As the work of Freud and Jung has shown, the *symbolism* of dreams—and surely this is not a misuse of the term—is of a vivid, immediate, dramatic character; and the dream symbols are not merely "about" something: such a discursive account of their content and meaning comes after the dreaming! The dream symbol, like the art

---

[45] Gurney, p. 227.

symbol, embodies what it is pointing to: it presents; it "is." And the difficulty of arriving at a satisfactory interpretation of many dreams indicates that often they do subsist, in Gurney's words, in a region where thought and language struggle in vain to penetrate.

Aside from all these considerations, however, no word can be rendered in all its connotations by any synonym: not, certainly, in the case of *symbol* by "sign," "representation," or any other approximation that comes to mind. If the term demonstrates a protean capacity for multiple meanings, as its heavy burden of connotations indicates, this may be the very recommendation we are looking for in our quest for appropriate language. Yet Gurney did not employ it; instead he coined the epithet *ideal motion*. Similarly, for what has been variously called the objective image, the symbolic analogue, the aural image, the Apollonian embodiment of the Dionysian, and so on, Gurney adopted the term *impressive*. The impressive, in Gurney's vocabulary, is that which can be objectively assessed. This is another usage which exasperated Hospers; yet in adopting it Gurney was not saying that music could not express anything, still less that it is meaningless. The distinctions Gurney makes between the categories *impressive* and *expressive* are the most subtle and difficult ones he brings to bear on his argument, and I hope I have understood them correctly. Impressiveness is that very quality which gives distance, objectivity, to the art work:

> The problem is indeed a staggering one, by what alchemy abstract forms of sound, however unique and definite and however enhanced in effect by the watching of their evolution moment

by moment, are capable of transformation into phenomena charged with feeling, and yet in whose most characteristic impressiveness separate feelings seem as fused and lost as the colors in a ray of white light.[46]

"Impressiveness" is what Schiller called *Schein,* what Clive Bell discerned in "significant form," what Susanne Langer described as "semblance." "Expressiveness," on the other hand, by which music may "suggest describable images, qualities, or feelings, known in connection with other experiences,"[47] is often *absent or only slightly present* in a great deal of impressive music. Gurney demonstrates, with considerable ingenuity, how the peregrinations of ideal motion can suggest tenderness, mysteriousness, caprice, passion, and humor—admittedly expressive qualities—but adds that "the very act of cataloguing a few of these definite emotional characters makes one feel how transient and uncertain they often are; how little they sum up the substance of the thing which is actually delighting us."[48]

Gurney makes three points having special relevance to those qualities of music which are analogous to life experience and thus lead to recurrent associations: music, or ideal motion, has infinite varieties and nuances which constitute the whole body of musical forms; musical motion sometimes displays general features suggesting physical motions in space; musical motion may, on occasion, suggest those human or extramusical emotions which physical motion, in a rough and general way, can sometimes give expression to without the aid of language. The supposed correspondence is then a reminder, a resemblance—which of course may be

[46] *Ibid.,* p. 316.   [47] *Ibid.,* p. 314.   [48] *Ibid.,* p. 336.

vivid—rather than direct expression. The ramifications of Gurney's distinctions are complex and copiously illustrated; they also have a high degree of intrinsic interest.

The *impressiveness* of the *ideal motion*—that unified presentation of the audible "image"—is what now concerns us. And this impressiveness is autonomous. The creating of symbols has often been called, since Carlyle, a building of "worlds." Here is Gurney's summary of that ideal activity:

> The central conception itself . . . is that the primary and essential function of music is to create beautiful *objective forms,* and to *impress* us with otherwise *un*known things, instead of to induce and support particular *subjective moods* and to *ex*press for us known things.[49]

I have assembled the main constituents of Gurney's theory within as small a space as feasible. The principal tenets of the ideal motion have been given, insofar as possible, in his own words. My juxtapositions of more or less synonymous words and phrases are intended to emphasize again and again the points of similarity among the thinkers we are examining. Actually, it is remarkable how close many of their formulations are to one another. A homogeneity of vocabulary is the very last thing we could expect; concepts, however, as we have compared them from Schopenhauer to Gurney show at times an amazing homogeneity. Consider, for example, the problem of distance and the "objectivity" of the image: the most profound essential agree-

[49] *Ibid.,* p. 490.

ment is manifested here. The "how," to be sure, remains mysterious. Insofar as the symbolic analogue—Gurney's musical impressiveness—is more than the sum of its parts, there is an element of mystery; the *Schein* is magical. The uniqueness of a particular image carries a suggestion also of strangeness, if not a touch of the exotic. But the impressiveness is the symbolic attribute which makes it generally accessible to the human understanding; it is precisely the transcendence of the particular in space and time that gives the relative autonomy to the art object. And again I say "relative" because art is a human creation and its import is realized only in a universe of human discourse. Since this environment may be assumed—although curiously it is sometimes necessary to make explicit acknowledgment of this human world, as of some very obvious thing we had forgotten about—we can say yes, the symbol is autonomous, *qua* art. Ideal motion, then, is objective—and we are not forgetting the peculiar character of the artistic matrix.

Impressiveness, it follows, is the distinctive mark in Gurney's thought of that objectivity. Gurney himself hints at the element of transcendence: but this, too, inheres in the objectivity of art, not in the vague subjectivity of individuals:

> True art is objective; and the definiteness in form which first-rate music presents to the hearing ear is compatible with a sense of mystery and infinity which no vagueness can emulate, and which will gain nothing from a score of possible (and very often entirely different) subjective interpretations.[50]

[50] *Ibid.*, p. 525.

Gurney's thought is in many respects close to that of Susanne Langer's; and the strong similarity that I find between them is the more remarkable in that she has not, to my knowledge, read him. "Art is the creation of forms symbolic of human feeling," says Professor Langer.

The correspondence of Gurney's theory with contemporary thought does not end there, however. Carlos Chavez, in his recent Norton lectures at Harvard University, affirmed that "the very nature of the musical medium, so utterly suitable to take on the shape of our emotions, makes music the ideal instrument of magic."[51] Note particularly the phraseology "take on the shape of our emotions" and its relevance to Gurney's hypothesis comparing ideal and physical motion in their relation to human feelings. Chavez also offers reinforcement to the organic thesis, which accords vitality to the ideal motion: "We want to make a creature with certain parts of its own that would make a coherent whole, because we ourselves rejoice in the contemplation of a unity. Man loves unities. That is how form has become the *sine qua non* of art as we conceive it nowadays."[52]

"Nowadays" will do, although we are separated by nearly a century from *The Power of Sound*. But Gurney's own explication of that power remains as timely as anyone's, and considerably more comprehensive—as well as more graceful—than most:

It must suffice here to mention in the briefest way the prime characteristic of Music, the *alpha* and *omega* of its essential effect: namely, its per-

[51] Carlos Chavez, *Musical Thought* (Cambridge: Harvard Univ. Press, 1961), p. 44.
[52] *Ibid.*, p. 28.

petual production in us of an emotional excitement of a very intense kind, which yet cannot be defined under any known head of emotion. So far as it can be described, it seems like a fusion of strong emotions transfigured into a wholly new experience, wherof if we seek to bring out the separate threads we are hopelessly baulked; for triumph and tenderness, desire and satisfaction, yielding and insistence, may seem to be all there at once, yet without any dubiousness or confusion in the result; or rather elements seem there which we struggle dimly to adumbrate by such words, thus making the experience seem vague only by our own attempt to analyse it, while really the beauty has the unity and individuality pertaining to clear and definite form. Even when the emotion takes on a definable hue, a kinship it may be to laughter or to tears, it still has the character of directing down these special channels a high-pitched excitement having its independent source at the general watershed of unique musical impression.[53]

It begins to appear that we have, in the *ideal motion* of musical symbolism, a phenomenon that is in some degree *archetypal*. If this is so, it will be necessary to undertake a more intensive investigation of symbolic structure.

[53] Gurney, p. 120. The reader will have observed, throughout this chapter, Gurney's emphasis on organic unity, which Chavez obligingly echoes. The concept is again exciting considerable interest in philosophic debates. See, for example, Catherine Lord, "Organic Unity Reconsidered," *JAAC*, XXII, No. 3 (Spring, 1964), 263–68.

* * * CHAPTER SEVEN

BACKGROUNDS AND FOREGROUNDS: HISTORIANS, SCIENTISTS, SEERS

* * * WARREN DWIGHT ALLEN, IN HIS *PHILOSOPHIES OF MUSIC HISTORY,* refers to the nineteenth-century concept of musical form as *organism* as a pseudomystical idea which has done more than anything else to postpone the modern scientific approach to musicology as a study of style. He suggests that we "abandon the 'single lofty point of view' of music as a mystic entity, in order to find a pluralistic method by which we may deal in a scientific way with different arts of music in different areas."[1] Yet Allen concedes that "while the musicologist is concerning himself with specific techniques in limited areas of inquiry, he has not yet formulated a general *method,* a philosophy with reference to the whole field."[2]

[1] Warren Dwight Allen, *Philosophies of Music History* (New York: Dover Publications, Inc., 1962), p. xxvi.
[2] *Ibid.,* p. xix.

Of course we must have both the general and the particular; the concept of "organism" itself makes this mandatory. I agree with Allen that we must define our terms and that the development of a sophisticated style criticism will aid in the dissemination of a broad musical culture, while the adherence to the narrow strictures of "form and analysis" as it has long been taught in our conservatories can hardly be expected to do so. Allen's canons of pluralistic style analysis, however, give us no means of throwing light on what music is. It may well be that the formulation of general theory, inside or outside official musicological circles, will finally entail something that may be construed as a "single lofty point of view."

The Romantic demand for syntheses may have to be resurrected. Professor Allen's book is itself a remarkable synthesis of many particulars, related to each other through his own unifying conceptions. The first part of his book is an examination of music histories; the second, a consideration of philosophies of music history. In his introduction to the second part he deals with the static and dynamic components of continuity; he places himself on the side of dynamism and challenges the traditional conceptual modes of historical thought; he wishes to promote the "emergent new." In his advocacy of a wide musical comprehensibility Allen favors "a return to the tolerant spirit of that great musician and scholar, Michael Praetorius, who could enjoy all kinds of music, ancient and modern . . . and music for all kinds of social use and communication."[3] He maintains

[3] *Ibid.*, p. 182.

that we should not impose standards. In this he is wholly in accord with Gurney, who castigates the fallacies of his day:

> My argument, so far as it is true, cuts the ground from under the sort of musical controversy which is most rampant and useless—the endless disputation and dogmatism about the comparative merits of composers and compositions—by showing how little tangible basis such disputation has; how utterly unconvincing it is doomed to be; and how the application of the only possible test distinctly points to the wisdom, in this region, of exceptionally wide tolerance.[4]

However, in abandoning the possibility of a single—and let us substitute "comprehensive" for "lofty"—point of view, Allen is conforming to recent orthodoxy. A powerful analytical method (even if addicted to pluralisms) may, as with Bertrand Russell, be taken for the whole: substituted, indeed, for that matrix out of which it was itself engendered. Russell states that logical analysts

> confess frankly that the human intellect is unable to find conclusive answers to many questions of profound importance to mankind, but they refuse to believe that there is some "higher" way of knowing, by which we can discover truths hidden from science and the intellect.[5]

We may discount the terms *conclusive* and *higher* in the above quotation: a scientific receptivity

[4] Edmund Gurney, *The Power of Sound* (London: Smith, Elder, & Co., 1880), p. ix.
[5] Bertrand Russell, *A History of Western Philosophy* (New York: Simon and Schuster, 1945), p. 835.

to evidence in no way obliges us, before the evidence is presented, to qualify it by the use of such adjectives. But the refusal to admit possibilities is, *qua* science, unacceptable; the refusal is a personal and temperamental bias, notwithstanding Russell's ideal of scientific truthfulness, "by which I mean the habit of basing beliefs upon observations and inferences as impersonal, and as much divested of local and temperamental bias, as is possible for human beings."[6] He is obliged, of course, to admit that it is human beings who make the observations and draw the inferences. The fixing of arbitrary limits will not serve a comprehensive theory, whatever the gains in lucidity, manageability, and convenience might be.

Allen is intrigued by Leibniz's *infinite divisibility of the continuous,* a concept which plunges us into the heart of the Zeno controversy. As a dynamist, Allen would be on the side of Bergson. Allen states that analogy has, historically, served static concepts. But why dispense with analogy, however dangerous it may be, as Allen implies that we should? The comparison of dynamic continuity with the single flight of the arrow is itself analogy—in the service, this time, of mobility. The singleness of a large motion—an overriding dynamism—may similarly be used analogically to suggest the purview, the inclusive compass, of comprehensive theory.

The difficulties of arriving at a comprehensive view—the prospect of inevitable mistakes and misinterpretations—cannot be yielded to without a serious impoverishment of speculation and hence theory.

[6] *Ibid.,* p. 836.

"Scale" is a relevant factor provided for in the comprehensive outlook: thus the principles of Newtonian mechanics, eminently workable within the range of thought that produced them, are inadequate to account for the phenomena observed in modern physics. Theory, or "construction," with its practical consequences, grows not only by speculation, as Jung attests in the passage that follows, but grows by what can only be considered as heresy from the standpoint of whatever orthodoxy may be in the ascendant:

> The analytic reductive method has the advantage of being much simpler than the constructive method. The former reduces to well-known universal elements of an extremely simple nature. The latter has, with extremely complicated material, to construct the further path to some often unknown end. This obliges the psychologist to take full account of all those forces which are at work in the human mind. The reductive method strives to replace the religious and philosophical needs of man, by their more elementary components, following the principle of the "nothing but," as James so aptly calls it. But to *construct* aright, we must accept the developed aspirations as indispensable components, essential elements, of spiritual growth. Such work extends far beyond empirical concepts but that is in accordance with the nature of the human soul which has never hitherto rested content with experience alone. Everything new in the human mind proceeds from speculation. Mental development proceeds by way of speculation, never by way of limitation to mere experience. I realise that my views are parallel with those of Bergson, and that in my book the concept of the libido which I have given, is a concept parallel to that of "élan vital"; my

constructive method corresponds to Bergson's "intuitive method."[7]

Bergson, by virtue of his emphasis on process, made a strong appeal to the pragmatists, particularly William James, who wrote to the author of *Creative Evolution:* "Oh, my Bergson, you are a magician and your book is a marvel, a real wonder . . . a pure classic in point of form . . . such a flavor of persistent euphony, as of a rich river that never foamed or ran thin, but steadily and firmly proceeded with its banks full to the brim."[8]

The richness and persistent euphony are facets, indeed, of what we are defining as the *musical symbol.* Clearly, I am making use of analogy. Martin Buber does the same when, using music as a point of departure, he says that true inwardness is a polyphony in which no single voice can be "reduced" to another. The intricacy, the richness, may in the apprehension of certain modes of experience—the hearing of a Bach fugue, for example—be the fact of the matter. Truth in such an instance is not to be found in ignoring (nor in ignorance of!) the complexity of the apprehension, nor will the pulling apart of various strands explain the Gestalt. But it is a fact of the experience that cognizance is also taken of those strands themselves or, holding the example of the fugue, its separate voices. "The con-

[7] C. J. Jung, *Collected Papers on Analytical Psychology,* trans. by Constance E. Long (London: Baillière, Tindall and Cox, 1920), p. 120.
[8] Quoted in Irwin Edman's "Foreword" to Bergson's *Creative Evolution,* trans. by Arthur Mitchell (New York: The Modern Library, 1944), p. ix.

structive comprehension also *analyses,"* says Jung, "but it does not reduce."[9]

Musical experience is empirical, not abstract. But the meaning of that experience is in the interaction between man and the musical image: the formal "sound" is objective; but the experience of it is inward, unrelated causally to the day, the year, or the hour. That a moment in historical time must provide the occasion is undeniable; but the musical apprehension itself is in no way conditioned by the choice of time—other things being equal—except by the necessary condition that an occasion be provided. Using that point of departure the experience of music moves into another dimension: the movement which constitutes its form is ideal; though actual time is used up, the essence of the dialogue, the human apprehension of the aural image, is nontemporal.

In the application of his pluralistic criteria of style, Allen would keep the art in "time"; from the standpoint of a historian this is necessary and feasible. But an essential understanding of music can only come about through a recognition of its own modality—a virtual one. Hence theory, beyond its stylistic analyses, must deal with the problem—and for the discursive reason it is surely a problem—of the virtual, even should this preoccupation finally entail that "single point of view" Allen would do away with. I will join him, however, in discarding the concept of "lofty," for this is surely an irrelevancy, no less than Russell's "conclusive" and "higher."

[9] Jung, p. 344.

Allen asks for an end to monistic philosophies of music history; this seems to me to be the expression of a personal and temperamental bias. Such philosophies may, so far, have been seriously in error; but what of a monistic view so all-encompassing that it recognizes an essence whose manifestations are infinite in themselves? I will not, however, press this point, since the problem is one of those ultimates susceptible (though, I suspect, for the very reason I have just suggested) to either a monistic or a pluralistic interpretation. It is not idle conjecture to propose that in the reading of phenomena, pluralistic criteria could be "contained" in a larger unity. Allen, nevertheless, enjoys the support of Bergson and James on this point—and, of course, that of John Dewey.

I have described the modality of music as virtual, nondiscursive, nontemporal in essence. The sphere of the actual, in which temporal processes occur and discursive reason initiates causal sequences, is distinguished from the subjective world, in which the meaning of objective form is realized by Jung who is also describing in psychoanalytical terms the "timeless" nature of that inner, subliminal world:

> To interpret Freud objectively, i.e., from the causal standpoint, is as though a man were to consider a sculpture from the historical, technical and—last but not least—from the mineralogical standpoint. But where lurks the *real meaning* of the wondrous work? Where is the answer to that most important question: what aim had the artist in mind, and how are we ourselves to understand his work subjectively? To the scientific spirit this seems an idle question which anyhow has nothing

to do with science. It comes furthermore into col-
lision with the causal principle, for it is a purely
speculative constructive view. . . .

But if we would approach to an understanding
of psychological things we must remember the
fact of the subjective conditioning of all knowledge. The world is *as we see it* and not simply
objective; this holds true even more of the mind.
. . . The causal understanding of Faust enlight-
ens us as to how it became a finished work of art,
but reveals nothing of the living meaning of the
poet. That meaning only lives if we experience
it, in and through ourselves. . . . The causal
standpoint reduces things to their elements, the
constructive standpoint elaborates them into
something higher and more complicated. This
latter standpoint is necessarily a speculative one.

Looked at from within . . . constructive understanding means redemption.[10]

He then quotes Nietzsche who said that "creation" is
the great redemption from suffering and easiness of
living. Nietzsche is here again acknowledging the necessity for that Apollonian embodiment of the Dionysian, to which Jung's "constructive understanding" is
analogous, that "ordering" of experience, both inner
and external, which accords reality to the symbolic image. The symbolic function of dream images has been
discussed. "The world is as we see it."

The automatic and profligate nature of dream
symbolism is testimony in its own sphere to Hayakawa's
assertion that the symbolic process requires the human
nervous system.[11] The world as we see it is conditioned

10 *Ibid.*, p. 123.
11 Cf. S. I. Hayakawa, "Art and Tension," *Language in
Thought and Action* (New York: Harcourt, Brace & Co.,
1949), p. 143 ff.

by our humanness. The world of our perceptions—artistic and otherwise—must be in large measure a human world. Herbert Read has this to say:

> The farther modern psychology has probed into the distinctive quality of the work of art, the more it has tended to recognize the presence of autonomous processes of organization within the nervous system, and to attribute to these processes the formal characteristics that constitute the aesthetic appeal of the work of art.[12]

Yet the creation of a work of art, he would agree, is a special kind of ordering, both for its maker and for the percipient. *Integration* is a term we are more accustomed to. If we raise the concept to another (loftier?) power we get, in the lexicon of Jung (and Nietzsche), *redemption*. Or, in Hayakawa's terms, the capacity to bear the unbearable.

"Far removed from their pain," said Schopenhauer of music in its relation to all the emotions of our inmost nature. Perhaps not so far, but at one remove certainly: and at that "objective" remove, irrevocably crystallized for contemplation in the musical symbol.

Causality is operative in actual time. Jung points out that causality is a statistical truth; there are real exceptions in space-time to its dominion, events that are observable but not provided for in the causal world view. These events are nevertheless meaningful and appear under the guise of a correspondence of

[12] Herbert Read, *The Forms of Things Unknown* (New York: Horizon Press, 1960), p. 55.

events unrelated causally; to such *meaningful coincidences in time* Jung gives the name *synchronicity*. The acausal phenomena which belong to this category of manifestation—such as precognition in dreams—relativize space-time. The analogues, which may be revealed in the human psyche to actualities (past, present, or future) in the world, take the form of images or phantasms; they are not actual but they correspond to actuality. These images have an objectivity, an autonomy; they have symbolic relevance to the mind of the percipient. The greater the number of meaningful coincidences and the more exact their correspondence to actuality, the less can they justifiably be looked upon as pure chance, and "for lack of a causal explanation, have to be thought of as *meaningful arrangements. . . .* Their 'inexplicability' is not due to the fact that the cause is unknown, but to the fact that *a cause is not even thinkable in intellectual terms.*"[13] Synchronicity, Jung explains, is no more baffling or mysterious than the discontinuities of physics:

> It is only the ingrained belief in the sovereign power of causality that creates intellectual difficulties and makes it appear unthinkable that causeless events exist or could ever occur. But if they do, then we must regard them as *creative acts,* as the continuous creation of a pattern that exists from all eternity, repeats itself sporadically, and is not derivable from any known antecedents. We must of course guard against thinking of every event whose cause is unknown as "causeless." This, as I have already stressed, is admis-

[13] Jung, *Psyche and Symbol,* ed., Violet S. de Laszlo, trans. by Cary Baynes and F. C. R. Hull (New York: [Anchor] Doubleday & Co., 1958), p. 281. (Italics mine.)

sible only when a cause is not even thinkable. But thinkability is itself an idea that needs the most rigorous criticism. Had the atom corresponded to the original philosophical conception of it, its fissionability would be unthinkable. But once it proves to be a measurable quantity, its non-fissionability becomes unthinkable.[14]

I suggested at the conclusion of the previous chapter that the musical symbol appears to have an almost archetypal character. We have now examined many ideas concerning the relationship of music to the emotions. It appears to be the consensus that there is such a relationship: the consensus, too, that the relationship is not direct. Some essence, as it were, of the life of feeling is objectified in the aural image and freed from the demands of the immediate. It becomes then an object of contemplation; it is meaningful for the psyche: it has relevance, in a formal and concentrated way, to life in its generality. The causal aspects of events in the empirical world are not, however, mirrored in the image; it is, in Jung's term, *acausal*.

That the analogue to feeling revealed by the aural image is close to Jung's concept of the archetype and its function should now be clear: "The archetype *is* the introspectively recognizable form of a priori psychic orderedness."[15] The forms of psychic orderedness, moreover, are—he maintains—*acts of creation in time*. It was remarked by Gurney, as it has been observed by Roger Sessions and others in our own day, that musical processes suggest in their lineaments similar movements in the physical world and in the human psychophysical organism. The archetype, says Jung,

[14] *Ibid.,* pp. 280–81.   [15] *Ibid.,* p. 278.

"reveals itself to psychic introspection—so far as inward perception can grasp it at all—as an image, or rather a type which underlies not only the psychic equivalences but, remarkably enough, the psychophysical equivalences too."[16] The archetype, he says, portrays ordinary instinctual events in the form of *types*.

The archetypal configurations of human consciousness are no doubt prior to, more universal, and more durable than any objective image—the creation of a single mind—that we would call a musical symbol. Nevertheless, there is unmistakable resemblance in terms of generality, relevance to human feelings, and relative independence of actual time. The "continuous creation" Jung postulates is causeless; he observes that a series of successive aspects of creation is also a manifestation of the one creative act—Zeno's arrow again!—and that what happens successively in time is simultaneous in the mind of God.

One of the most exciting results of this study, and one that could not have been foreseen, has been the reinforcement of particular ideas that has come sometimes from the most unexpected sources. Support for one's central conceptions is always welcome and particularly when, as one hopes, this is forthcoming from colleagues in one's own or related fields. But there is a special delight, too, in observing a still wider applicability of the same principles. I hope that such reinforcement has already been evident; there are other examples to follow. What strikes me as significant is not the ascription of origins a particular writer will

[16] *Ibid.*, p. 277.

make, nor the vocabulary he uses to express his insights, but the fact that there is wide essential agreement on *the existence of certain processes.* The interpretation of these processes, as we are discovering, is far from homogeneous: but that a process of what I call symbol building (though it may be called by other names) is there—in the world of human discourse—and may be observed is attested to by an impressive number of reputable witnesses, themselves widely scattered in time and space, reporting from the most disparate vantage points, not excluding those breeding grounds of personal and temperamental bias.

Theory follows observation and is abetted by speculation; the ratio of one element to the other is never fixed. But theory must ultimately depend for whatever cogency it possesses upon referents in the world of human actuality, which provides its empirical laboratory. Insofar, then, as a reading of phenomena is based on observations which may be shared by others, the acceptance or rejection of a particular conceptual framework in which an investigator chooses to enclose his observation is an optional matter and need not invalidate the empirical data. Thus one need not be a Catholic to find valid—because testable—insights in the writings of Maritain; one may, for that matter, be inclined to an intuitive approach to experience both in life and art without any theological presuppositions whatsoever.

Coomaraswamy, one of the most erudite men of our century, called one of his lectures "The Christian and Oriental, or True, Philosophy of Art." His espousal of Plato and Aristotle was no less fervent than his en-

dorsement of what he regarded as the "true" principles
of art to be found in Eastern and Western religious
traditions; he reiterated the view that what he offered,
what he believed, was not his "own." But the pronouncements he makes which are directly applicable,
for example, to music may be examined at that level of
relevance; I cannot admit, for my purposes, Coomaraswamy's further claim that his entire framework is necessarily presupposed. When we confine ourselves to the
immediate relevance of empirically testable data, we
see that we are confronted, in these words of Coomaraswamy, by concepts which are now familiar: "What is
implied by contemplation is to raise our level of reference from the empirical to the ideal, from observation
to vision, from any auditory sensation to audition."[17]
Coomaraswamy is an Apollonian: we perceive art not
through the feelings but by the intellect; true art is
rational. But art reflects ultimates and is therefore only
partially accessible to the discursive reason; it is symbolic: "We have no other language whatever except
the symbolic in which to speak of ultimate reality."[18] In
defiance of Dwight Allen he claims that the unmani-
fested can be known by analogy. (Such analogical
knowledge is inherent in the musical symbol.) A symbol, he says, is a mystery—and here he echoes Carlyle—
which half reveals, half conceals. Coomaraswamy is a
traditionalist; he is also a transcendentalist. But his assertion that artistic invention is "the entertainment of
ideas; the intuition of things as they are on higher than

[17] Ananda K. Coomaraswamy, *Christian and Oriental Philosophy of Art* (New York: Dover Publications Inc., 1956),
p. 37.
[18] *Ibid.,* pp. 50–51.

empirical levels of reference"[19] could have been made by Schopenhauer. Works of art, Coomaraswamy tells us, are supports to contemplation: "They are such adequate analogies as to be able to remind us, i.e., put us in mind again, of their archetypes."[20] Here he strikes a Jungian chord.

And so does Jacques Maritain in these lines from "The Internalization of Music":

> I have considered what is, to my mind, the prime and most genuine way in which the immediately illuminating image arises—I mean as drawn by poetic intuition from the ocean of images which are part of the preconscious life of the spirit and connatural instruments of the Illuminating Intellect.[21]

Poetic intuition for Maritain is knowledge through emotion, but an emotion corresponding to Gurney's special musical sense: an emotion that causes us to *see*—gives us *vision*—puts us *there*. "There" is the domain of the virtual. And "there" we experience liberation from the immediate exigencies of life; we are "far removed from their pain." Conceptual knowledge of poetic intuition is gained from translation; poetic intuition itself yields "the music of imaginal and emotional pulsions." The pulsions are dynamic. They are inward: "We must listen," says Maritain, "to the interiority of the work."[22]

Robert Frost says a poem begins with a "lump

[19] *Ibid.,* p. 35.
[20] *Ibid.,* p. 10.
[21] Jacques Maritain, *Creative Intuition in Art and Poetry* (New York: [Meridian] Pantheon Books, Inc., 1955), p. 229.
[22] *Ibid.,* p. 209.

in the throat"; Maritain, that its origin is in "a kind of musical stir, of unformulated song, with no words, no sounds, absolutely inaudible to the ear, audible only to the heart, here is the first sign through which the presence of poetic experience within the soul is recognized."[23] A full store of images and "emotional movements" are present in the inner self, in a state of virtuality. Meaning is set free in a motion capable of inflicting that "immortal wound" that Frost referred to.

But the primordial stir must become more explicit: images "awaken." Their aspects are intelligible, though nonconceptual; Maritain's Illuminating Intellect is wider ranging than the discursive reason. This Catholic apologist could be referring to the Zen experience of *satori* when he says the final poetic aim is "a mysterious *flash of reality* which has been grasped without concept and which no concept can express."[24] The completed process is "objective": "The poetic intuition demands to be objectivized and expressed in a work. It is enough that the work exists, that this kind of a world is created."[25] The work reveals both the subjectivity of the creator and the "ontologic mystery" of the world; when the work—the completed symbol—presents itself to contemplation, there is a "communication" of intuition, from the *creative* to the *receptive:* "What matters is that something be perceived of what was contained, even virtually, in the inexhaustible intuition from which it proceeds."[26] The symbol captures an essence and delivers it formally—that is to say, objectively. Here, then, is the presentational symbol. And

---

[23] *Ibid.,* p. 203.
[24] *Ibid.,* p. 212.

[25] *Ibid.,* p. 208.
[26] *Ibid.,* p. 209.

its nature is acausal: "The supreme law of expression is no longer the law of rational and logical connections, it is the law of the inner connections between intuitive pulsions, and of the unconceptualized intelligibility of which the images quickened by poetic intuition are the vehicles."[27] Coomaraswamy says the symbol half reveals, half conceals; Maritain, that the poem "is an engine to make us pass *through* or *beyond* things." The symbol reveals *in* and *through;* it is transcendent.

Maritain speaks of the music of intuitive pulsions; in his view of poetry, music underlies words. He is, as we shall see, close to the *symbolistes* in his postulation of a word-music, a poetry that aspires to the condition of music. That music, to which Mallarmé alludes, is in its "first transient and tendential stage" inaudible within the soul. But although Maritain throughout his essay "merges the modalities," as it were, of music and poetry, he finally grants an expressive—and nonverbal—ascendancy to music, in words which echo Tagore:

> Of every music it is true to say that the song begins where the word stops, as a bursting forth of a spiritual and emotional stir or exultation of the subjectivity—too deeply subjective, too existentially singular, too incommunicably affective to be possibly conveyed by any meaning of words.[28]

The musical "stir" itself, leading finally if it is "realized" to a capture of reality, is "entirely condensed, embraced, or caught in that deep and sovereign actuation." Although Maritain, like Molière's gentleman, is writing prose, he is using words—and poeti-

<hr/>

[27] *Ibid.*, p. 215.   [28] *Ibid.*, p. 294.

cally—to point in the direction of transcendence; he is
attempting (what I believe any writer can understand)
to make words outdo themselves; they are inadequate
for the task. There is more meaning than can be expressed, and it is not illusory. Hence the repetitions,
the profligacy, the search for synonyms and verbal correspondences of all kinds, the shifts and restatements.
It is nevertheless a joyous exercise; and it is, next to
immersion in the symbolic modality, the nearest one
can come. Words themselves are seeking a transcendence, in a correspondence of their own to the symbolic
mode. When the musical "stir" is "so rich in intuitive
virtuality or emotive power" that the symbol is unable
to capture it, there is an overflowing, or what Maritain
calls an *in plus*. This superfluity may be compared to
grace; it is "free" and it "makes a game of art": very
much in the manner, it occurs to me, in which the
Divine, according to the Hindu concept, takes sport in
His creation in an everlasting play, or *Lila*.

The superfluity, the *in plus*, is felt as magic. It
is "free with the pure freedom of the nocturnal depths":

> And it overflows also the power with which the
> work attains intuitively the listener. More things
> that are unknown and unseizable stir in a deeper
> and more expansive way his energies of emotion,
> intelligence, and imagination, poetry strikes him
> in more obscure darkness, he is more completely
> and defenselessly taken hold of by it. It is be-
> cause the work is thus endowed with greater
> power, born in night and operating in night, that
> the word magic seems appropriate, despite its
> ambiguity.[29]

[29] *Ibid.*, p. 295.

Richness and ambiguity, I have already observed, characterize the symbol. Maritain looks upon music as one realm of poetry, and magic is not the prerogative of music alone. Music, however, can manifest this quality—which, it must be emphasized, is a quality of transcendence—more intensively than any other art, since music "has the peculiar privilege, as we have observed, of expressing—beyond any possible meaning of words—the most deeply subjective, singular and affective stirs of creative subjectivity, too deep-seated to be possibly expressed by any other art."[30] Music may express thoughts that lie too deep, Wordsworth might have conceded, not only for tears—but for poetry as well.

And the expressive always assumes form, acquires objectivity. It is, we have seen, the objective expression of a work of art that makes it generally accessible to human beings: this is its symbolic aspect, embodied *in* the work, shining *through* it. Like stars, symbols vary considerably in brightness, in magnitude. But it is the capture, in some measure, of a reality in the universe of human discourse that gives them an abiding relevance to that world, that provides the avenue away from it and back to it. The nature—and the extent—of the reality "caught" will determine the power of its virtuality and hence its persistence in time; this measure of the "size" and quality of the reality (or *essence*) is also the measure of the symbol. Many metaphors, flaming out like supernovae, eventually fade; others appear to shine eternally in a quieter planet light.

The symbol, like life, is an alloy; no refine-

[30] *Ibid.*

ments can make it altogether pure; but the degree of its purity is the criterion of its strength. Purity in this sense is not intended to evoke any sexual analogues. The purity of the symbol is its formal (hence expressive) cogency: a cogency which may be compatible with any number of "radical juxtapositions." The Apollonian embodiment of the Dionysian may present, as we know, an unchaste image; but it may nevertheless be pure. It follows "the law of the inner connections between intuitive pulsions."[31]

The phenomenon of *catharsis* is related to the objectivity of the symbol: and the degree of catharsis to its universality. It is essential in investigating aesthetic experience that levels of that experience be recognized and admitted. Only that which has been objectified can be contemplated, can be understood. Even before any consideration of levels becomes pertinent, we must get beyond the precognitive musical stir. The effectiveness of catharsis—and here even its possible moral benefits may be admitted—would appear to be related to the clarity with which images are presented to the understanding: presented not merely to the discursive understanding, but to what Maritain calls the "Illuminating Intellect." Obviously, the less opaque the image, the greater its cogency for the perceiver. Along with the condensation and concentration that characterize symbolic structure, there must also be reduction in the sense that no image can be formed without it. Many possibilities may be realized, given form, in a single image; but not every possibility can be.

[31] *Ibid.,* p. 215.

An Apollonian mirroring must inevitably be a narrowing of the infinite, so that it becomes perceptible to human vision. A "something more," a hint of magic, will remain. But the Dionysian, the nonhuman, the diabolic, the divine—whatever the infinite contains—receive measure in the symbol; and the symbol, however much it may embody the irrational, is a rational construct. The infinite is not humanly comprehensible, not humanly manageable; yet man yearns for it. The symbol through its quality of transcendence brings the "something more" into a manageable human context; the symbol suggests more than it is; the symbol radiates an aura; but the symbol itself is finite. As a rational structure—though picturing what it will—the symbol is good; this is a peculiarly Greek notion, as is the notion of the catharsis which is presumed to follow upon an understanding of that good.

But the existence of certain processes can be detected by any qualified observer. Patterns of human experience are not a provincial patrimony; they have universality. Thus we find the equivalents of Maritain's free "delight," the Greek notion of "catharsis," and the concept of "aesthetic distance," in these lines of Sri Aurobindo:

> For the universal soul all things and all contacts of things carry in them an essence of delight best described by the Sanskrit aesthetic term, *rasa*, which means at once sap or essence of a thing and its taste. It is because we do not seek the essence of the thing in its contact with us, but look only to the manner in which it affects our desires and fears, our cravings and shrinkings that grief and pain, imperfect and transient pleasure or indiffer-

ence, that is to say, blank inability to seize the
essence, are the forms taken by the Rasa. If we
could be entirely disinterested in mind and heart
and impose that detachment on the nervous being,
the progressive elimination of these imperfect and
perverse forms of Rasa would be possible and the
true essential taste of the inalienable delight of
existence in all its variations would be within our
reach. We attain to something of this capacity for
variable but universal delight in the aesthetic re-
ception of things as represented by Art and Poetry, so that we enjoy there the Rasa or taste of
the sorrowful, the terrible, even the horrible or
repellent; and the reason is because we are detached, disinterested, not thinking of ourselves or
of self-defence, but only of the thing and its essence.[32]

We are far from their pain. . . . There is
something more, however, in Aurobindo's analysis that
is helpful for our purposes. The habit of "missing the
essence" of an objective image in its contact with us and
looking only to the manner in which it affects our
desires and fears, our cravings and shrinkings—the habit,
in short, of being preoccupied with our own reactions to
the symbol: this is the response of the aesthete, who
moves in a virtual world of textures and surfaces, reacting sensitively, aware and proud of his own reactions.
Seeking the essence of a thing, in contrast, is an act of
identification—following the Bergsonian injunction to
"enter into" an object and possess it through intuition.

The *existence of certain musical processes* is
what concerns us here: those processes themselves, and
the "how" of their recognition by human beings. The

[32] Sri Aurobindo, *The Life Divine* (New York: E. P. Dutton,
1951), p. 101.

modality of this recognition, I am proposing, is peculiar to musical apprehension; I regard it as a symbolic modality, but symbolic purely in a tonal—or what Leonard Meyer would call a "nonreferential"—sense. That music *qua* music is by definition nonreferential should by now be obvious, but the point needs pressing. I do not object to the term *revelation* applied to the apprehension of meaning attained through this unique modality; yet I do not insist upon it. There are so many trivial examples of musical composition that such a description of the musical experience should be reserved for those pinnacle occasions when a new symbolic meaning—a musical microcosm—is grasped.

Theory is concerned with what happens and why it happens. Theory is not necessarily plausible to common sense; but it must take into account the observable evidence if its hypotheses are to be entertained at all. Jung adumbrated an hypothesis of continuous creation of archetypal patterns that appear again and again without apparent cause in human consciousness. "Continuous creation is to be thought of not only as a series of successive acts of creation, but also as the eternal presence of the *one* creative act."[33]

The reader may be tempted to dismiss such speculation, even in a person of Jung's stature, as wild fancy; but a very similar idea is seriously cultivated by a prominent contemporary group of astrophysicists: the distinction being that Jung is dealing with an inner universe of human consciousness, the astrophysicists with the macrocosm. Fred Hoyle states the case for the scientists of his persuasion: "I find myself forced to

[33] Jung, *Psyche and Symbol,* p. 280.

assume that the nature of the Universe requires continuous creation—the perpetual bringing into being of new background material."[34]

The correspondence of ideas in the two theories is, in itself, an example of that "synchronicity" which Jung postulated—though he, in point of time, was precursor. But the reinforcement Hoyle provides does not end with this coincidence in descriptive terminology:

> The most obvious question to ask about continuous creation is this: Where does the created material come from? It does not come from anywhere. Material simply appears—it is created. At one time the various atoms composing the material do not exist, and at a later time they do. This may seem a very strange idea and I agree that it is, but in science it does not matter how strange an idea may seem so long as it works—that is to say, so long as the idea can be expressed in a precise form and so long as its consequences are found to be in agreement with observation.[35]

Obviously, a refusal—positivistic or whatever—to consider what is there is unscientific in spirit, whether the phenomena consist of hydrogen atoms in interstellar space or recurrent archetypal figures in dreams. One need not, of course, be predisposed to a particular hypothesis. Hoyle explains the "big bang" theory held by many eminent scientists regarding the creation of the universe and explains his own preference for "continuous creation":

[34] Fred Hoyle, *The Nature of the Universe* (New York: Mentor Press, 1955), p. 111.
[35] *Ibid.,* p. 112.

On scientific grounds this big bang assumption is much the less palatable of the two. For it is an irrational process that cannot be described in scientific terms. Continuous creation, on the other hand, can be represented by precise mathematical equations whose consequences can be worked out and compared with observation. On philosophical grounds too I cannot see any good reason for preferring the big bang idea. Indeed it seems to me in the philosophical sense to be a distinctly unsatisfactory notion, since it puts the basic assumption out of sight where it can never be challenged by a direct appeal to observation.[36]

The point I wish to make is that Jung and Hoyle are both postulating ultimates that are acausal. It appears likely that their hypotheses can neither be proven nor disproven at this juncture. But as comprehensive theorists in two disparate fields their speculations have brought them very close together. Their speculations, moreover, were prompted by what they observed and were shaped into theory in order to account as satisfactorily as possible for those observations; hypotheses are tenable only so long as they do, in fact, find support in actuality. The importance of valid intuition in science, as well as in art, is too often lost sight of. In his search for a unified field theory Einstein exemplified the speculative mind that imposes upon itself continuously the rigors of empirical testing and verification. But speculation must anticipate empirical possibilities, and the disparity between theory and practice is one of the conditions of progress in any department of human activity: the tardy verification of Einstein equations is testimony to this. Verification, it need

[36] *Ibid.*, p. 113.

hardly be added, does not always follow theory. Fred Hoyle, it should be pointed out, has now abandoned his theory of continuous creation, because he finds it unsupported by the most recent astronomical observations.

The relevance of all this to musical theory may not, at this point, be apparent. Let me say, then, that I am seeking in this study of musical meaning something analogous to a "unified field" theory. My intuition is that of an ultimate musical monism. I think we can predicate a matrix that will provide all the pluralisms Warren Dwight Allen could desire: a proliferation of styles that will go on without end, like the creation of galaxies in space.

The creation of music, unlike the making of celestial bodies, is a human enterprise; yet in the sonorous symbol man achieves something transcendent: a "virtual" object or image. One does not, of course, make full entry into the timeless realm with so fragile an icon—but he may, if he is lucky, get his foot in the door. The symbol, however the stirring of its components may originally have been actuated, is forever removed in function from a universe of causality; this is why its necessity cannot be utilitarian. And this is why the yardsticks of mundane utility alone—whether applied according to the canons of *Gebrauchsmusik,* conventional decorum, Soviet reality, or whatever—must always be, finally, a degradation of the art. The fixing of explicit limits means the extinction of musical possibilities.

Jung called causeless events "creative acts."
The creation of music is observed in time, but it conceals a mystery. The creation of even a single composition is never finished; the form is there potentially, but
it always awaits realization in performance.

The musical form that awaits performance is
archetypal. Every actual performance is measured
against it. The belief in the potency of the archetypal
form—Langer calls it the "commanding form"—is implicit in the mind of the performer who strives to make
his interpretation measure up to the conceptual ideal;
and it is believed in also by the perceptive critic who
measures the performer's efforts against that same ideal
as he, the critic, conceives it. The Platonic overtones of
this phenomenon must be remarked here. One does not
think of a musical composition as an object at all, temporal or eternal; yet as that special kind of dynamic
image, the musical symbol, it might be so construed.
The deployment of actual-virtual time are attributes of
the musical object so that the object itself acquires a
further dimension absent in the other modalities, at the
same time sacrificing a characteristic dimension the
other modalities share: that of space.

The musical performance itself leaves no trace:
nor do a thousand performances. Yet no one doubts
the existence of the B Minor Mass. The work may be
assessed historically, but its peculiar mode of being is
transhistorical. Historical assessments are the province
of historians; similarly, philosophies of music history
are within the historical purview. Professor Allen's
prerogative of dealing "in a scientific way with different
arts of music in different areas, with different peoples

made up of different individuals"[37] is uncontested. But
this prerogative does not usurp the right of philosophy
nor nullify its obligation to investigate a mode of being.
"Think in other categories," said Gurdjieff to one of
his disciples. The modality of music is "another"
category, its practice a "thinking."

The discursive treatment of musics of the
world is necessary and desirable. Professor Allen's
study shows that historical works on music have not
only been appearing recently in greater numbers but
have evidenced an expanding scope and finer scholar-
ship; his own book is a monument of comprehensive-
ness. Hugo Leichtentritt's *Music, History, and Ideas*
is another contribution to comparative stylistic analysis,
covering an extended period of time. And Paul Henry
Láng's *Music in Western Civilization* is a highly significant and panoramic examination of music in the
contexts of successive cultural milieux. The knowledge
of particular epochs (as well as the stimulus to comparative musicology) consolidated in these and other
contemporary studies—notably those remarkable contributions to the Norton series by such scholars as Reese,
Bukofzer, Grout, and Alfred Einstein—is of inestimable
value to the student of music and to the professional
practitioner.

But the musician is seeking something more
than description; he seeks insight. Receptivity to symbolic meaning is a subjective condition he must bring

[37] Allen, p. xxvi.

to the enterprise of music making, whether he is a listener or performer. A viable work of art must also be present; the symbol is a transmitter, yet it remains whole. The peculiar dynamism generated under these circumstances is of an assured, proven kind, though still capable, at one pole, of a failure of current, and at the other, of spontaneous incursions of new elements. The interpreter who brings off this second kind of performance is called inspired.

The composer, however, makes the enterprise feasible, plays the seminal role. He is not the custodian of a pilot light, nor keeper of the kiln. He is the governor of a fiery furnace, and his earth has not cooled; he seeks to shape, in that burning matrix, a form destined to endure: a sonorous symbol whose impulsions of sound will be transmitted with no diminution of its own integrity.[38]

The completed symbol is musical order in a new configuration. Charles Seeger, writing "On the Moods of a Music-Logic," asks the crucial question which must give perennial pause to the historian: "What is the extent of correspondence, then, between the original construction (a music-rationale) and the

---

[38] It may be argued that Cage and other composers who incorporate random elements into their works do not want "a form destined to endure." I have said that the musical symbol is a recognizable entity which may be "realized" repeatedly in performance. Those highly protean "compositions" which claim for their own whatever accidental sounds may be available at a given performance time are rather far removed from my own concept of *musical idea*. So-called "aleatory music" suggests a radical pragmatism which, in my view, denigrates the conceptual role of the composer. Anything goes; Cage's cooperation with this "going" may take the form (as, on occasion, it has) of a directive to the performer to "play what you wish."

re-construction of it (speech-rationale)?"[39] Semantic subtleties, one is tempted to suggest, will get us nowhere. Description of music is, at most, a pointing toward what is there. Even Bergson's command to "enter into," dramatic and direct though it is, is no more than such a pointing. "Like this, like this"—that technique of description, whatever its rationale—may whet the appetite for confrontation; the pointing may be, beyond description, an invitation to listen.

[39] Charles Seeger, "On the Moods of a Music Logic," *JAMC*, XIII (1960), 225.

CHAPTER EIGHT

THE SYMBOLIST POETS
AND THEIR INFLUENCE

* * * THERE IS MUCH TALK, AT THE TIME OF THIS writing, of *communication* or *communications*. But whether singular or plural the term belongs to a world of utilitarian discourse. What is communicated in that world are statements and what Whitehead called "scraps of information." The term *information* has recently acquired a more inclusive sense through the development of "information theory," which Leonard Meyer (as we shall see in the next chapter) has been investigating for musical purposes. We shall therefore transfer the onus from musical information to *statements about music.* Whatever the terms, the problem remains the same: primacy belongs to the word. In the utilitarian world poetry itself is expected to yield propositions in the prose vernacular. (One thinks of the recent rewriting of *Hamlet,* intended to make Shakespeare more accessible and palatable to contemporary readers.)

A century ago it was thought proper to apply Comte's principles of positivism to the anatomy of art by means of the exhaustive analysis of particular works, using techniques recognized as valid for scientific investigations. Taine, in his *Philosophie de l'art,* assumed that the data of the arts bore sufficient resemblance to the data of botany or zoology to be susceptible to similar treatment. Accordingly, classification of works and a rational interpretation of them took precedence over immediate perception; historical and biographical considerations were highly honored, as were the facts of physiological response—for instance to music—insofar as these could be ascertained. Sensuous perception, therefore, was relevant to the extent that it was measurable. Taine, following Comte's lead, looked upon art as a human activity in the service of a positivistic sociology and not significant in its own right; his yardsticks were utilitarian. Yet Taine postulated for art, beyond its role of imitation of life, a *caractère essentiel.* But if the essential character of a work can be rendered in words, as Taine assumed, then why the work of art? A. G. Lehmann, in *The Symbolist Aesthetic in France,* points out that Taine created difficulties which need never have arisen.

As we have seen, the difficulties were prevalent before Taine, and they are with us still. The crux of the problem is the confusion of modalities. Beyond this confusion of modalities per se is the misunderstanding of the functional character of music in human discourse; for music, I believe we can show, is necessary without being utilitarian. Any view that accords to music a merely instrumental importance—as does Soviet ideology, notwithstanding the strong support given approved artistic enterprises—fails to recognize its fundamental necessity. That music, an art of intrinsic human significance, may also be put to multifarious uses is obvious.

It is ironical that at the very time when the search for knowledge for its own sake was so widespread and productive in the sciences, a misappropriation of laboratory techniques (and a too exclusive reliance upon them) was to inaugurate all kinds of mischief in modes of discourse, notably the arts, where other methods of investigation were demanded by the very nature of the evidence. I have reiterated that musical experience is essentially empirical; yet it is the truth of the "experience" that nineteenth-century positivists refused to deal with; and they have passed on to the twentieth century their legacy of obfuscation.

Even at the time when positivistic canons enjoyed their greatest vogue, however, there were strongly opposed views. Hanslick occupied a somewhat anomalous position; he supported the concept of music as *autonomous,* yet he was clearly influenced by scientific reductionism: he sought to find some lowest common denominator. Gurney, in contrast, elaborated a more comprehensive, *psychological* theory of music and its effects; he anticipated the Gestaltists in his recognition of functional apprehension; and he made the facts of such apprehension, such musical experience, relevant to his theory.

In France an apotheosis of art in its uniqueness was celebrated by that group of late nineteenth-century poets—among whom were Laforgue, Rimbaud, Ver-

laine, and Huysmans—known as the *symbolistes.* They
were theorists as well as poets, and their predilection for
establishing a quasitheological framework for their crea-
tions was responsible in no small measure for the spread
of the symbolist canons outside France. Mallarmé, one
of the least prolific of fine poets, was their most articulate spokesman; Symons refers to him as a priest. The
influence of the symbolist gospel, in the promulgation
of which Symons himself and subsequently Yeats played
an important part, has continued to make itself felt in
the twentieth century, particularly in the works of
James Joyce and T. S. Eliot.

Carlyle, the pre-Raphaelites, and even Edgar
Allan Poe were early contributors of ideas that coalesced
in the *symbolisme* doctrines. Mystical elements were
emphasized by Carlyle, Ernest Heller ("L'art est le
souvenir de la présence de Dieu."), and Baudelaire.
Carlyle, in *Sartor Resartus,* finds the artistic symbol to
be mystically transcendent: ". . . let but Eternity look,
more or less visibly, through the Time-Figure *(Zeit-
bild!)* . . . . Of this latter sort are all true Works of art:
in them (if thou know a Work of Art from a Daub of
Artifice) wilt thou discern *Eternity looking Through
Time; the God-like rendered visible.*"[1] Compare this
with Symons' description of Mallarmé's teaching as
being along the lines "of that spiritualising of the word,
that perfecting of form in its capacity for allusion and
suggestion, that confidence in the eternal correspondences between the visible and the invisible universe."[2]

---

[1] Thomas Carlyle, "Symbols", *Sartor Resartus* (Chicago:
Hooper, Clarke & Co., n.d.), Book 3, Chap. 3, p. 220. (Second italics mine.)
[2] Arthur Symons, *The Symbolist Movement in Literature*
(New York: E. P. Dutton and Co., 1958), p. 75.

How close, too, this concept is in intent to the capture of the timeless in Eliot's lines:

> Sudden in a shaft of sunlight
> Even while the dust moves
> There rises the hidden laughter
> Of children in the foliage
> Quick now, here, now, always—
> Ridiculous the waste sad time
> Stretching before and after.[3]

Baudelaire was the spiritual father of the symbolist poets and showed in his own life and work that transcendence may be downward as well as upward. What concerns us here, however, is not the attainment of heaven or hell, nor yet the question of which is the more desirable, but the explication of the symbol, and the borrowing from the *symbolistes* of whatever ideas may be viable for our own musical purposes. These poets, we shall see, gave themselves free access to music, as they freely construed it. Baudelaire wished art to be clearly distinguished from propaganda of all kinds; he attacked "philosophical art" and inveighed against the distinction between content and form.

Lehmann points out that the chief difference between the positivist and symbolist views of art lay in the fact that for the symbolists, art was distinguished from science through the indispensable element of form. Croce echoes the symbolist position when he says that the whole

> is that which determines the quality of the parts. . . . The difference between a scientific work and

---

[3] T. S. Eliot, "Burnt Norton," *Four Quartets* (New York: Harcourt, Brace and Co., 1943), V, p. 8.

> a work of art, that is, between an intellectual fact
> and an intuitive fact, lies in the difference of the
> *total effect* aimed at by their respective authors.
> This it is that determines and rules over the sev-
> eral parts of each, not these parts separated and
> considered abstractly in themselves.[4]

The intuitive fact, musically speaking, would be what the listener "experiences."

Croce differs from the symbolists in that for him form and content are not identical; he associates form with *ex*pression, content with *im*pression, and speaks of the "raising of the content to the dignity of form." But since he holds that we can know nothing about content until it has "determinable qualities," and becomes "actually transformed," he is saying that we apprehend content through form. This is the symbolic mode: eternity made visible, virtual time made audible. In any event Croce's distinction between form and content is an exceedingly tenuous one, since he certainly postulates a formal unity: "Aesthetic expression is *synthesis*."[5]

The problem of the "intelligible proportions" of the symbol has been touched on in earlier chapters. Comprehensible formal unity is the criterion of an independent, organically complete symbol, which Lehmann calls (unhappily, in my opinion) an "aesthetic monad." The symbol may satisfy this condition of autonomy, other things being equal, whether it is "large" or "small." Croce gives helpful elucidation to this thesis, at the same time distinguishing the aesthetic

[4] Benedetto Croce, "Intuition and Expression," *Aesthetic*, trans. by Douglas Ainslie (London: Macmillan and Co., 1922), Chap. 1, pp. 2–3. (Italics mine.)
[5] *Ibid.*, "Intuition and Art," Chap. 2, p. 19.

from the analytic view, and reinforcing the concept of the work of art (very much in the manner of Gurney) as an organism:

> Expression is a synthesis of the various, or multiple, in the one. . . . The fact that we divide a work of art into parts, a poem into scenes, episodes, similes, sentences, or a picture into single figures and objects, background, foreground, etc., may seem opposed to this affirmation. But such division annihilates the work, as dividing the organism into heart, brain, nerves, muscles and so on, turns the living being into a corpse. It is true that there exist organisms in which division gives rise to other living beings, but in such a case we must conclude, maintaining the analogy between the organism and the work of art, that in the latter case too there are numerous germs of life each ready to grow, in a moment, into a single complete expression.[6]

Croce looks upon language as a vehicle of Expression. The products of language in its highest manifestations are what we call works of art. These works—can we doubt that they are symbols?—are "acts of becoming aware carried to the point of extreme and dazzling lucidity."[7] Croce is obviously not confining language to the uses of the discursive reason. Indeed, discursive thought, which he identifies as the *reflective consciousness*, is essential, he says, to the historian or critic, but not to the artistic genius. No doubt Croce would admit, then, a "language" of music; but this language would be not too vague and ambiguous for dis-

---

[6] *Ibid.*, p. 20.
[7] Quoted in A. G. Lehmann, *The Symbolist Aesthetic in France 1885–1895* (Oxford: Basil Blackwell, 1950), pp. 133–34.

cursive treatment, but too precise, as Mendelssohn
suggested, for words.

The symbolist poets sought—I believe the
phrase is Angelo Bertocci's—an exactitude in the grasp
of the ineffable in feeling. The works of Debussy,
Ravel, and other musical Impressionists pursued a similar aim: the capture of an evanescence in sound—an
Apollonian rendering of fleeting (and usually refined)
sensation. "Apollonian" is particularly apt here because the creative impulse in these composers, as in the
symbolist poets, is classical in its quest of ordered rendering. It is a conscious and deliberate art, exhibiting a
passion for perfection: demanding of its authors lucidity, consummate technique, and highly developed powers of analysis and self-criticism. The choice of themes,
to be sure, was often Romantic in the extreme; but the
treatment had a controlled rationale—wonderfully
French—that produced a predetermined effect. Mallarmé's poem provided Debussy with the title of his
symphonic poem *L'Après-midi d'un faune,* which, according to Symons, interprets the poem faultlessly. But
the dreamy nuances of the piece were achieved by an
art of the greatest calculation. Debussy, who often visited Mallarmé's salon, wrote many songs to symbolist
poems, particularly those of Verlaine. He insisted upon
the most punctilious observance of whatever directions
he had written into his scores. Maggie Teyte tells of
the severe discipline the composer imposed when he
coached her for the role of Mélisande. Complaining of
artists who—unlike Miss Teyte—are unequal to such
rigorous demands, Debussy says:

> Resolutely turning their backs on their youth
> they are lulled to sleep by success. They are never
> able to rise to a fame happily reserved for men
> whose lives, consecrated to the search for a world
> of ever-renewed sensations and forms, have ended
> in the joyous confidence of a noble task accom-
> plished.[8]

The interpreter, like the composer, must carry awareness "to the point of extreme and dazzling lucidity."

One sees how the deliberate technique of the
symbolist poets in securing desired effects influenced
the procedures of Impressionist composers as it did those
of their contemporary painters; or it would be more accurate to say, the myriad manifestations of art reflected
those central preoccupations that were in the air. The
affinities of theme and technique offered testimony to
Baudelaire's theory of correspondences and seemed to
demonstrate the feasibility of that *synesthesia* he hypothesized: there was much talk of the colors of sounds,
the music of words. One sees, too, how Poe's criteria as
set forth in *The Philosophy of Composition*—the subordination of all elements to a singleness of effect and
the "rhythmical creation of beauty"—would make their
appeal to Baudelaire, whose own ideals of sadness, mystery, and nostalgia as elements of the beautiful were
close to Poe's.

The reveries of "The Raven" and "Ulalume"
are scarcely a match for anything in the corpus of the

---

[8] Claude Debussy, *Monsieur Croche: The Dilettante Hater,*
trans. by B. N. Langdon Davies (New York: Lear Publishers, 1948), p. 65.

symbolistes; yet in his insistence upon music as the prime element of poetry, Poe is second only to Mallarmé. All art aspires constantly toward the condition of music, said Pater. Mallarmé would agree; but he used the term in a very special, generic way. No more than for Keats in the "Ode on a Grecian Urn" need the music be sounded. Any actual music making, like the writing of a poem, can only be a pale reflection of the Idea to which the mind has access in contemplation. Let there be ditties, then, of no tone: and poems, finally, to be read like a musical score and not uttered: a species of *Augenmusik*. An "ideal music" appealed to Mallarmé because he regarded music as the most expressive of artistic modalities, the least susceptible to those intellectual falsifications visited upon poetry. In *Un Coup de Dés*, says Lehmann, Mallarmé suffers the tragic dilemma of a creative spirit aspiring to an Absolute but possessing only the means to a relative mastery of expression. Or, in the terms of Dorothy Sayers, Mallarmé's Trinity is scalene: the Father is strong, but the Son is not permitted a full incarnation; he is scarcely fleshed.

Recognizing the ever present threat of falsification—chiefly through the activities of the discursive reason—Mallarmé nevertheless sought to achieve a merging of artistic modalities. For Wagner there had been the *Gesamtkunstwerk;* for Mallarmé there was the "Book." Though his production was no match for Wagner's, his dream of artistic synthesis was more uncompromising, and of course, even less susceptible than Wagner's to actualization in the world.

But Symons credits Mallarmé in two of his poems—*L'Après-midi d'un faune* and *Hérodiade*—with

the attainment of Wagner's ideal, "that 'the most complete work of the poet should be that which, in its final
achievement, becomes a perfect music': every word is a
jewel, scattering and recapturing sudden fire, every
image is a symbol, and the whole poem is visible music."[9] Of his ultimate artistic purpose, Mallarmé said:

> We are now precisely at the moment of seeking,
> before that breaking up of the large rhythms of
> literature, and their scattering in articulate, al-
> most instrumental, nervous waves, an art which
> shall complete the transposition, into the Book, of
> the symphony, or simply recapture our own: for,
> it is not in elementary sonorities of brass, strings,
> wood, unquestionably, but in the intellectual
> word at its utmost, that, fully and evidently, we
> should find, drawing to itself all the correspon-
> dences of the universe, the supreme Music.[10]

And this is a music, we may assume, no longer
relevant to the world of human actuality. Mallarmé
apprehends something akin to Maritain's "musical stir,"
but it remains archetypal in his consciousness: "I say:
a flower! and out of the oblivion to which my voice con-
signs every contour, so far as anything save the known
calyx, musically arises, idea, and exquisite, the one
flower absent from all bouquets."[11]

Here, surely, Mallarmé is vulnerable to the
charge of a far-out aestheticism: much more frenetically
than Shelley is he beating his wings in the intense inane;
he has carried the concept of the virtual to further attenuations of its own disembodied realm. Mallarmé is
no advocate of "communications"; he burns his virtual

[9] Symons, p. 69.   [10] *Ibid.*, p. 73.   [11] *Ibid.*

bridges behind him. But words, when they are artistically most salient, accomplish what music can do more easily: capture the dynamic essence of Zeno's moving arrow at the very apex of its trajectory. Mallarmé described poetry as the language of a state of crisis; all his poems, says Symons, are the evocation of a passing ecstasy.

At the end of the second chapter I suggested that the modality of musical discourse would be the clue to our understanding of its meaning. What is the chief peculiarity of that modality? It is distinctly auditory: music must be heard, either actually or in the imagination. An imaginative hearing, whether reconstructed from memory or constructed new from knowledge and experience, presupposes many actual performances which provide the constituents for imagined renditions. The imaginative listener may also hear performances of music which has not yet been performed in actuality, possibly on instruments which do not yet exist and which may never come into existence; the listener who pursues the activity just described is *composing,* whether he ever puts these musical thoughts on paper or not. The truly creative composer, I venture to say, must be a listener in this radical sense; his concern with calligraphy—if he is concerned with it at all—is secondary. The world in which a creative musician apprehends "ditties of no tone" is a virtual realm; this music, a silent music only in actuality, has had an origin as idea. It is still subject to whatever manipulation may be desired, even before its notation on paper has begun. This is, to be profoundly redundant, an *ideal* procedure; Mozart seems to have followed it more successfully than any other composer of whose methods we have knowledge. Most composers resort to a good bit of empirical testing as they write, so that the manipulation goes on, as it were, both in and out of time: both in actuality and imaginatively, or virtually. Beethoven is a strong exemplar of the latter procedure. If there is a loss of perfection in this way of creating music, there is often a gain in earthiness, in pungency and immediacy. In composing as in listening there must be, in any event, a measure of correspondence between the actual and the virtual.

The modality of music is auditory. The famous educator who made the ingenuous and fervent pronouncement, "Music is sound; if it isn't sound, what is it?" was on solid ground. But *mutatis mutandis,* the correspondence between actual and virtual may be discerned in any art. Moreover, just as there are degrees of actuality there are gradations of the virtual: some imaginative forms are more *possible,* in terms of actual manifestation, than others; and these more possible ones are more real than those forms comparatively remote from our space-time continuum. It is that continuum which is the determinant of what we call actuality; we must, I think, accept this as fact, and not as a moral judgment. Possibilities are capable of being arranged in a hierarchy, given sufficient knowledge. In terms of our space-time world, impossibilities, even those that can be imaginatively envisaged, must qualify as sheer fantasy.

I submit that the imaginative artist (and the unimaginative artist should be a contradiction in terms) has a pretty wide compass to range over. He may choose to be "close in," "far out," or on any point of the scale in between; or he may, like Stravinsky, resist all classification.

The practice of an art takes place in the actual world. Artists who are also theorists like Mallarmé may finally forsake practice for theory; they are usually tempted to do so, particularly when those ideas which they manipulate so fluently in the realm of imagination are repeatedly frustrated and vitiated in being actualized. After many struggles to create viable forms, and many partial or utter failures, it may seem better to take refuge in the idea which no actuality, after all, can adequately realize. This appears to have been the course Mallarmé pursued. Yet he still had the power to inspire others to write. His mode was the word, despite all his talk of music. And despite his gradual withdrawal from the actual word—so that the white space of the paper and the placing of letters in a kind of word dance on the page absorbed his imagination more and more—he remained essentially a poet and a teacher of poets.

As a master of the virtual realm he can still teach us something of what happens in aesthetic contemplation. Having achieved, himself, so many attenuations of the virtual, he can report something of the territory he has traversed, measure its distance.

There is no direct correspondence between the life of feelings and their symbolic analogues in art. We are "far removed from their pain." In the art of Mallarmé there may be only a memory of a memory of pain; the poet moves in astral, mental, and spiritual realms, leaving brute physicality far behind. The release Mallarmé offers is gentle, ephemeral, disembodied, like the music he extolled. "This ecstasy," Symons explains, "is never the mere instinctive cry of the heart, the simple human joy or sorrow, which, like the Parnassians, but for not quite the same reason, he did not admit in poetry. It is a mental transposition of emotion or sensation, veiled with atmosphere, and becoming, as it becomes a poem, pure beauty."[12]

According to Lehmann, the symbolist poets succeeded in establishing canons for the very kind of poetry they themselves were writing in Paris near the end of the nineteenth century. They failed in breaking down the limitations of circumstance and history:

> The symbolists emphasized *the essentially expressive character of formal unities* or, as they preferred to call them, *symbols;* but did not see that this datum of aesthetic stretched far outside the boundaries of mystic traditions, linguistic novelties, and the German romantic art-myth which for the moment occupied the artistic stage.[13]

I think Lehmann is right. But the artistic canons the symbolists promulgated have been tenacious of life. And it must be remembered that they were canons rather than a canon. Moreover, the *symbolistes* did not so much originate concepts as they served as a center of force, energizing the ideas they entertained. Goethe, much earlier, had described the symbol as the "concrete universal." Carlyle, like Baudelaire, had emphasized its quality of transcendence. What the symbolists did was to provide a unique laboratory for prac-

---

[12] *Ibid.*, p. 67.   [13] Lehmann, p. 303. (Italics mine.)

tice and theory, in which certain closely related ideas recurred again and again—suggesting that special technique, as practiced by Gerard de Nerval, whereby a poem using a cluster of related images is uniquely suggestive: *le symbole*. Lehmann offers a number of definitions of the symbol, drawing only on meanings that have actually been ascribed to it at one time or another; he is not confining himself to the aesthetic of the symbolist poets. One of these definitions, close to the concept of *le symbole* just adumbrated, was subscribed to by Valéry: "a formal construct or poetic image of great force which constantly recurs in the poet's work as his mind circles around a certain predominant attitude." Another prevalent concept which would have satisfied both Goethe and Gide (who saw the symbol as coeval with formal artistic unity) is that of the symbol as "any work of art at all, considered as a formal unity, or embodying an aspiration to formal unity." Lehmann's own view of the symbol is that of the aesthetic unity of created art, which is—at once—unity of form and unity of content.

In 1831 Carlyle said that in a symbol

> there is concealment and yet revelation: here therefore, by Silence and by Speech acting together, comes a double significance. . . . There is ever, more or less distinctly and directly, some embodiment and revelation of the Infinite; the Infinite is made to blend itself with the Finite, to stand visible, and as it were, attainable there.[14]

Whitehead, writing one hundred years later, but using a more recondite vocabulary, delineates the virtual:

[14] Carlyle, p. 217.

In what sense can unrealized abstract form be relevant? What is its basis of relevance? "Relevance" must express some real fact of togetherness among forms. The ontological principle can be expressed as: All real togetherness is togetherness in the formal constitution of an actuality. So if there be a relevance of what in the temporal world is unrealized, the relevance must express a fact of togetherness in the formal constitution of a nontemporal actuality.[15]

But there is the interplay of "actual" and "virtual," which Whitehead acknowledges: "The things which are temporal arise by their participation in the things which are eternal."[16] In this statement, true, Whitehead is not suggesting a symbol. But his definition of an *entity* would correspond to the aesthetic monad of Lehmann and equally well to that unity of form and content postulated for the symbol. One senses at once, moreover, that Baudelaire and Mallarmé would approve:

> In the complete particular "givenness" for an actual entity there is an element of exclusiveness. The various primary data and the concrescent feelings do not form a mere multiplicity. Their synthesis in the final unity of one actual entity terminates its becoming in one complex feeling involving a completely determinate bond with every item in the universe. . . . Thus in an actual entity the balanced unity of the total "givenness" excludes anything that is not given.[17]

[15] Alfred North Whitehead, *Process and Reality* (New York: [Torchbook] Harper & Brothers, 1960), p. 48.
[16] *Ibid.*, p. 63.
[17] *Ibid.*, pp. 70–71.

The correspondence to be noted among such disparate figures as Carlyle, Baudelaire, Mallarmé, Croce, and Whitehead lies in their *recognition of certain processes.* The explanations they give of those processes differ. But the feasibility of certain recurrent aesthetic apprehensions on the level of empirical experience are repeatedly attested to in their different vocabularies. The process can be observed, whatever names may be given to them, whatever cosmology assumed. Cosmologies may be fascinating in themselves: and the fact that the world view of Baudelaire proves to have resemblances to that of Whitehead might be called an *in plus,* to appropriate Maritain's term, of this investigation. But it is the processes themselves we are here concerned with; although it is my own view that primary value inheres *in* these human aesthetic apprehensions, even though this belief must follow (*if* it follows) the "recognition" of them. I am far from regarding the acceptance of any particular world view as a condition for the understanding of music; I think the facts make it clear that valid musical experience may occur for the listener whatever his beliefs concerning the universe and human destiny. Those beliefs, of course, are likely to influence the associations music will acquire for him, as well as any theoretical rationale he may construct. But if the empirical processes are in some measure respected for what they actually are in experience, and not automatically categorized and subordinated to the service of conceptual presuppositions, they will be seen to function with recognizable similarity within (or without) any metaphysical system whatsoever, as do the demonstrably human functions of walking and talking.

Any supposed occult tradition, therefore, as reflected in the work of Yeats or even Eliot, does not provide the key to the understanding of their work: only their poetry does that; the poem is the *given;* the poem *is* the work, *is* its meaning. It is the observable artistic actuality that makes it a symbol; and a symbol, regarded as amalgam of actual and virtual, makes the best of both worlds. This does not mean that the study of theosophical and other influences in their work will not be of value; such study will have considerable interest and value in its own right, and it may be a help in the poetic confrontation of such artists as Baudelaire and Rimbaud. But there is no obligation to look upon the poet as magus or seer, notwithstanding John Senior's contention, in *The Way Down and Out,* that we are "saved" through the occult symbolism of poetry. A genuine seer may be a bad poet; or a great poet may be, in his capacity of Deliverer, a fake. I shall not try to fix the proportions in Yeats, though of his poetic stature there can surely be no doubt. It seems to me, however, that the best of him is in his poetry which has evidently transmuted, in many instances, some of his very tedious numerological and other preoccupations into the gold of the authentic symbol.

Musical numerology offers, to some minds, a fascinating study; I have known theorists who devoted their entire lives to it. We have observed past manifestations of this mode of thought: the ascription to number, for example, of that imagined "harmony of the spheres" as the concept recurs throughout history. Some recent variations on the theme of music as number are the Schillinger system of composition; appropriations of the "dynamic symmetry" theses of Hambedge; and even

12-tone or "serial" composition to the extent that its exponents are preoccupied with numerical permutations—a manipulation which appears in some instances to be the underlying rationale or idea, and not merely one aspect of technique. The apotheosis of technical procedures, like the glorification of idea, can become a mystique, but with less glamorous results.

What I am saying is that all such considerations—theological, mystical, moral (as in Tolstoy), or social—are tangential to an examination of music as a functional entity. We do not experience music in those ways, except secondarily via conceptual associations. Particularly, I should like to say, we do not experience music in terms of the components to which analysis can reduce it. Every listener implicitly brings to the experience his particular "cosmology," yet he need not be insulated thereby from what is happening. If we examine the phenomenon of listening to music, both as it recurs in ourselves and in others (to the extent we are able to judge empathically and through analogous extension), we will become more consciously aware of the modality of musical discourse, its unique "how." We are experiencing a process; we are also observing it. Now—and there's the rub—we must describe it.

Those who have given names to the facts of aesthetic experience have used a variable terminology; they have usually sought new terms. Even when the very modality of the art is words, as with the symbolist poets, we have seen their struggle, in describing their artistic concerns, to force language to yield adequate insights, to give some clue to the nature of their intuitions.

Let us take the concept of the ideal. I am dealing here with the ideal as a recognizable realm to which the imagination and the fantasy as well have access; this may, indeed, be their natural home. It is the abode of memory, the matrix of concepts and unrealized possibilities. All this is demonstrable, and it has a special relevance to the orderings of art. The ideal, whatever name we give to it, refers to a world of human experience; its existence is a matter of knowledge through recurrent, valid apprehensions. For Plato it was the realm of eternal forms; he imbued his concept with lasting power. ("The safest general characterization of the European philosophical tradition," says Whitehead, "is that it consists of a series of footnotes to Plato.")[18] Theologians call it the Eternal; others may prefer a small "e." For Jung the ideal world is acausal and archetypal. Some idealists call this realm the real, others the timeless, others the virtual. Bergson, who was no Platonist and posited no eternal, nevertheless had to hypothesize a *durée* to account for the facts of intuition. His "real duration," in its relevance to music, corresponds to Gurney's "ideal motion." Nietzsche posited an Apollonian ordering; Santayana, "pleasure objectified."

Santayana speaks of "essence," which "visits time but belongs to eternity." He arrives at his essence through the mediation of the senses: "First we suffer, afterwards we sing. An interval is necessary to make feeling presentable, and subjugate it to that form in which alone it is beautiful."[19] In Santayana's theory eternity itself appears as aesthetically valid but otherwise somehow nonexistent, because immaterial, though nevertheless a realm of ultimate human values. Scho-

---

[18] *Ibid.*, p. 63.
[19] George Santayana, *The Sense of Beauty* (New York: Crowell-Collier, 1961), p. 157.

penhauer, for whom the "extracted quintessence" of music is expressive of a real eternity, begins not with suffering, but with the timeless singing: "Our imagination is so easily excited by music, and now seeks to give form to that invisible yet actively moved spirit-world which speaks to us directly, and clothe it with flesh and blood, i.e., to embody it in an analogous example."[20] In both views the resultant is that fusion of actual and virtual which we call the symbol.

I suggested that Santayana's eternity was somehow nonexistent. Yet the dialogue which I have predicated between the worlds of human actuality and virtuality has been nowhere expressed with more poignancy than in these lines:

> The sun is not now unreal because each one of us in succession, and all of us in the end, must close our eyes upon it; and yet the sun exists for us only because we perceive it. The ideal has the same conditions of being, but has this advantage over the sun, that we cannot know if its light is ever destined to fail us.[21]

It is the acknowledgment of the virtual, under whatever name and whether implicit or explicit, that makes artistic creation possible; the objective image can endure only if it possesses "real duration." Its quality of being "there" is predicated upon a transcendence of the here and now; an immediate perception of the image thus yields a sense of "something more"; and this sense,

[20] Arthur Schopenhauer, *The World as Will and Idea,* trans. by R. B. Haldane and J. Kemp (Garden City, N.Y.: [Dolphin] Doubleday & Co., 1961), p. 273.
[21] Santayana, p. 180.

in turn, is something more than a half-conscious awareness that the experience is repeatable, that the image—visual or sonorous—may be grasped again and again. In authentic symbolic apprehension the awareness of transcendence is present, even if the experience is unique. Assuming repeatability as the norm, however, successive encounters will not be identical. Intensity varies. But the virtual objectivity of images is the condition of aesthetic apprehensions.

These recurrent apprehensions, whatever they are called, are humanly valid. It is not my concern to determine the suitability of small or capital letters in referring to the "ideal," nor to indulge in futile speculation on its extent or myriad possible subdivisions; it is enough to recognize it as "other" in its polarity with our space-time actuality. *Virtual* is my choice because of the relative neutrality of the term.

Sir James Jeans pointed out that no verbal statement of any kind can be equated with reality. Whitehead, in *Process and Reality,* explicitly repudiates the trust in language as a satisfactory expression of propositions.

> It is merely credulous to accept verbal phrases as adequate statements of propositions. The distinction between verbal phrases and complete propositions is one of the reasons why the logicians' rigid alternative, "true or false," is so largely irrelevant for the pursuit of knowledge. . . . Language is thoroughly indeterminate, by reason of the fact that every occurrence presupposes some systematic type of environment.[22]

[22] Whitehead, pp. 17–18.

Music presupposes, first of all, a human environment. A particular world music may—as we have observed in the East-West dichotomy—presuppose a certain cultural (if not historical) milieu. Comprehensive theory, however, must be capable of accounting for the practices of all world musics throughout history.

How does music mirror the complexities of human societies? Will its distinctive mirroring be susceptible to verbal explication? Can we define its role and give reasons for its importance? Is musical experience, any more than love, essentially a reasonable matter?

Music, as a human creation, may be expected to exhibit an internal logic, for logic itself is a peculiarly human manifestation. But the logical rationale of music as an artistic form is a different logic from that of the discursive reason. And the discursive reason cannot account in its own terms for the logic appropriate to other modalities such as music and painting. The prevalence of all the arts bespeaks their necessity; and the endless proliferation of forms could only occur in an activity of joy. Necessity and delight characterize all essential human activities. Art, therefore, is not really an optional human enterprise; there is no need, then, to question its importance. Great art, moreover, brings to the percipient a sensation of inevitability: *this is how it is.*

According to Ernst Cassirer:

> Reason is a very inadequate term with which to comprehend the forms of man's cultural life in all their richness and variety. But all these forms are symbolic forms. Hence, instead of defining

man as an *animal rationale,* we should define him as an *animal symbolicum.* By so doing we can designate his specific difference, and we can understand the new way open to man—the way to civilization.[23]

Joseph Wood Krutch in his excellent essay, "Experience and Art," reminds us that we construct our sciences, our philosophies, and our arts: they reflect us, and we reflect them. We render nature into human terms, and we cannot do otherwise. "We think and we understand—not with things—but with words, with symbols, and with syllogisms. Our minds cannot work until objects and phenomena have been translated into mental terms; but translation always implies deformation."[24] Art, science, and philosophy arrange the materials of nature into patterns which are humanly intelligible. This "setting apart" is the whole meaning of aesthetic distance; the setting apart, the "presentation," is virtual. The ordering which art gives to the objects and phenomena of our experience sets them apart for our contemplation: "*For it is, in the end, contemplation which makes things real* and it is the ability to contemplate which constitutes the distinguishing characteristic of the human mind."[25]

Santayana, speaking of contemplation, strikes a Bergsonian note: "This passage into the object, to live its life, is indeed a characteristic of all perfect contemplation."[26] Aesthetic forms, for Santayana, are finite

[23] Ernst Cassirer, *An Essay on Man* (New Haven: Yale University Press, 1944; [Anchor] Doubleday & Co., n.d.), p. 44.
[24] Joseph Wood Krutch, *Experience and Art* (New York: Crowell-Collier, 1962), p. 73.
[25] *Ibid.,* p. 74. (Italics mine.)
[26] Santayana, p. 168.

and exclusive: the highest aesthetic good would be "the greatest number and variety of finite perfections."[27] These forms possess the exclusive *given* of which Whitehead speaks.

Santayana delivered his lectures on aesthetics at Harvard College from 1892 to 1895: the very period consecrated in Paris to the symbolist poets. He complained of an absence of form, "in which, as in the writings of the Symbolists of our time, all the significance is kept back in the individual words, or even in the syllables that compose them. . . . The descent is easy from ambiguity to meaninglessness."[28] He goes on to suggest that the indeterminate in form is also indeterminate in value.

Music is a symbolic mode of human discourse, in which meanings are aurally apprehended through auditory entities. The very starting point of comprehensive theory is the proposition that all *musical* import is auditory; yet musical symbolism is nonverbal.

Artistic modalities do gravitate toward one another; they do tend, often, to merge in practice. All of them doubtless originate in impulsions or "musical stirs" that are prior to their separate manifestations. I am not crusading for purity of the modalities; I am saying that in a theory of music we must think straight. Let us mix what modalities we choose, however we choose, but consciously; let us distinguish clearly between musical and extramusical manifestations. If we can make these elementary distinctions, then any construct, whether it be an ultimate *Gesamtkunstwerk* or a penul-

---

[27] *Ibid.*, p. 109.   [28] *Ibid.*, p. 105.

timate, still visible "Book," will gain, rather than lose, in intensity.

Despite the scope of their imaginations and their capacity for generalizations, the symbolist poets were of no help in this department. In fact they encouraged what proved to be a hopeless confusion of artistic modalities. Music, as always, was the most popular sacrificial modality; long accustomed to being regarded as a kind of celestial mathematics, the art was now appropriated by poetry as its very own. Gide, if he did not take the torch direct from the hand of Mallarmé, nevertheless kept it burning:

> Musical! The word should be allowed to express not merely the flowing caress or the harmonious impact of the verbal sonorities through which poetry may please even a foreigner with a musical ear, but no knowledge of the language: but also that sure choice of expression which is dictated not by logic alone, and which escapes logic, by which the "musical" poet succeeds in formulating, as exactly as a definition would do it, the essentially indefinable emotion.[29]

One finally comes to the realization that in the shifting sands of such usage the art of music suffers a real neglect, if not debasement. These men who are not musicians use the term *music* to recognize or to inculcate in their own art elements that are imitative or

[29] André Gide, "Baudelaire and M. Faguet," *Reflections on Literature and Morality,* Justin O'Brien, ed., trans. by Angelo P. Bertocci (New York: [Greenwich] Meridian Books, Inc., 1959), pp. 156–72. The essays in this volume are translations from the following French works: *Prétextes* and *Nouveaux Prétextes,* published by Mercure de France, and *Divers* and *Incidences,* published by Gallimard.

suggestive of musical qualities. This kind of transfer can be enormously effective; and it may be more than transfer. The rendition of poetry, like chanting, is close to song; and when the interpreter adds distinct pitches to the inherent rhythmic structure, there is music. Even in such instances, however, the music is secondary and derivative; the primary modality is verbal.

Perhaps this is no very serious warfare. One wonders, sometimes, what autonomy remains for the integral, wordless music when the poets get through with it. They are men of words, and they have the advantage; they *must* speak. The musician's business, too, is sound, but of a different order. He needs no defense, really, though he stands in awe of the word: the word moves him as it moves all men. If he is to make music, others must occasionally be silent; the wordless musical symbol may then be brought into being.

CHAPTER NINE

RECENT PHILOSOPHIC THEORISTS

* * * "ULTIMATELY ALL CONFUSION OF VALUES proceeds from the same source:—neglect of the intrinsic significance of the medium."[1] These are the words of John Dewey. No transcendentalist, he keeps his attention fixed on the actual processes of human experience. And though the results of that scrutiny are couched in still another vocabulary, we discern the corresponding elements of artistic activity, the recurrent facts—if you will—of experience. Dewey does not refer to revelation or transcendence, but to "the sense of disclosure and heightened intelligibility of the world."[2] He nowhere refers to a *symbol* in the sense in which I use the term, yet he says the point of all art is the unity of form and matter. Only in reflection can a distinction be made be-

---

[1] John Dewey, *Art As Experience* (New York: [Capricorn] G. P. Putnam's Sons, 1958), p. 319.
[2] *Ibid.*, p. 289.

tween them; Dewey grants the critic and theorist this prerogative. The work itself, however, is "a way of envisaging. . . . Hence there can be no distinction drawn . . . between form and substance. . . . The act itself is exactly *what* it is because of *how* it is done. In the act there is no distinction, but perfect integration of manner and content, form and substance."[3] He accords the symbol its unique objectivity when he speaks of the "qualitative novelty that characterizes every genuine work of art."[4] And concerning the objectification of the emotions—Langer's "symbolic analogue of emotive life"—Dewey observes that "our appetites know themselves when they are reflected in the mirror of art, and as they know themselves they are transfigured."[5]

Here once more, in the mirror of another mind, are constituents we have seen again and again: the *processes* of the aesthetic experience. And it is the human experience of the process that concerns Dewey primarily: "Contemplation designates that aspect of perception in which elements of seeking and of thinking are subordinated (although not absent) to *the perfecting of the process of perception itself*."[6] The dynamic view which Dewey takes of the act of contemplation itself is a view peculiarly appropriate to the modality of music: "A contemplation that is not an aroused and intensified form of attention to material in perception presented through the senses is an idle stare."[7]

Perceptual experience of this kind incorporates both desire and thought. If desire to possess or use is dominant, there can be no disinterested enjoyment.

[3] *Ibid.*, p. 109.
[4] *Ibid.*, p. 288.
[5] *Ibid.*, p. 77.
[6] *Ibid.*, p. 253. (Italics mine.)
[7] *Ibid.*, p. 255.

Dewey's recognition of this essential "distance" recalls Santayana's dictum: "We cannot venerate any one in whom appreciation is not divorced from desire."[8] It is detachment which makes full participation possible. Though he imagines no incursion from "above," Dewey looks upon experience of art as bringing about a heightening and concentration of one's powers, a greater inclusiveness of conscious elements. He refers to Bergson's concept of "entering into" the object of contemplation. "Perception that occurs for its own sake," says Dewey, "is full realization of all the elements of our psychological being."[9]

Dewey's comprehensive naturalism does not exclude ideal possibilities; he admits the role of imagination in bringing possibilities into artistic actuality, injecting that indispensable element of the new—in the manner of Whitehead's novel prehensions—which is a condition of artistic vitality. With Dewey we get once again the analogy of the art work to an organism: "Only by progressive organization of 'inner' and 'outer' material in organic connection with each other can anything be produced that is not a learned document or an illustration of something familiar."[10]

Recognition of the intrinsic significance of a particular modality is fundamental. Dewey states as clearly as could be desired the limitations of verbal discourse:

> If all meanings could be adequately expressed by words, the arts of painting and music would

[8] George Santayana, *The Sense of Beauty* (New York: Crowell-Collier, 1961), p. 166.
[9] Dewey, p. 256.
[10] *Ibid.*, p. 75.

not exist. There are values and meanings that
can be expressed only by immediately visible and
audible qualities, and to ask what they mean in
the sense of something that can be put into words
is to deny their distinctive existence.[11]

Since it is one of my major theses that music
is a nonverbal symbolism, I will defend the integrity of
its distinct modality, particularly against the charge of
anti-intellectualism. Charges and recriminations, however, are irrelevant, unless it can be shown that I am
falsifying processes which are, after all, public property
and can be tested by anyone who fulfills the necessary
conditions. So far as the intellect is concerned, I see no
need to confine its activity to traffic in verbal propositions; the tendency so to restrict it reflects rather narrow and utilitarian concerns, even in the use of language
itself. Poetry is capable of yielding meanings beyond
language; yet great poetry is the apotheosis of language.
Whether this apprehension of further meanings is "intellectual" or not is perhaps a moot point; it is certainly
a matter of definition. Bergson speaks of an "intellectual intuition," whereas intellect and intuition are
often regarded as antithetical. Dewey does not admit
a transcendence of the world but nevertheless refers
to aesthetic experience—including the experience of
poetry—as participation which in its fullness and
immediacy "transcends" the intellect.

So far I have touched only on those aspects of
Dewey's thought which apply with equal cogency to all

[11] *Ibid.,* p. 74.

the arts. But he has insights into the distinctive modality of music which have the greatest pertinence to its
unique *dynamism*. He begins with allusions to rhythm,
to the rhythm of existence, to the rhythm that underlies
all art: "Underneath the rhythm of every art and of
every work of art there lies, as a substratum in the
depths of the subconsciousness, the basic pattern of the
relations of the live creature to his environment."[12]
(Langer speaks of the "forms of sentient being.")

Dewey makes the remarkable statement that
where there is a uniformly even flow, without variations
of intensity or speed, there is no rhythm. This is true,
and my agreement is not prompted by my profound
respect for the subtleties of rubato only. Even those
"natural" models which are extolled and pointed to as
our rhythmic guides—the movement patterns of the
heavenly bodies, the human heartbeat and respiration—
have their peculiar deviations within a given order.
But on the level of musical art it is often an understanding of the underlying rhythmic dynamism of a composition that means the difference between a live performance and a dead one. The sense of tempo—and not
merely the dutiful recurrence of accents—is crucial
rhythmically, while intensity of the beat is communicated only if the actual playing is relevant to an inner,
and virtual, infallibility. Only the virtual perfection
makes rhythmic liberties admissible; the artist measures
his freedom in each performance against it. A sense of
the beat may be innate for most people, but only the
artist has rhythm. "Rhythm," says Dewey, "is ordered
variation of changes."[13]

[12] *Ibid.*, p. 150.   [13] *Ibid.*, p. 154.

The permutations of emotional energy in the matrix of art are more vividly described by Dewey than by any other writer I have encountered. Sessions does this to a degree. But Dewey makes the forces he describes analogous to humanly felt realities of both a physical and psychological nature. Gurney cited instances in which music could suggest spatial analogies— "up" and "down"—by means of melodic contours. Frivolity, nostalgia, and other psychological apprehensions, he acknowledged, may also be susceptible of suggestion through musical means; but especially relevant are those similarities of music and pace as it is physically experienced: tempo and its modifications—ritardandos, accelerandos, and so on—being the source of the closest parallels between music and life. Dewey, emphasizing the cardinal role of rhythm in this process, gives an energetic account, providing for both objective "distance" in the transformation of rhythmic-sensuous elements and the intimate nature of the musical experience:

> Music . . . gives us the very essence of the dropping down and the exalted rising, the surging and retracting, the acceleration and retardation, the tightening and loosening, the sudden thrust and the gradual insinuation of things. *The expression is abstract in that it is freed from attachment to this and that, while at the same time it is intensely direct and concrete.*[14]

He also gives an explanation of rhythm which would be rendered in the Freudian lexicon as *sublima-*

---

[14] *Ibid.,* p. 208. (Italics mine.)

tion, though it is no less plausible when viewed simply as that setting apart which is essential for artistic ordering: "The resistance offered to immediate expression of emotion is precisely that which compels it to assume rhythmic form. This, indeed, is Coleridge's explanation of meter in verse."[15] The pyschological analogues which music embodies are carried a step farther with the addition of melodic counterpoint: "Music complicates and intensifies the process of genial reciprocating antagonism, suspense and reënforcement, where the various 'voices' at once oppose and answer one another."[16]

Dewey points out that in its essential dynamism music expresses "stir, agitation, movement, the particulars and contingencies of existence," and is thus at the opposite pole from the sculptural, which depicts "the enduring, the stable and universal."[17] Yet he holds that there is a common substance which the various arts draw upon, their differences being of emphasis only, so that music may be said to be temporal, the plastic arts spatial, though elements of time and space may be found in both. "Each possesses what the other actively exploits." This would appear to be not strictly true, since the "space" of music, functionally speaking (which is to say musically speaking), is a concept only. Langer deals successfully with the problem, I believe, when she assigns to each art its *primary illusion;* each art, to be sure, may have secondary ones. "Illusion" in her terminology does not mean artistically unreal, still less what Sachs refers to in the barbarism "illusionistic"; the primary illusion is the projection of a work in its own virtual

<hr>

[15] *Ibid.,* p. 156.   [16] *Ibid.,* p. 236.   [17] *Ibid.*

modality. In examining music Dewey has come very close to capturing its essential dynamism in the discursive modality of words:

> Music, having sound as its medium, thus necessarily expresses in a concentrated way the shocks and instabilities, the conflicts and resolutions, that are the dramatic changes enacted upon the more enduring background of nature and human life. The tension and the struggle has its gatherings of energy, its discharges, its attacks and defenses, its mighty warrings and its peaceful meettings, its resistances and resolutions, and out of these things music weaves it web.[17]

It will be helpful to my argument to point out, at this juncture, that the dynamic qualities just enumerated are at the very core of what we call *life*. These sensations, described in such general terms, are deeply felt at one time or another by every human being and many times by any person who is intensely alive. Yet it is only this general—or universal—*dynamis* which in the ways Dewey has described is musically expressible. It is not, as Schopenhauer clearly understood, this or that particular joy, or sorrow, or pain; but joy, sorrow, or pain themselves in their essential nature—"to a certain extent in the abstract."

But this essential character of an emotion or complex of feelings is musically depicted by humanly observable analogy—and not through the embodiment of a mystically intuited Will, though this is a compelling poetic metaphor. Schopenhauer was confusing the modalities. But music itself does more than suggest;

[17] *Ibid.*

like a poem, it *is*. It maintains its own integrity, more-over, despite suggestion: just as a person whose eyes may remind you of another's retains his vision whole.

Music may thus be considered metaphor, manifesting the quality of *allusion* as a secondary and inevitable concomitant. If music, however, is metaphorical in its own modality, it will not be susceptible of explanation—*qua* metaphor—by means of verbal recognition of its allusive qualities. This is where Donald Ferguson makes his fundamental error in his essay on music *as* metaphor. That music can and does suggest myriad ideas and pictorial associations to most listeners is demonstrable; but recourse to these disparate and secondary aspects of the listening experience as argument for musical metaphor is to subordinate the essential feature—the primary illusion—to these elements which in our culture are bound to be predominantly verbal in character. A metaphor gives meaning: the pairing of opposites, when apposite, may yield a flash of insight. If the term *metaphor* is applicable to music at all, then we have a right to expect in the modality of music—as we expect in poetry—that, however radically dissimilar they may originally have been, the constituents will be made one; the whole unites and transcends the parts. The whole is the *symbol*. And it is the musical ear that must attend.

The "simultaneous expression of opposites" is within the power of music, as Langer and other theorists have noted. Rendered in terms of feeling as ambivalence, this simultaneous expression of opposites could also be regarded—as Dewey seems to view it—as "indeterminacy." Dewey advances a particularly intriguing

notion in connection with the emotional force of the
indeterminate:

> Sound is the conveyor of what impends, of what
> is happening as an indication of what is likely to
> happen. It is fraught much more than vision with
> the sense of issues; *about the impending there is
> always an aura of indeterminateness and uncer-
> tainty—all conditions favorable to intense emo-
> tional stir.* . . . It is sounds that make us jump.
> . . . In reality the intellectual range of hearing
> although enormous is acquired; *in itself the ear is
> the emotional sense.* . . . Sounds have the power
> of direct emotional expression. A sound is itself
> threatening, whining, soothing, depressing, fierce,
> tender, soporific, in its own quality.[18]

We turn now from Dewey, firmly rooted in
empirical reality, to Karl Jaspers for whom "the world
as a whole and in every individual feature shows infinite
depth."[19] Reality—Being—is transcendent; we ourselves
at our "boundaries" express, as we are surrounded by,
the Encompassing: "The world and everything that
occurs in it is a mystery."[20] That mystery is read by
symbols—or *cyphers,* as Jaspers calls them; and the multiplicity of humanly apprehended symbols makes up the
cypher-script. Symbolic meaning cannot be discursively
rendered, for "no given interpretation suffices"; the
symbol does not offer a content of knowledge apart from
itself.

---

[18] *Ibid.,* pp. 237–38. (Italics mine.)
[19] Karl Jaspers, *Truth and Symbol,* trans. by Jean T. Wilde,
William Kluback, William Kimmel (New Haven: College
and Univ. Press, n.d.), p. 37. From *Von der Wahrheit*
(Munich: R. Piper & Co., 1947).
[20] *Ibid.*

Again, we are dealing with truth as metaphor; or if this seems an overstatement, with the truth of metaphorical experience. Symbolic meaning is apprehended in its *presentness*—would this differ from "presentational immediacy"?—and is not to be referred to something beyond itself, nor reduced to its constituents. But though the symbol makes eternity accessible in the now, imbues time with the timeless, the actual human world is its field of manifestation: "Within empirical existence itself the symbol speaks: in the concreteness of existing things we experience the essential reality of the symbol."[21]

Radically different as Jaspers' interpretations of the world are from Dewey's, he is faithful, on the side of empirical observation, to what he sees and to what others may likewise see. In other words, *certain processes* are being affirmed yet again. Dewey admits the inadequacy of language for the grasp of other symbolic modes; Jaspers states that "no thought is adequate to the symbol." He says succinctly that "talk" of the symbol, though it must go on, will not "give" us the symbol. These lines are peculiarly relevant to music:

> *The cypher is listened to, not cognized. All talk about it,* so unavoidable because the cypher only steps forth more clearly in communication, *is already mistaken in its roots.* For this reason the character of the cypher is only encircled but not reached if, in metaphor, we call it speech.[22]

Viable symbols are "transparent"; the timeless quality (Jaspers calls it the infinite) is projected through

[21] *Ibid.,* p. 40.   [22] *Ibid.,* p. 41. (Italics mine.)

that transparency. But there is a suspension, such as the simultaneous expression of opposites presupposes, an indeterminacy: a suspension of the subject-object polarity. The modes of subject (Being) and object (the empirical world) are both essential to its realization; the awareness, the apprehension of meaning, depends upon the polarity, the balance between the worldly constituents and the presence of the Other apprehended within the symbol. The withdrawal of Being—and for Being I would postulate a characteristic quickness to acknowledge the unique dynamism as well as the empirical instability of the symbol in the world—leaves the cypher opaque; simultaneously, the Other loses that particular form of expression in the world. The quick has, to empirical observation, become the dead.

Although Jaspers' explanations of symbolic transformation interest me enormously, it is with the processes he describes that I am mainly concerned here. Jaspers' apprehension of Being corresponds to those concepts of the Ideal, the virtual, the eternal, the time-less—what you will—which are employed to give verbal expression to recurrent facts of human experience. Art has the capacity to give the impression—no matter whether it may be called illusory or not—of transcendence of the here and now; yet universally its efficacy is in the immediate. But whether we take *eternity* as the starting point, as did Plato, or *process,* as did Bergson and Dewey, there is an indispensable polarity between the unseen (in whatever conceptual terms it may be presented to us) and observable activity. Possibility inheres both in the virtual and the actual and presupposes both; it may be said to hover over the world as a spirit to which the imagination of man has access, or perhaps as an energizing force that may be tapped by either side and made to unite them in a new concretion. Theologically we have in what I have just described the Trinity of Father, Son, and Holy Ghost. Whatever our ultimate beliefs, all language is a pointing; and the very existence of other modalities is testimony to its incompleteness.

For all observers the symbol is grasped, if it is grasped at all, in the here and now; even a memory is present now, as are anticipations of a possible future. The evocation of "something more" into the immediate data of consciousness is an enlargement or—there is no way of avoiding the term—an *enrichment* of what is presently apprehended. This incursion of "something more" is provided by the viable symbol; and *transcendence,* for the observer, need mean nothing more than this. For both Dewey and Jaspers the given object is sensuously concrete; this is symbolically the way we can receive the meaning it encompasses—through itself. We "enter into" its modality if we can. But the very sensuousness of the symbol is made viable for Jaspers through its "transparency":

> Transparency of sensuousness signifies at the same time disassociation from sensuousness as such. Absolute adherence to the sensuous draws one into the darkness of transparentlessness. The grasping of the content of Being in adherence to the sensuous goes beyond the sensuous.[23]

"We cannot venerate anyone in whom appreciation is not divorced from desire," said Santayana. Jaspers, in his explication of transparency, is accounting

[23] *Ibid.,* p. 44.

for the "distance" we require in the mirrorings of art. Here we are once more close to the "how"; yet Jaspers, though he is not excluding the cypher-script of art, is speaking of symbolic transformation in general. Jaspers does not look with favor upon a contemplation which is merely aesthetic, in which we live only vicariously through forms; the conscious aesthete whom he deprecates would be one addicted hopelessly to the Apollonian picture world, content with that immutable realm, secure in the enjoyment of his own feelings, resistant to change, lost to action. He calls the aesthetic attitude a "slipping into detachment."

Transparency in the symbol may be lost. Symbols may degenerate into mere things with static referents; they may become "mere" images, "collapse into fixed forms" and "henceforth provide no real support." I have spoken several times of faded metaphors. In any dynamic form a failure of power is possible if not, in the long run, inevitable. Jaspers sees this loss of power as the result of an attempt to break down the genuine unity of the symbol:

> The material of their appearance stems from the world of sensuous observations and of conceivabilities. But to lead the symbols back to this material is to misunderstand their essence and becomes a genetics which dissolves them.[24]

We must, then, be Gestaltists in our apprehension of symbols, or their meanings for us will perish. In this sense, then, though he never intended it, Hanslick was correct in stating that "music means itself." It

[24] *Ibid.*, p. 50.

means itself in the sense that it cannot be explained; music is to be fully heard, fully listened to.

What Jaspers says of the meaning of symbols—and again it is a general statement—seems to me to be particularly applicable to the apprehension of meaning in the arts. I want to conclude my brief summary of Jaspers' thought with these lines, and in quoting them I have keenly in mind the wide terrain our investigation has taken us over:

> Genuine symbols cannot be interpreted; what can be interpreted through an "other" ceases to be a symbol. On the other hand, the interpretation of symbols through their self-presentation penetrates into them but does not explain them. Such interpretation encircles and circumscribes, penetrates and illuminates. It becomes itself at once a part of the symbol. By interpreting, it participates in symbol-status. The symbol is not passed over by being understood, but is deepened and enhanced by being meditated upon.[25]

Dewey spoke of "the sense of disclosure and heightened intelligibility" which aesthetic experience yields; in Jaspers' terms this would be the reading of a particular cypher-script: "Universal research must lead to the boundary where the highest astonishment and the most penetrating cypher-script become possible."[26]

It is no accident that comprehensive theory is best served by thinkers of extraordinary stature. In assembling evidence for a general theory of music as a nonverbal symbolism, I have had recourse to Schopenhauer, Nietzsche, Bergson, Jung, Whitehead, Dewey, and Jaspers. These men are not philosophers of music,

[25] *Ibid.*, p. 53. [26] *Ibid.*, p. 71.

and three of them scarcely make even passing mention of the art. Yet it is in their ideas—as well as in philosophies of art such as those of Gurney, Croce, Santayana, Maritain, Langer, and Read—that we will find the basis of viable theory, rather than in the writings of specialists. There is among them—notwithstanding their profound differences—a common recognition of the dynamics of the human mind, including both conscious and unconscious aspects; a receptivity to new evidence as it occurs in the constellations of human experience, as well as an appetite for novelty; and the allowance—even while they are subjecting process to the most careful scrutiny—for possible influences which, though difficult to categorize and perhaps in some instances incalculable or altogether beyond reach, may nevertheless have a profound relevance to what occurs in the world. This much they have in common even when one has contrasted the archetypal realm of Jung with the turbulent mysticism of Bergson; each is presenting his experience of the transcendent. All these philosophers indeed mirror truths through their distinct temperaments: we cannot altogether separate the observer from what he observes, nor the person from his intuition. The attempt to do so, certain to fail even in discursive investigations, is pernicious in art, as much present-day research demonstrates.

The only two investigators of the explicitly musical whom I have dealt with at any length, Hanslick and Gurney, were respectively critic and psychologist. Hanslick, despite his gifts, did not succeed in divorcing speculation from the personal axes he had to grind; even so, he contributed the most durable essay in musical philosophy of the past century. With Gurney it was the very breadth of his thought as a nonspecialist that has given such timeless cogency to his theory and such rapport between his thought and that of the nineteenth- and twentieth-century philosophic giants whom we have been examining. The eclipse of his remarkable book can only be a temporary one; in fact, Basic Books, Inc., republished *The Power of Sound* early in 1967, with an introduction by Edward T. Cone.

What of musicians themselves? Are there not artists of extraordinary stature? Of course. They are not, however, and have not been, theorists. Let us consider one composer whose stature is beyond cavil: Johann Sebastian Bach. He was a master in the modality of music—a realm other than the discursive; he did not write learned treatises. Yet the consummate contrapuntal skill he displayed was the product of a musical imagination in comparison to which the discursive faculties pale into insignificance. The imagination of Bach, as anyone who is willing and able to fulfill the necessary conditions can discover, is a world of lofty order and—yes, knowledge.

But I am not attempting to defend Bach or any other great artist who stands in need of no defense. The mastery of one mode of human expressiveness is more than most men will ever accomplish. We will see in the next chapter that several contemporary musical masters have proved themselves verbally articulate as well, and the pronouncements of artists themselves should always be entitled to a special hearing. Even today, however, such pronouncements tend to be at best scattered and fragmentary. They do not add up to a system of thought. That we have them at all is thanks to the widespread verbal sophistication of our century. The musical judgments of Schumann, aside from the literary talent they evinced, were naive by present-day canons; even his versatility, so often noted, would be less remarkable today.

The composer now has the added temptations, occasionally lucrative, of the lecture platform, the classroom, and the conductor's podium. If he delivers the Norton lectures at Harvard during one academic year, it is necessary to weigh that gain to the discursive understanding of his hearers (and later his readers) against the loss of his musical productivity for the same period; for, unless he is a true Renaissance man and something of a Mozart in the bargain, there will be a diminution of his composing during the period that he is writing and delivering his lectures.

The composer will follow his own dictates but I, for one, am not proposing that he become a philosopher of music. It is better—far better—that he be a composer if he has the equipment; and if he must, in order to live, let him teach composition and theory. Philosophy—through philosophic spokesmen—may be expected in time to produce a cogent theory of a kind that can now only be aspired to. In the development of such a purview, the insights of artists and their reflections as well must constitute a large portion of whatever evidence is assembled. It is the business of philosophy, says Susanne Langer, to make sense of experience. And with no disparagement of other modalities and their meanings, she means discursive sense.

Gurney complained of the musical conversation of his day, which centered around the exploits of virtuosi and comparisons of their performances. The situation among executants remains unchanged one hundred years later. Professional preoccupations—even on the plane of contrapuntal, harmonic, and structural analysis, the present demesne of official theory—cannot be the starting point of fruitful speculation.

"The study of philosophy is a voyage towards the larger generalities," says Whitehead. "The primary method of philosophy is descriptive generalization."[27] Further, "morality of outlook is inseparably conjoined with generality of outlook.[28] He points out that any definite entity (and a musical composition will answer that description) depends upon a "systematic universe" for its status. Our familiar, though still mysterious, world of human discourse may be said to satisfy that condition. Our theory, then, will be relevant to that kind of entity in that kind of universe wherever it may occur; its validity will not depend upon particular circumstances of time and space but upon what occurs musically whenever the symbol is presented; and theory must, in its generality, provide for just that unique expression.

There must be no deprecation of specialists upon whom the life of art depends; an artist is such a specialist, raised to a higher power. The symbolist poets were a group of such artists who did not deal only with the obvious. They invoked the spirit of music, though they were disciples of the word. Mallarmé as the conscious aesthete remained, however, a victim of overspecialization, for all his theorizing. Baudelaire, who

[27] Alfred North Whitehead, *Process and Reality* (New York: [Torchbook] Harper & Brothers, 1960), pp. 14, 15–16.
[28] *Ibid.*, p. 23.

viewed the universe as an organism, very nearly qualified as a theorist with a capital "T." But all the mem-
bers of this highly interesting cluster, of whom Baudelaire was precursor, were artists. I have said they
confused the modalities—and this includes Baudelaire,
their strongest artist-philosopher. But this mixing, this
transposition, this syncretism—however articulate they
were in their espousal of it—was a metaphorical fusion;
analogy was implied but the metaphor itself was nevertheless given without reservation or qualification.
"Enter into the object," Bergson advised. How? By an
"intellectual act of intuition." The answer must suffice,
insofar as we have recourse to the artist. If Baudelaire
was artist-philosopher (or very nearly so), Bergson was
the philosopher-artist par excellence.

The business of philosophy is no doubt to
make sense of experience, including the experience of
art. The business of art is to present configurations of
another kind to human perception. Having given birth
to them, human intelligence may be expected to encompass whatever modalities of discourse are presented
to the consciousness. It may be the function of an artist,
in a particular instance, to merge two or more modalities, to effect a veritable synesthesia. Theoretically,
there cannot be any holds barred. But the function of
the philosopher of art will be to study the result of the
artist's efforts, account for it to the extent that he can,
and even examine constituents that go into the symbol.
He need not, however, mistake the parts for the whole.
And when verbal analysis is inadequate for the task, he
must say so. The philosophical interpreter may "cir-
cumnavigate" the symbol in an examination which he

hopes will "encircle and circumscribe, penetrate and illuminate" although, as Jaspers is careful to stipulate, "we circumscribe it in order to keep ourselves free for this truth, not in order to know what it is."[29] As philosophical theorist, the observer not only cannot, therefore, "enter into" the symbol but he is obliged to point out the literal impossibility of doing so. The impracticability, however, is an actual one; the implicit mode of the ingression is virtual. The theorist must recognize this and distinguish between modalities as the artist is under no obligation to do. What is not feasible on one level may be so on another; yet it may be (as with Bergson) an important dramatic advantage to the artist not to admit the difference. The artist's apprehension of his reality, moreover, may be so vivid, so intense, that he is unable to make such practical distinctions. Such inability in the philosopher is an incapacity. The philosophical theorist makes necessary distinctions; but he does not deny nor destroy the metaphor unless he is incompetent. A literal-minded interpretation cannot invalidate the "primary illusion" of a work of art.

Monroe Beardsley, whose "controversion theory" of metaphor with its principles of *congruence* and *plenitude* comes very close to my concept of the symbol, allows for that quality of "thickness" that I have characterized as richness and ambiguity.[30] A metaphor, he says, "is a miniature poem, and the explication of a metaphor is a model of all explication. . . . All the connotations that can be found to fit are to be attributed

[29] Jaspers, p. 43.
[30] Monroe C. Beardsley, *Aesthetics* (New York: Harcourt, Brace & World, Inc., 1958), pp. 134–47.

to the poem: it means all it *can* mean, so to speak."[31]
Auditory metaphor—a term which here occurs to me—
indeed conveys much of the quality of the musical symbol. But the modality of music is not verbal; and if I
read Beardsley correctly, this would make the use of
either "metaphor" or "symbol"—in describing music
itself—inappropriate. Like Hospers, he resists the distinction between "signal" and "symbol" that Langer
makes and finds the concept of a "presentational" or
"non-discursive" symbol unacceptable. Again like
Hospers, Beardsley would require that a symbol in some
way "stand for" something else: "I cannot find in her
discussion . . . any answer to the question why we
should take the music as referring to anything beyond
itself, any more than we take a chair or a mountain that
way."[32] Susanne Langer, however, is not concerned with
music as referring to things which it does not in itself
evoke: hence her fondness for such terms as *picture,
vital import, sentience.* She appears to be in agreement
with Douglas Morgan that a "proposition" must be a
statement in words: if so, music does not contain propositions. I have emphasized the nonverbal character
of music; I have also referred to it as a symbolism. Even
within the semantic restrictions imposed by Beardsley,
however, in considering whether or not music can refer
to anything beyond itself, one might suggest that "it
means all it *can* mean." But if meaning itself can only
refer to statements about things, we may need to speak,
as Susanne Langer does, of its "vital import."

I think we need not end in a semantic cul-de-
sac, even if Beardsley is less generous with "symbol"

[31] *Ibid.,* p. 144.   [32] *Ibid.,* p. 361.

than with "metaphor." (I believe that symbol will prove as viable for musical theory as metaphor is for poetic. There is long precedent for my extraordinary demands on the symbol. I will indicate how my requirements for concretions of meaning in the musical symbol go beyond Langer's.) Beardsley, indeed, is not trying to circumscribe musical art. He speaks eloquently of music as possibly

> the closest thing to pure process, to happening as such, to change abstracted from anything that changes, so that it is something whose course and destiny we can follow with the most exact and scrupulous and concentric attention, undistracted by reflections of our normal joys or woes, or by clues and implications for our safety or success. Instead of saying that music can be no more than this, we ought to say that music can be all of this, as nothing else can be.[33]

Yet Beardsley, acknowledging that we are somehow "abstracted," separated from "actuality" in the musical experience, does not maintain the integrity of the objective image: "Music . . . is no symbol of time or process, mental or physical, Newtonian or Bergsonian: it *is* process."[34] How can this be?[35]

It has been apparent from the first that the search for the meaning of (or acquaintance with) music is impeded by terminological roadblocks. Beardsley seems to me to be in agreement with Gurney, Bergson,

[33] *Ibid.,* pp. 338–39.
[34] *Ibid.,* p. 338.
[35] It must be acknowledged that music in performance is a process and, to be sure, participates in process itself; but music does not thereby become process, nor is it synonymous with process to begin with. Susanne Langer's treatment of Bergson (*Feeling and Form* [New York: Charles Scribner's Sons, 1953], p. 113 ff.) is pertinent here.

and Langer on many points; but their different vocabularies present serious difficulties—and a too frequent recourse to classification does not help the matter. Thus, it is an oversimplification to refer to Langer as an exponent of the "signification theory" of music; and the assignment of both Hanslick and Gurney to the "formalist theory" is destructive of those nuances of thought that separate them.

Several years ago Langer spoke of the confusion that surrounded such terms as *symbol* and *meaning:*

> A symbol may be a myth, a root metaphor, or a clinical symptom. "Meaning," likewise, is neither signification nor denotation. It is anything from a stimulus-response relation, to the wish behind a dream. . . . There is little the poor epistemologist can do about such encroachments of the jungle on his garden. All he can say is that these are loose and illicit uses of the words "symbol" and "meaning." . . . The fact is that several major lines of thought have arrived almost simultaneously at the recognition of the basic mental function that distinguishes man from nonhuman creatures—the use, in one way or another, of symbols to convey concepts.[36]

Since those lines were written, Leonard Meyer has been exploring the ramifications of "information theory" for music. He finds a syntactical relevance, in terms of which two kinds of meaning are to be distinguished: "designative" and "embodied." He quotes

[36] Susanne K. Langer, "On a New Definition of 'Symbol,'" *Philosophical Sketches* (New York: Mentor Press, 1964), pp. 55–56.

Morris R. Cohen's definition of meaning: "Anything acquires meaning if it is connected with, or indicates, or refers to, something beyond itself, so that its full nature points to and is revealed in that connection."[37] This definition recalls Whitehead's emphasis, in his lectures on symbolism, upon relevance amidst independence, unity in diversity. A word itself is a symbol: "its *meaning* is constituted by the ideas, images, and emotions, which it raises in the mind of the hearer."[38]

Applying such elements of information theory as "uncertainty" and "probability," Meyer arrives at this: "Musical meaning arises when an antecedent situation, requiring an estimate as to the probable modes of pattern continuation, produces uncertainty as to the temporal-tonal nature of the expected consequent."[39] The possibilities of this line of thought for musical theory are exciting; and they are pertinent equally to composer, interpreter, and listener. According to information theory, deviations, delays, and ambiguities increase the amount of information: greater information is related to greater uncertainty and to greater freedom of choice. I have said that richness and ambiguity characterize the musical symbol, as they characterize Beardsley's *metaphor;* if nonverbal "meaning" resides in modalities other than the verbal, then nonverbal "knowledge" is a possibility: and symbols, like metaphors, mean what they *can* mean. And it is more

[37] Morris R. Cohen, *A Preface to Logic* (New York: Henry Holt & Co., 1944), p. 47.
[38] Whitehead, *Symbolism* (New York: [Capricorn,] G. P. Putnam's Sons, 1959), p. 2. (Italics mine.)
[39] Leonard B. Meyer, "Meaning in Music and Information Theory," *JAAC*, XV, No. 4 (June, 1957), 416.

meaning, not meaning stripped bare, that is the condition of symbolic power. The meaning that Beardsley allows metaphor is something more than literal statement, as the meaning that I ascribe to music is more than designative.

In its relevance to organic and dynamic processes the musical symbol has nonverbal designative meanings; it is these that constitute Langer's "analogue to emotive life." But at the same time the musical symbol embodies meaning: it "has" something of what it "refers to," and more. The musical symbol is only partially abstract: it is a configuration that has power precisely because of its formal integrity; it can point or remind or signify only incidentally or peripherally. Its function is whole: the abstract is concrete. Actual and virtual in the symbol are one.

I have thus far in scattered references given most of the constituents of Susanne Langer's theory of art. I want now to summarize that theory, inviting attention both to our areas of agreement and to our differences.

According to Langer, each art has its particular *virtual* mode of manifestation, by means of which it projects its peculiar "primary illusion." The virtual is a department (or creative organization) of the conceptual realm wherein the expressive form is set apart: this setting apart is a condition of the "life" of the objective image, a condition of the essential aesthetic "distance." (Thus Beardsley's statement that music *is* process confuses the actual and the virtual.) The primary illusion of music is achieved in virtual time, that of painting, sculpture, and architecture in their appropriate modes of virtual space. (My own term *modality,* which I defined earlier, refers to that characteristic complex of sensuous-structural elements which are at once the materials and the limiting conditions of a particular "virtual mode.") Artistic creation is the creation of *significant form:* "Art is the creation of forms symbolic of human feeling." Music she describes as "a tonal analogue of emotive life."

Langer's idea of semblance follows from the concept of significant form. *Semblance* is the autonomous form assumed by the artist's creation, its mode of being *qua* art, its quality as image, its identity in "otherness," in detachment from actuality. Langer speaks of the semblance of an art work as its direct aesthetic quality, and she refers to Schiller's recognition of this quality as *Schein.* Semblance is that crucial factor of illusion which characterizes in significant form the articulate symbol of feeling.

According to her theory an art can exhibit only one primary illusion: this would invalidate the concept of the *Gesamtkunstwerk*—invalidate it, that is to say, in terms of what Wagner intended it to be. But this is not to say that secondary illusions may not be borrowed from other arts:

> The fact that the primary illusion of one art may appear, like an echo, as a secondary illusion in another, gives us a hint of the basic community of all the arts. As space may suddenly appear in music, time may be involved in visual works. . . . The primary illusion always determines the "substance," the real character of an art work, but the possibility of secondary illusions endows it with the richness, elasticity, and wide freedom of

creation that make real art so hard to hold in the meshes of theory.[40]

In describing what happens in the recognition of artistic import—the apprehension of significant form—Langer points out that intuition is fundamental; even the understanding of a syllogism is dependent upon an intuition of meaning: "all discursive reasoning would be frustrated without it."[41] She postulates a "basic intellectual act of intuition."[42] Art is a projection of subjectivity; the act of intuition is the recognition, *in toto,* of a mode of emotive life which the symbol has made articulate. "For, although a work of art reveals the character of subjectivity, it is itself objective; its purpose is to objectify the life of feeling."[43] Even the so-called nonobjective types of art will be objective in their essential expressive forms (as structured, symbolic analogues of emotive life).

At this point, Langer's concept of the "commanding form" must be examined. The commanding form is that original conception, the general Gestalt, which seeks to maintain its identity, to preserve its original purposes, as the artist brings his work into being. It is that whole by which the organization of the parts is regulated:

> I stress this objectivity and potency of the commanding form in a piece of music so heavily because I believe it is the key to almost all the moot problems of performance, understanding, adaptation, and even that dry old bone of contention,

---

[40] Langer, *Feeling and Form,* p. 118.
[41] *Ibid.,* p. 378.
[42] *Ibid.,* p. 375.
[43] *Ibid.,* p. 374.

self-expression. From the matrix, the greatest movement, flows the life of the work, with all its contingencies, its powers and perils in the community of human minds.[44]

But there may be degrees of correspondence between the commanding form and its realization; and any failure of correspondence would be a loss of semblance to the same degree. While this relationship between commanding form and semblance seems to follow logically from the implications of Langer's theory, it is my own interpretation and is not so stated by her. How much such a concept as "commanding form" owes to Platonic tradition is clear. What interests me more, however, is its relevance to those aspects of information theory which Leonard Meyer has appropriated.[45] Information theory, notwithstanding its horrendous technical vocabulary, may be expected not only to reinforce some intuitions (and no doubt to discredit others) but to provide further refinements where needed. Information theory does not appear to operate on the principle of Occam's razor.

Langer's theory, indeed, oversimplifies: it appears to me that "commanding form" is an intuition of a kind of probability system. But if every detail is, in fact, envisaged before the form itself appears, then certainty is too great. From the musical interpreter's standpoint such fixity would result in a petrified performance, and so frozen a concept would be equally undesirable in the composer. The commanding form itself must be flexi-

[44] *Ibid.*, pp. 131–32.
[45] See especially Meyer's discussion ("Meaning in Music and Information Theory") of *stochastic* and *Markoff* processes.

ble if the symbol is to have life. Probabilities will suffice initially and to a different degree, in the "realization" itself. Meyer distinguishes between "desirable" and "undesirable" uncertainty—a distinction pertinent, I think, to a consideration of contemporary aleatory music which exploits random elements—and states that "undesirable uncertainty arises when the probabilities are not known."[46]

In her zeal to separate the realms of the actual and the virtual, Langer fails to do justice to the dynamic interplay between them, the constant shifts, the gradations "in and out" of time: the organic fusion of conceptual and actual. The very limiting of the domain of the art symbol—the expressive form—to "emotive life" is an oversimplification; the component of *mind* in the symbol is equally important. (The dichotomy of thought and feeling is an arbitrary splitting which we now seem to accept without question.) Her theory does not give us enough information; she establishes categories but she does not measure intensities.

The conceptual is the matrix of that realm which Langer refers to as the virtual. In music making the indissolubility of conceptual (or virtual) and "active" processes may be observed at any point: in the very process of composition as well as in the preparation of a performance. In listening to music, the apprehensions of the intellect, the response of the senses, the immediacy of the symbol—all may be unified in an experience of dazzling lucidity; or, more probably, there may be jerks and shifts in the listener's attention, so that he is now "here," now "there."

[46] Leonard B. Meyer, "Some Remarks on Value and Greatness in Music," *JAAC*, XVII, No. 4 (June, 1959), 491.

Langer's failure to distinguish gradations in artistic apprehension or in works of vital import is also a failure to provide any kind of yardstick for making comparative judgments concerning particular compositions. (Information theory appears to provide a means of doing so: "the banal is the most probable course toward the most probable end.") There are degrees of virtuality; the strongest (hence most abstract) musical idea is that which is least dependent upon immediate circumstances of time and place—and least dependent, therefore, upon physical time for its identity.

Langer does not chart the departments of the virtual. In the final chapter of the book I have undertaken a rough exploration of some territory in that conceptual realm.

* * * CHAPTER TEN

TWENTIETH-CENTURY COMPOSERS AS SPOKESMEN

* * * THE VERBALLY ARTICULATE MUSICAL GIANTS whose pronouncements follow are unquestionably specialists; more than this, they are artists. To some extent all are philosophers as well, if we acknowledge their predilection for those very canons Whitehead proposes:

> The useful function of philosophy is to promote the most general systematization of civilized thought. There is a constant reaction between specialism and common sense. It is the part of the special sciences to modify common sense. *Philosophy is the welding of imagination and common sense into a restraint upon specialists, and also into an enlargement of their imaginations.* By providing the generic notions philosophy should make it easier to conceive the infinite variety of specific instances which rest unrealized in the womb of nature.[1]
>
> [1] Alfred North Whitehead, *Process and Reality* (New York: [Torchbook] Harper & Brothers, 1960), pp. 25–26. (Italics mine.)

248

We are inclined to listen with special interest, and rightly so, to what a composer himself says about his art. In the figures of Schoenberg, Stravinsky, Hindemith, and Sessions, we have examples of verbal sophistication in the creative musical artist—a sophistication which is for the most part a late nineteenth- and twentieth-century phenomenon. Because of the wide dissemination of technical knowledge, the means of proficiency and a comprehensive knowledge about music—its structure, the craft of composing it—technique is not esoteric. It is not easily acquired but the means of acquiring it are at any rate generally within reach.

Composers have a great variety of techniques to choose from; they can make their choices deliberately, self-consciously. Their responsibility is therefore enormous, and the variety of styles they—and their listeners—have access to is a source of great confusion as well as enrichment. A composer may seek to fix boundaries of his own, as Hindemith did in his theories; he may have recourse to the forms of earlier times, as in the neoclassicism with which both Stravinsky and Hindemith have been identified; he may make a virtue out of necessity, as Hindemith did with his concept of *Gebrauchsmusik;* or observing what he believes to be the bankruptcy of major-minor tonality, a composer may organize the twelve semitones of the octave into arbitrary rows, as Schoenberg did, providing a theoretical framework for this technique.

Being verbally articulate, the composers so far named can defend what they do, should they consider it necessary; and they can contribute helpful explanations of their intentions as well as interesting interpretations of contemporary music in general. Whether they secure our approval or not, these men are musical forces to be reckoned with. The missing giant on this list is of course Bartók, a major influence of our century. However, unlike the others, Bartók wrote music only, no books; we have recourse to his music for his essential message. An austere and dedicated artist, Bartók did not leave any legacy of systematic pronouncements on music. (The best biography and listing of his works is still that of Halsey Stevens.)

Their merits and defects aside, these men provide convenient guideposts by which we can evaluate and compare trends. Schoenberg, Stravinsky, and Hindemith—and of course Bartók—would constitute the key figures for a large-scale investigation of the problems of tonality in the twentieth century. That is too vast a subject to be incorporated in the present study. But a brief summary of what happened to tonality in the late nineteenth century will be a useful introduction to the panorama of developments which these composers exemplify and concerning which they have voiced such decided opinions.

The extreme chromaticism of late Romanticism carried traditional major-minor tonality, as one observer expressed it, to "the edge of chaos." Yet despite constant modulation and the increase in dissonance through the presence of nonharmonic tones, the secure home base of a key center remained implicit, even in the works of Wagner and Richard Strauss, the two giants of the dying century. Tonality was like quicksand—the instability of this element is evident in the disparate idioms of such composers as Franck, Brahms, and Reger—but its foundations, though weakened, had not been destroyed. I am reminded of Browning's poem "Abt Vogler," in which he describes the far-ranging tonal peregrinations of a master organist who nevertheless returns to "the C Major of this life" when his far-out musical improvisations are done.

It remained for Schoenberg, whose early works are so suggestive of the Wagnerian idiom, to take the decisive—and, for him, logical and inevitable—step away from what fixity had survived and to disclaim any tonal priorities or allegiances whatsoever. All twelve tones of the octave were to be equal, and none more equal than others! For this reason, once the serial technique had been devised following a period of free atonality, it was bad form for its exponents to arrange a succession of tones that would be reminiscent of the outmoded system, though in theory any order is permissible. Gradually the rigors of the new ideology were relaxed somewhat. The relative accessibility (I mean to the general public) of the Berg Violin Concerto, which in its choice of a "row" does hint at triadic structure, is a case in point.

From our present vantage point we see that Debussy, whose tonal experiments so outraged his contemporaries, made no real break with traditional tonality, nor even with the fundamental practice of the Romantic style. His recourse to certain exoticisms—medieval modes, pentatonic and whole-tone scales, and the use of arresting timbres for new color effects—was a thoroughly Romantic tendency. This is not to deny the distinct originality of his style; it was a highly personal art. But so was that of Fauré, whose gentler twilight reveries seemed—when Debussy first burst upon the musical scene—a far cry from the astringencies of Impressionism. The tonal disparity between them today does not appear so very great.

Dissonance does not refer to any tonal absolute. The dominant seventh chord, still classified as a dissonance, once had a dissonant effect on the human ear; it can hardly be regarded today as functionally dissonant. "Every definite entity requires a systematic universe to supply its requisite status," says Whitehead. That systematic universe, to which consonance and dissonance have reference, has been—practically speaking—the traditional harmony as taught in European conservatories and the many schools in other parts of the world modelled after them. That particular universe, which seems to have exploded in the twentieth century, was already expanding rapidly in the nineteenth. Beethoven's delight in the seventh chord, which could manifest itself for many pages in some of his sonatas, could not be sustained in his composer heirs several decades later. The seventh became "old hat," a faded metaphor: and even ninth, eleventh, and thirteenth chords were to lose their savor following the initial novelty.

The tempo quickens. In the eighteenth century Voltaire was able to say that it takes a whole generation for the human ear to grow familiar with a new musical style. The varieties of composition in a single generation of our century truly exceed the capacity of the human ear to cope with them, though the dedicated and sophisticated listener may hope to comprehend several contemporary idioms. But even though he be a music lover of strong appetites and physical stamina, who can do justice to the sheer quantity of new works to which we now have access with the help of electrical reproduction? Langer has been impelled to speak of the "madhouse of too much art." But the listener himself, as well as the composer, seeks novelty. Sir James Jeans, in *Science and Music,* states that "the sated ear forever demands new harmonies which it will fast learn to tolerate, and then dismiss as threadbare and uninteresting."

Nevertheless, no specialist can encompass it all. The six Bartók quartets are looked upon by some experts as carrying on—or carrying forward the implicit possibilities of further development of a particular kind—where the late Beethoven quartets left off. It is a defensible thesis; an isolated page of a late Beethoven quartet can easily be mistaken on cursory examination for a Bartók score. I am thinking here of the sheer visual aspect of the score, though the resemblance is no less striking on the basis of tonality and—especially— handling of the motivic elements, both melodic and rhythmic. Yet how many active listeners can honestly claim to have exhausted the late Beethoven quartets, really to have explored and to have done with that final testament in the way many of us may legitimately claim to have reached the final limits of what we needed, or will ever need, from Tschaikowsky's Fifth Symphony—if not Beethoven's own Fifth? When, for most of us, are the late quartets likely to become a "faded metaphor"? And the Bartók quartets similarly make rigorous demands; they do not yield everything even on repeated hearings; they are extraordinarily viable symbols.

Notwithstanding these facts of musical experience, as they apply to all but the most avid (and perhaps supersophisticated) consumers, I have heard the opinion expressed not infrequently that Bartók has already had his day. "No one," a composer of electronic music recently remarked to me, "really wants to listen to that any more. It's passé." I suspect this opinion reflects, more than anything else, a preoccupation with the machinery of composing.

Jeans's remarks about the human ear and its demand for novelty correspond closely to Schoenberg's account of what he observed in the European musical milieu of his own youth:

> The ear had gradually become acquainted with a great number of dissonances, and so had lost the fear of their "sense-interrupting" effect. One no longer expected preparations of Wagner's dissonances or resolutions of Strauss's discords; one was not disturbed by Debussy's non-functional harmonies, or by the harsh counterpoint of later composers. This state of affairs led to a freer use of dissonance: comparable to classic composers' treatment of diminished seventh chords, which could precede and follow any other harmony, consonant or dissonant, as if there were no dissonance at all. . . . What distinguishes dissonances from consonances is not a greater or lesser degree of beauty, but a greater or lesser degree of *comprehensibility.*[2]

Here, Schoenberg is treating music not merely in terms of its structure but as "idea." Here he approaches philosophy.

[2] Arnold Schoenberg, *Style and Idea* (New York: Philosophical Library, 1950), pp. 103–4.

The validity of his method is not something we can determine here. The general question I want to raise is that of his vocabulary and—using his own term—the *comprehensibility* of the musical results that depend upon that vocabulary. Whatever the listener may finally decide on that score there can be no question of the composer's right to devise a new method, if he chooses, or to eschew deliberately all traditional ones. Gurney, it will be remembered, speaks of the endless disputation regarding the comparative merits of composers and compositions as the most useless sort of musical controversy; he pleads for the wisdom of an exceptionally wide tolerance. It is not only wisdom but a practical necessity to examine musical works in this spirit, remembering that comprehensibility is not dependent upon the use of any particular *modus operandi;* if it were, the concept of a healthy musical appetite could not even arise. So far as the technical means considered in isolation are concerned, every serious student of music has examined works which may be structural paragons but inspire no more than an academic interest. Comprehensibility is a yardstick which each listener must apply according to his own canons of intelligibility (on the rational level) combined with those immediate responses he has found to be a reliable guide. The experience of music is a Gestalt; the particular vocabulary is not irrelevant to the experience. But in a discussion of Schoenberg—or serial composition in general—there is a tendency to deal with musical comprehensibility in terms of that vocabulary alone, because of its far out auditory characteristics. (Again, I am thinking of that hypothetical general listener.)

Particularly, there is confusion surrounding that movement called Viennese Expressionism because, even after more than half a century of repeated hearings and indefatigable support in influential circles, its musical import has made little impression upon a wide musical public and gives as yet small promise of taking hold among the uninitiated. This is in striking contrast to the fate of other important idioms (such as Impressionism, early Stravinsky, and even—to a degree—neoclassicism) which, after evoking initial hostility, achieved the status of staples and finally of faded metaphors—the inevitable result of having arrived. Expressionism—a label that promises much—has been around for a long time; it has fervent advocates; but so far, it resembles certain highly interesting biological specimens in the history of nature which, after reaching a state of relative perfection and durability, at length disappeared: off-beat, experimental by-products, not in the mainstream of evolution, but possessing, nevertheless, inherent interest and value. I am not saying this is to be the fate of serial technique; perhaps it will survive in modified form or contribute a few genes to a musical organism destined to endure, which has not yet emerged from the matrix. The serialists surely are an influential group and verbally articulate; but their pronouncements have more often been relevant to the technical *processes* of their composition than to elucidation of musical *ideas;* and they have contributed, therefore, not a little to the confusion of which I spoke. Before I return to Schoenberg let me point out that present-day twelve-tone composers need not be equated with him; there have been as many divisions among his spiritual heirs as among the various exponents of the Marxist ideological patrimony. Many contemporary serialists are thoroughgoing pragmatists who would vehemently reject any suggestion of a *mystique*. What is disturbing, however, is that some of them exhibit in their writings singularly little concern for musical ideas.

Schoenberg belonged to the Expressionist school. As the high priest of that persuasion he was a Romanticist, and I agree with those of his followers who maintain that the expressive content of his work remained intense, regardless of what technical means he employed. Curt Sachs and other observers have allowed Schoenberg's shift in techniques to confuse them on matters of musical meaning; they confuse structural processes with ideas. A shift of technique may of course lead to an inaccessibility of the work; and to a great extent this has happened with Schoenberg. We might compare Schoenberg to James Joyce; both were men of genius; their works are significant, even if not wholly successful by some canons. The pertinent question in regard to their respective techniques is this: how far— how radically—can the artist change his vocabulary and still be read, still be listened to?

There is a pronounced difference between early and late Beethoven, as there is between Schoenberg's tonal and atonal periods. The crucial difference is that an organic relationship is clearly discernible throughout the evolution of Beethoven's style, so that the final works are implicit in his earliest production— the unity of form and content persisting all the way. Schoenberg maintains that a similar unity characterizes his own creative life; what many observers have looked upon as a great "leap" away from tonality he regards as a logical "next step." It is at least permissible to raise the question of whether a different situation from Beethoven's may not prevail here. I feel impelled to a different interpretation of these two giants, because Schoenberg's conscious adoption of a principle of organization not previously employed in his writing was to constitute the guiding rationale of all his subsequent work. In a sense the serial technique compensated structurally for the loss of explicit tonality, while other elements of composition—rhythmic devices, general expressive indications, even the formal architecture of musical works— were subjected to no such reorganization.

What I am suggesting is that Schoenberg himself in the formulation of his system may have provided the basis of a dichotomy between feeling and form, so that a single component of the musical symbol—in this instance the organization of tonality—becomes elevated to a position of paramount importance. Such a radical change of emphasis in the constellation of elements making up the symbol, particularly when the new order is imposed consciously from the outside, might be expected to produce some of the results which have actually followed upon his innovations. One might easily get the impression from a sampling of the available literature on the subject that the devices of serial technique were the *raison d'être* of the musical works which exemplify them.

The kind of confusion which can result from a failure to distinguish technical devices from musical meaning is reflected in a statement made by Portnoy in reference to Reger: "He was concerned with technical values of tone and form and, because of his zeal for purism, misinterpreted his idol Bach by emphasizing the musical symbol rather than the emotion which the symbol represents."[3] Reger, who still has devout followers in Germany, was a Romanticist who developed a highly complex, chromatic style; he imagined himself to be a kind of successor to Bach whose work he was carrying forward! Reger, as Portnoy suggests, may not have been successful in communicating emotion in his work; I am inclined to share a widely held belief that his technical prowess overshadowed his inspiration. But in musical symbolism we cannot separate the symbol and the emotion it represents in the way Portnoy attributes such a separation to Reger. Because emotion is integral to music itself, music is a true symbol, and not merely a sign referring the listener to something extraneous.

Of Schoenberg's integrity and stature as an artist there can be no doubt. There remains, however, a dichotomy between the period of his composition represented by *Verklärte Nacht,* and those works written after he had abandoned traditional concepts of tonality altogether. Admittedly, the twelve-tone works, the products of his maturity, appear more original than those Wagnerian-like compositions of his early, formative years. But there is the plain fact of the inaccessibility of his mature vocabulary, except to initiates. I do not say that the more esoteric art must justify itself to all, though Schoenberg himself was very defensive in regard to serial technique. Certainly the more limited

---

[3] Julius Portnoy, *The Philosopher and Music* (New York: Humanities Press, 1954), p. 205.

range of the later works—more limited in terms of the number of listeners they can reach—must be attributed to the profound shift in compositional technique, and not to rather sudden, inner changes in Schoenberg himself. It is significant that his disciples speak repeatedly of the emotional intensity, the concentrated feeling, of his twelve-tone works. If these are valid intuitions, as they may well be, then Schoenberg was an Expressionist to the end; and it is plausible to expect there would therefore be a unity of spirit behind the disparate works, whatever their period. But some listeners who have sought with hope for such a continuity audible in the works themselves—a continuity plainly discernible in Beethoven—have been disappointed. With due allowance for their incapacities (which are, I am afraid, rather widespread), there is an unfortunate blocking of the channels of communication between composer and audience. For these listeners the mature Schoenberg appears to be beyond musical reach. The mature Schoenberg was a great theorist and teacher, as well as composer, and his claim to eminence does not depend upon any single facet of his labors. But an artist who, after more than a half-century of productivity during which his name becomes familiar to every serious student of music, still does not break through to an audience commensurate in size with his own stature cannot hold that audience altogether responsible.

Speaking of his first efforts in his new style around 1908 and similar works by his pupils Webern and Berg, Schoenberg recalls that "the foremost characteristics of these *in statu nascendi* were their extreme expressiveness and their extraordinary brevity."[4] Idi-

---

[4] Quoted in Sam Morgenstern, (ed.), *Composers on Music* (New York: [Bonanza] Pantheon Books, Inc., 1956), p. 379.

oms aside, Schoenberg is attesting to indissolubility of form and content when he adds: "At that time, neither I nor my pupils were conscious of the reasons for these features. Later I discovered that our sense of form was right when it forced us to counterbalance extreme emotionality with extraordinary shortness."[5] Exhibiting that faith in "the infallibility of one's own fantasy" which he held to be essential to the artist, Schoenberg made this prediction: "The time will come when the ability to draw thematic material from a basic set of twelve tones will be an unconditional prerequisite for obtaining admission into the composition class of a conservatory."[6]

Schoenberg's rigorous self-discipline, his concern to achieve a *rapprochement* between practice and exalted theory, suggests that rigid control and distillation of the materials of his craft which Mallarmé sought in poetry:

> The restrictions imposed on a composer by the obligation to use only one set [of twelve tones] in a composition are so severe that they can only be overcome by an imagination which has survived a tremendous number of adventures. Nothing is given by this method; but much is taken away.[7]

It is a rigorous and austere concept, artistically arduous, assuming—as did Mallarmé—that what is left out is also crucial. There can be no doubt that Schoenberg was in quest of the objective musical symbol. But it was to be a supersymbol of dazzling lucidity.

[5] *Ibid.*
[6] *Ibid.*, p. 384.
[7] *Ibid.*, p. 383. (From Schoenberg's essay, "The Composition with Twelve Tones," 1950.)

There can also be no doubt that his music increasingly was destined to be an exclusive music, on which only a jury of his peers could pronounce judgment. For that elite, however, his symbolic gift was to be a musical organism of heightened intelligibility:

> Composition with twelve tones has no other aim than comprehensibility. In view of certain events in recent musical history, this might seem astonishing, for works written in this style have failed to gain understanding in spite of the new medium of organization. Thus, should one forget that contemporaries are not final judges, but are generally overruled by history, one might consider this method doomed. But, though it seems to increase the listener's difficulties, it compensates for this deficiency by penalizing the composer. For composing thus does not become easier, but rather ten times more difficult. Only the better-prepared composer can compose for the better-prepared music lover.[8]

Until quite recently, Schoenberg and Stravinsky represented opposing points of view. In turning his protean talent to the challenge of serial technique, Stravinsky has demonstrated once again his utter unpredictability, his sovereign disregard of his public's expectations.

Schoenberg was essentially Romantic; Stravinsky is fundamentally a classicist in his leanings. What Stravinsky has to say relevant to a philosophy of music is said most cogently in his *Poetics of Music,* the Norton lectures which he delivered at Harvard in 1939–

---

[8] *Ibid.,* p. 378.

40. In these lectures he reaffirms the Nietzschean dichotomy of Apollo and Dionysus, clearly stating his own preference for the Apollonian side, which represents balance, restraint, order: the Greek classical ideals.

It is important to observe in Stravinsky himself a steady movement toward Apollo as he grows older. The early works—*Petrouchka, Rite of Spring, Fire Bird*—inspired by their ballet settings and written in collaboration with Diaghilev, were to a great extent—is it not obvious?—Dionysian in character. Let us not forget that the composer himself was at that juncture in his life when those very qualities in his own nature would be most compelling in their demand for expression. With their savage vitality, overpowering quantity of sound, and rhythmic intensity, these early compositions are still Stravinsky's most popular works. He introduced certain innovations of an experimental nature—the use of bitonality, for example—none of which singly could define the essential character of his work nor be exalted to the role of a cardinal principle. His ballet compositions, *in toto,* evoked the most fervent reactions of delight and outrage; and they have survived as intact unities, with or without the dance they were meant to serve.

I am far from imputing to Stravinsky a lessening of his creative powers following the first spectacular period of his career. Surely, however, the paring down of resources that accompanied the neoclassic essays from *L'Histoire du soldat* on was not the act of an unhatched fledgling, but of a mature craftsman possessed of "an imagination which has survived a tremendous number of adventures." Aldous Huxley remarks somewhere that hedonism is a philosophy that recommends itself to the young rather than the aged; one's most abstract ideals may reflect, beyond inherited temperament, his time of life and state of health. Aside from the ageless characteristics he has exhibited throughout his career, Stravinsky was no doubt an old soul at his birth. The power of conception that is so strong in the sensuous works of his youth is also the source of their durability; even then he was providing the necessary objectivity. It is still significant that the growing preoccupation with art as patterns of order brought him to the tone-row—but only at an advanced age. I shall not make any sweeping generalizations from his example. It should nevertheless be noted that both Schoenberg and Stravinsky identified themselves more and more with the Apollonian mirroring after they had drained the cup of experience. I am of course referring not to their personal activities, of which I have no knowledge, but to their imaginative identifications.

The very distrust of excess emotion which Stravinsky exhibits reveals the volcanic force of his own creative life and leads him (as it led Schoenberg) to the search for suitable principles of organization and control. He does not, however, appear to be in search of any single absolute. Curious and voracious, he gives his allegiance only provisionally to any canons; there is no ultimate fixity, unless it be Apollonian order itself, from which all patterns—even the exquisite calligraphy of Stravinsky's scores—are derived.

The necessity for the ordering of music prompts Stravinsky to restrict the license of performers. Unlike many other composers, he seems to deny a creative function to the interpreter; one gets the impression that if Stravinsky could eliminate the human element in performance he would gladly do so. Admittedly, every live performance is a risk; each interpreter introduces new Dionysian possibilities which the composer may expressly wish to exclude. Stravinsky takes every precaution, through the detailed instructions in his scores, to insure as faithful an adherence as possible to his intentions. Once the image is crystallized in his imagination he hardly dares entrust it to the world.

Copland, in contrast, sees the interpreter as an important—indeed, indispensable—intermediary between composer and public; the interpreter is one who can bring a work to life, or bury it. Copland concedes that an interpreter may even discover in a score nuances which the composer had not consciously intended but which he may be joyfully surprised to hear. If Copland is capable of delighted surprise at a new reading of one of his works, he is equally capable of the opposite reaction and has doubtless been inspired in that negative direction on many occasions; this is a necessary condition of the risk. I gather that Stravinsky has seldom been pleased by an interpreter's efforts that did not closely coincide with his original intentions.

Stravinsky, who studied under Rimsky-Korsakov, rebelled strongly against the prevalent Romanticism of his youth, though it nevertheless helped to form him. It is interesting that notwithstanding this general rejection he has retained a great admiration for Tschaikowsky, a composer he believes to have been badly underrated. Tschaikowsky, of course, is rich in the very element Stravinsky is weakest in: melody.

The astringent, austere quality of Stravinsky's thought, as expressed in *The Poetics of Music,* has a tonic effect; it is "truth through a temperament." He is rational; and true to his Apollonian tendencies he echoes the Greek concept of the finite as good, the infinite as evil, when he postulates an ordering of the Many, a harmony of varieties: "How much more natural and more salutary it is to strive toward a single, limited reality than toward endless division!"[9] The problem of unity in variety he regards as the essential question: an *inquiry of an ontological order.* My own question, "What is music?" with which the book opens, is such an inquiry. Stravinsky assumes a transcendent meaning for music, as well as a universe of human discourse: "Music comes to reveal itself as a force of communion with our fellow man—and with the Supreme Being."[10] He sees the creative process as both rational and unconscious; it becomes intelligible (becomes a symbol) in the formal unity of the objective image: "It seems that the unity we are seeking is forged without our knowing it and establishes itself within the limits which we impose upon our work."[11]

I spoke of his experimental creativity and his appetite for novelty. As Stravinsky redefined for himself and refined the guiding concepts of his developing classicism, the process was reflected—much as with Mallarmé—in a gradual alteration of the work itself, particularly in its gross material aspects. The direction of his thought led him away from the pursuit of myriad

[9] Igor Stravinsky, *Poetics of Music* (New York: Vintage Books, 1956), p. 145.
[10] *Ibid.,* p. 146.
[11] *Ibid.,* p. 145.

color effects, away from an infinity of orchestral or other sonorous resources. He has been able to keep alive an interest in viable and original ideas and to draw upon those instrumental and vocal media best suited to a succinct musical rendering. The preoccupation with idea, though it gradually unfleshed his work, saved him from that endless multiplication of sound textures cultivated for their own sake, so characteristic of many contemporary works in which color is the chief element. Sound sensation leads to a music which—in the absence of the sustaining power of thought, which I think we may acknowledge as the very source of *legato*—can only be described as atomistic. Sensation, from its forceful immediacy in *Rite of Spring,* undergoes a metamorphosis in Stravinsky's hands:

> For myself, if my own tendency leads me to search for sensation in all its freshness by discarding the warmed-over, the hackneyed—the specious, in a word—I am nonetheless convinced that *by ceaselessly varying the search one ends up only in futile curiosity.* That is why I find it pointless and dangerous to over-refine techniques of discovery.[12]

The search for new experience, then, dominated by strong conceptual power, does not degenerate into the discovery of new sounds that can be produced by rubber bands, paper clips, or other impromptu instruments (in conjunction with a piano or in any other juxtaposition whatsoever, or in isolation). Although the renunciation of color by one so gifted in its use seems to me wasteful, Stravinsky has saved his work from that most terrible of all deprivations, sensation without

[12] *Ibid.* (Italics mine.)

intelligibility. Without conceptual power no objective image can appear; at no time in his long career has Stravinsky been wanting in the power to give form.

One further insight, another reinforcement to my thesis, appears in the *Poetics.* I have presented the concept of music as subsisting in *virtual time.* Stravinsky, in his lecture "The Phenomenon of Music," has this to say: "Musical creation appears . . . an innate complex of intuitions and possibilities based primarily upon an exclusively musical experiencing of time— *chronos,* of which the musical work merely gives us the functional realization."[13] Exactly. The musical realization of time *is* the virtual.

"What is musical vision?" Hindemith asks in *A Composer's World.* His answer is one of the most arresting accounts of musical inspiration to be found:

> We all know the impression of a very heavy flash of lightning in the night. Within a second's time we see a broad landscape, not only in its general outlines but with every detail. Although we could never describe each single component of the picture, we feel that not even the smallest leaf of grass escapes our attention. We experience a view, immensely comprehensive and at the same time immensely detailed, that we never could have under normal daylight conditions, and perhaps not during the night either, if our senses and nerves were not strained by the extraordinary suddenness of the event.
> Compositions must be conceived the same way. If we cannot, in the flash of a single moment, see a composition in its absolute entirety, with every pertinent detail in its proper place, we are not

[13] *Ibid.,* p. 31.

> genuine creators. . . . Not only will he [the com-
> poser] have the gift of seeing—illuminated in his
> mind's eye as if by a flash of lightning—a complete
> musical form (though its subsequent realization
> in a performance may take three hours or more);
> he will have the energy, persistence, and skill to
> bring this envisioned form into existence, so that
> even after months of work not one of its details
> will be lost or fail to fit into his photomental
> picture.[14]

This was written by a composer of dissonant counterpoint, a neoclassicist. It was a classicist, Mozart, who gave a similar account of total vision of a work, for which the writing down process was merely a matter of calligraphy:

> All this fires my soul, and, provided I am not
> disturbed, my subject enlarges itself, becomes
> methodised and defined, and the whole, though it
> be long, stands almost complete and finished in
> my mind, so that I can survey it, like a fine picture
> or a beautiful statue, at a glance. Nor do I hear
> in my imagination the parts *successively*, but I
> hear them, as it were, all at once (*gleich alles
> zusammen*).[15]

Beethoven, whose laborious transmogrifications of thematic material were remarked upon earlier, described the final crystallization of his musical concepts in similar terms:

> I change many things, discard others, and try
> again and again until I am satisfied; then, in my
> head, I begin to elaborate the work in its breadth,

---

[14] Paul Hindemith, *A Composer's World* (Garden City, N.Y.: [Anchor] Doubleday & Co., 1961), pp. 70–71.
[15] Quoted in Brewster Ghiselin, *The Creative Process* (New York: Mentor Press, 1955), p. 45. From Edward Holmes, *Life of Mozart* (New York: E. P. Dutton, 1912). The authenticity of this letter is in doubt.

its narrowness, its height, its depth and, since I
am aware of what I want to do, the underlying
idea never deserts me. *It rises, it grows, I hear
and see the image in front of me from every angle,
as if it had been cast like sculpture, and only the
labor of writing it down remains. . . .* [16]

These instances give a remarkably homogeneous account of that phase of the creative process in
which a total envisagement of the work takes place: the
objective image itself—the symbol—is apprehended by
the composer in its final unity of form and content; he
has only to record it. Mozart and Beethoven are in
agreement on the mysterious origin of the ideas.
"Whence and *how* they come, I know not; nor can I
force them," said Mozart.[17] And Beethoven: "You may
ask me where I obtain my ideas. I cannot answer this
with any certainty: they come unbidden, spontaneously
or unspontaneously."[18] Hindemith adds his corroboration: "Something—you know not what—drops into
your mind—you know not whence—and there it grows—
you know not how—into some form—you know not why.
This seems to be the general opinion, and we cannot
blame the layman if he is unable to find rational
explanations for so strange an occurrence."[19]

The material of *A Composer's World* was first
presented as the Norton lectures a decade after Stravinsky occupied that chair at Harvard. The opening
chapter, "The Philosophical Approach," seeks to isolate

---

[16] Quoted in Morgenstern, p. 87, taken from a written conversation with Louis Schlösser dating from 1822 or 1823.
(Italics mine).
[17] Ghiselin, p. 44.
[18] Morgenstern, p. 87.
[19] Hindemith, p. 67.

in "the more esoteric realms of our musical nature" those enduring values that transcend the deaths (and occasional resurrections) of particular pieces; these are values, he suggests, that may be found in music; yet he can hardly refer to musical values when he proposes that if we want "to recognize and understand such values, we must perceive music not as a mere succession of reasonably arranged acoustical facts; we must extricate it from the sphere of amorphous sound, we must in some way participate, beyond the mere sensual perception of music, in its realization as sound."[20] Here we are headed, once more, for the archetypal idea, for the soundless music beyond music that is actually (and merely) *heard;* we are headed for the Platonic realm of eternal objects, where our conceptual reach exceeds our audible grasp. The dynamic modality of music is denigrated.

Hindemith refers to the *De musica* of St. Augustine and the *De institutione musica* of Boethius, which he describes as the two extremes: "The Augustinian precept, in which our mind absorbs music and transforms it into moral strength; and the Boethian precept, in which the power of music, its ethos, is brought into action upon our mind."[21] Hindemith's distinction, which seems to me a somewhat arbitrary one—giving two readings of what is essentially a single process—is that the Augustinian view accords greater autonomy to the mind, the Boethian to music. And when music is in the ascendancy, the mind is passive. He gives credence to both readings of musical experience, suggesting that we must accept one or the other

[20] *Ibid.*, p. 3.   [21] *Ibid.*, p. 13.

alternative unless we can achieve "their forceful unifi-
cation in one single act of will power."[22] He quotes the
opening sentence of *De institutione musica:* "Music is
a part of our human nature; it has the power either to
improve or to debase our character." Why Hindemith
implies that Augustine would not hold a similar view
is not clear; but his statement, "The idea of musical
ethos in its extreme Platonic form is in strict opposition
to Augustine's musical attitude,"[23] is quite indefensible.
Hindemith also attempts to make a distinction in inter-
preting Plato between the *ethical power* of music (which
he says Plato acknowledges) and its capacity to effect the
moral improvement of the soul. Wherein is the
difference?

When I say that Hindemith denigrates (and
this is strange) the dynamic modality of music, I mean
that he is embracing the Augustinian canons of the
"noble, superhuman, and ideal" whereby music will be
converted into moral power:

> It is our own mind that brings about this con-
> version; music is but a catalytic agent to this end.
> The betterment of our soul must be our own
> achievement, although music is one of those
> factors which, like religious belief, creates in us
> most easily a state of willingness towards this bet-
> terment. In short, we have to be active; music,
> like humus in a garden soil, must be dug under in
> order to become fertile. Composers, performers,
> teachers, listeners—they all must outgrow the mere
> registration of musical impressions, the superficial
> and sentimental attachment to sound.[24]

[22] *Ibid.,* p. 14.   [23] *Ibid.,* p. 11.   [24] *Ibid.,* p. 6.

In his "Philosophical Approach" Hindemith fails completely to define what is distinctly musical in this purview; he finds cogency in the tradition of musical numerology, the concept of music of the spheres, and the rest: "It may well be that the last word concerning the interdependence of music and the exact sciences has not been spoken."[25] He can only be referring, here, to a felt harmony of numbers, a soundless mathematical correspondence. Hindemith acknowledges the fact, which I have also alluded to, that the composer is not called upon to develop a musical-philosophical system. But Hindemith's basic misunderstanding of what a philosophy of music would be, and the source of his own confusion, is clearly indicated in these lines:

> Since in venturing into the realm of philosophy we all enjoy freedom of choice, we may concentrate on the works of certain writers and entirely neglect others. We can exercise our prerogative of emphasis or bias without forgetting that our primary concern is, after all, not philosophy, but music.[26]

Yet in referring to "that science which deals with the essence, the effects, and the history of music," Hindemith is delineating precisely the demesne of musical philosophy.

A Composer's World has chapters on the intellectual and emotional perception of music; the author recognizes the fact that our experience of music is

[25] Ibid., p. 9.   [26] Ibid., p. 3.

both. He says, moreover, that music is "meaningless noise unless it touches a receiving mind." Not surprisingly, Hindemith speaks with most authority when he refers to those aspects of musical experience that he knows intimately and that can be repeatedly verified in the empirical world—the creative process both as inspiration and craft, apprehension of the objective symbol, and its relationship to virtual time and motion. Though he fears, as much as Stravinsky, the degenerative possibilities of that which is sensuous and material, there is no other field in which his work can be realized: the musical symbol, like any other, is sensuously concrete—Goethe's "concrete universal." Here is Whitehead's testimony: "An actual entity is concrete because it is such a particular concrescence of the universe."[27]

Hindemith, in speculative vein, believes he observes "a growing tendency to replace the predominantly materialistic methods of the past with ways of research and communication the impulses of which stem from a closer inclination towards an Augustinian interpretation of music and its functions."[28] Perhaps so. But I do not see the evidence for this and I am inclined to shrug at such a prediction.

But when Hindemith, out of his own profound knowledge, adds further testimony to the concordance we have been building (when he says, for example, that "music does not express feelings but merely releases images of feelings"[29]), we know that we are receiving

[27] Whitehead, *Process and Reality*, p. 80.
[28] Hindemith, p. 15.
[29] *Ibid.*, p. 49.

the evidence of a master. Similarly, when he tells us that "it is only with the memory of feelings in our mind that we can have any feelinglike reaction caused by music,"[30] we get the equivalent of Wordsworth's "emotion recollected in tranquillity," but of course, independently arrived at.

In trying to account for the psychological and physiological connections between the feelings and music—or between what we distinguish as "life" and "art," the "actual" and the "virtual"—Hindemith offers this equation: "Actual motion on the one side equals feeling of motion on the other side."[31] Let me invert and paraphrase the equation: Symbolic emotion in music equals—or refers to—experiences of actual emotion stored in the memory of the self.

One of the most verbally articulate of living composers is Roger Sessions. In *The Musical Experience,* which consists of six lectures first presented at the Juilliard School in 1949, he offers a succinct and compelling testament. The opening lecture, "The Musical Impulse," deals successively with the composer, the performer, and the listener: the three types of human beings who may be said to enter into relationship with music. The composer's relationship is simple, direct, primary; the performer's—a more problematical, complex relationship—is a reproductive, interpretative, and projective one; and the relationship of the listener (a newcomer, the product of a late stage of musical sophis-

---

[30] *Ibid.,* p. 46. [31] *Ibid.,* p. 49.

tication) is more complex still. The active listener—
not one who merely hears the sounds—is a participant.
"But the essential is that music is an activity: it is something done, an experience lived through, with varying
intensity, by composer, performer, and listener alike."[32]
        Sessions displays more concern for the essential
dynamism of music than Schoenberg, Stravinsky, or
Hindemith. Like them, he pays heed to crucial elements of *idea,* the realm of musical conception; but he
gives primacy to the actual processes, the facts of musical
experience. He is more of a Bergsonian than a Platonist.
He looks upon rhythm, which has its origin in organic
processes, as the primary fact: "The subject of rhythm
is a vast one, and indeed an adequate definition of
rhythm comes close to defining music itself."[33] Musical
experience is human; it has to do with the listener's
relationship to the sound he hears. The basic characteristics, then, of that experience are not to be sought in
the science of acoustics. He makes a necessary distinction (which Hindemith fails to do) when he acknowledges that music and physics touch at points but are
fundamentally different spheres of discourse.
        Rhythm is fundamental. Sessions is in accord
with Hindemith in referring to breathing as our first
and most lasting experience of rhythm, reflected
musically in upbeat and downbeat, arsis and thesis, and
so on; what we call a musical phrase is a musical breath.
Those organic sources of music that Sessions emphasizes
are to be found in humanly apprehended experience,

[32] Roger Sessions, *The Musical Experience of Composer,
Performer, Listener* (New York: Atheneum Publishers,
1962), p. 8.
[33] *Ibid.,* p. 16.

and not in physical facts of sound and rhythm; Sessions keeps music in a world of human discourse; it is functional. He speaks, as Cassirer does, of those elements of tension and relaxation present in music as in life and which contribute to the emotional analogue the former can provide: "What we may call the raw, formal materials of music are also the expressive elements, and these, again, have their basis in certain of the most elementary, intimate, and vital experience through which we live as human beings."[34] He refers to those inner human gestures which embody our deepest and most intimate responses: these are not yet art, but the material from which it is made. Sessions suggests that "a melodic motif or phrase is in essence and origin a vocal gesture; it is a vocal movement with a clearly defined and therefore clearly expressed profile."[35]

The clear definition (form) and expression (emotion) make up the *objective image* we have been alluding to under various names; *profile* is nicely descriptive of its symbolic modality, which sets it apart for contemplation. Gurney and others have pointed out analogous movements between music and life. Sessions gives the example of "agitated breathing," which is reflected in agitated melodic and rhythmic movement: "or conversely, sharp, irregular accents, or successive violent contrasts in pitch will call forth subconscious associations suggesting the kind of agitation which produces violent or irregular breathing."[36]

The emotive analogues of music are enormously complex in comparison with such fundamental processes; but all the refinements, all the "distance" in

[34] *Ibid.,* p. 19.   [35] *Ibid.,* p. 18.   [36] *Ibid.*

the world, do not deprive music of its essential human relevance nor result in the necessity of art for art's sake or the culmination in a music that means only itself. "Artistic values remain, and remain in the last analysis, identical with human ones. We must ask of the artist what we ask of human beings in general, and assign to him values that are of general relevance."[37]

The objective image, the musical symbol, is dynamic. Musical gestures are expressed through time and motion. Though Sessions does not use the terms *ideal* or *virtual* for the realm of symbolic discourse, he clearly recognizes and provides for the peculiar characteristics and exigencies of that dimension as they are expressed in music. Far from deprecating sound as its primary modality, Sessions explains why music is the art of sound:

> For of all the five senses, the sense of hearing is the only one inexorably associated with our sense of time. The gestures which music embodies are, after all, invisible gestures; one may almost define them as consisting of movement in the abstract, movement which exists in time but not in space, movement, in fact, which gives time its meaning and its significance for us. If this is true, then sound is its predestined vehicle.[38]

Sessions's concept of musical time is strongly Bergsonian: "Sound, at least in our experience, is never static, but invariably impermanent; *it either ceases or changes. By its very nature it embodies for us movement in time,* and as such imposes no inherent limits."[39] And

---

[37] *Ibid.,* p. 120.   [38] *Ibid.,* p. 19.   [39] *Ibid.* (Italics mine.)

he adds in a proposition Bergson himself might have stated: "The experience of music is essentially indivisible."[40]

Sessions takes pains to emphasize the fact that music is what it expresses—it is this ascendancy of metaphor over simile that testifies to its integrity as a symbol, although, like any work of art, the musical symbol also suggests and reminds the percipient of things outside itself.

> Music not only "expresses" movement, but embodies, defines, and qualifies it. . . . In embodying movement, in the most subtle and most delicate manner possible, it communicates the attitudes inherent in, and implied by, that movement; its speed, its energy, its élan or impulse, its tenseness or relaxation, its agitation or its tranquillity, its decisiveness or its hesitation. It communicates in a marvelously vivid and exact way the dynamics and the abstract qualities of emotion, *but any specific emotional content the composer wishes to give to it must be furnished, as it were, from without, by means of an associative program.*[41]

What music embodies is for Sessions, as for Mendelssohn, definite and precise, but nonverbal. Extramusical associations are adventitious. Music presents what it presents with an exactitude that no alien modality can equal. Its permutations are too precise, rather than too vague, for words. But if the musical experience is nonverbal, it does not follow that it is also unvocal. The experience of vocal sound, like the experi-

[40] *Ibid.*   [41] *Ibid.*, p. 22. (Italics mine.)

ence of the fundamental rhythms of life, is universal and intimate. Sessions points out that even unmusical persons undergo a complex vocal education, not so much through conscious powers of discrimination as through emotional response to experience: "the kind of response that is instinctive and that precedes discrimination and possibly even precedes consciousness."[42] He says that it is from the vocal impulse that we derive the sensitive response to differences in pitch; melodic feeling itself springs from the vocal impulse:

> In simple terms, when we raise our voices we increase the intensity of our vocal effort, a rise in pitch implies an increase in tension, and therefore an intensity of energy, or, in other terms, of expressiveness in one direction. When we lower our voices we make a different kind of effort, and gain an intensity of a different and more complex kind. Similarly, an increase in volume denotes, not only in terms of the physical effort of production, but in the sympathetic effort of response, also an increase in tension and hence of intensity.[43]

From such origins a musical edifice of great complexity and refinement ultimately evolves. The fundamental vocal responses carry over into instrumental music: the concepts of "singing" tone, of "breath" control for intelligible rendering of phrases, and so on, apply with equal strength to all performance media. Instrumentalists, as a matter of fact, neglect vocal concepts to their peril; a pianist who cannot "sing" at his instrument is deficient both in musicality and technique. Many of the color images which singers

[42] *Ibid.*, p. 17. [43] *Ibid.*

employ could also be profitably borrowed by instrumentalists—as, indeed, they occasionally are. One sometimes hears a skillful string player refer to a "whitening" of tone to achieve a certain effect; his more clinically minded colleague may feel that playing *sans vibrato* is an adequate means for getting the desired result. One concept, however, at least shows an awareness of color in the tone; the other is a mechanical rule of thumb. So far as most instrumentalists are concerned, undisciplined vocalists have infected all singers with guilt by association. It should be remarked, however, that in the absence of the impulse to sing, a mere adherence to the correct pitch and meter is woefully insufficient no matter how impeccable it may be.

Even in listening to music there is the unconscious adjustment of the vocal cords to changes of pitch, a process that goes on in the untutored as well as in the musically erudite. This is an experience in which the physical organism is integral; and, one suspects, this intimate participation must always be an element of the human apprehension of music on whatever level it may occur.

"It is not easy to determine the nature of music," said Aristotle. What is music? The results of our inquiry so far are not conclusive. It is apparent that music is connected in some way with the emotional life of man: but the "how" continues to elude us. Sessions states the problem fairly: "No one denies that music arouses emotions, nor do most people deny that the values of music are both qualitatively and quantitatively connected with the emotions it arouses. *Yet it is not easy to say just what this connection is.*"[44]

Sessions, nevertheless, contributes significantly to the weight of evidence which comes close to defining the musical symbol as productive of a particular kind of experience which, in the juxtaposition of actual and virtual, is present in any musical apprehension whatsoever. The sonorous image is set apart; it is a unity of form and content; its emotional import—a quality which is really there—is available only in that unique symbol, though it may have residual, associative, reminiscent, and other peripheral meanings as well. "A musical gesture," says Sessions, "gains what we sometimes call 'musical sense.' It achieves a meaning which can be conveyed in no other way."[45]

The Apollonian mirroring holds the image; we look upon the permutations of the emotional life; we see "how feelings are" but we are far from their pain. Music, according to Sessions, embodies a certain kind of movement; it does not define feelings. (The percipient contributes to the analogue he intuits.) Here Sessions is very close to Cassirer, as well as to Langer: "Once more, music embodies the attitudes and gestures behind feelings—the movements, as I have said, of our inner being, which animate our emotions and give them their dynamic content."[46]

This concept corresponds, also, to Gurney's *ideal motion.* The musical symbol subsists in a universe of virtual time and motion; though coexistent with the

[44] *Ibid.,* p. 21. (Italics mine.)   [45] *Ibid.,* p. 24.   [46] *Ibid.*

world of actuality, its own possibilities are already realized: those possibilities have taken shape in the sonorous image. The symbol endures—a real duration, or durée, in the ideal—and is there, always in the present tense, for contemplation.

CHAPTER ELEVEN

MORPHOLOGY OF THE MUSICAL SYMBOL

* * * IF IT IS TO BE COMPREHENSIVE, A THEORY OF music must accommodate very general manifestations of art, insofar as these are relevant to music as well as to other modalities, and must provide in particular for the peculiarities and uniqueness of music itself. Music is one modality of art. In an investigation of the symbolic morphology of music—and this is what I have undertaken—it is to be expected that certain characteristics of symbolic expression will apply to modalities other than music; some aspects, indeed, may apply universally. There is a tendency among aestheticians to use the term "art" *sui generis* and to make generalizations that are intended to be valid for painting, music, sculpture, the dance, and poetry. That there is considerable danger of confusing their distinct modalities has already been demonstrated by Maritain. For him *poetry* is the generic term, but even poetry aspires to

the condition of music. His intuition of an inner correspondence between modalities must be respected; in a very general way, *qua* symbol, the relationship doubtless exists, though it is beyond the scope of this study to consider the problem of unity in the arts. Such unity is in any case a substratum, a homogeneity perhaps of fundamental impulse, that exists prior to form, that gives rise to forms in their peculiar modalities; such an underlying force or tendency would approximate very closely Maritain's inchoate "musical stir."

There are, nevertheless, general features of art and its meaning in human discourse that the various modalities share through the media of their distinct objective images. (Here, of course, "image" is a metaphor.) The fact of the objective image itself, realized in its appropriate modality as a unity of form and content, is a self-evident aspect of art; the relevance of that image to a world of human discourse is another; the formalized dynamics of emotive life, with its concomitant distance from actuality, is still another. These propositions are hardly subject to debate; they have been agreed upon by the most disparate observers, and even the terminologies used by these expositors have shown remarkable similarities. These general characteristics of art are components of the symbol—any art symbol—as I define it. There are, however, two other ingredients of the symbol which I should insist upon but concerning which there is no widespread agreement: these are the characteristics of *transcendence* and *necessity*.

There is a further consideration of great importance to symbolic theory: I refer to the question of the possible effects of musical apprehension on the listener in terms of what has been called *catharsis*. This phenomenon, already alluded to a number of times, is related to all the general characteristics of the symbol and may be described as what happens to the attentive listener when artistic dialogue, or symbolic realization, is consummated. The problem is one which requires extensive treatment: for *what happens* in listening is what the music *means* to the hearer.

I have summarized very briefly the salient axioms of a comprehensive symbolic theory. All of them apply as cogently to music as to any other modality of art. The recognition of these fundamental postulates must precede any detailed examination of the unique modality; but only through that modality can a distinctly musical meaning be apprehended. Since knowledge of these postulates is far from general and acceptance of them all is even more restricted, I have, as support for my theoretical views, given them considerable attention. The necessary frame of reference—the context for my particular theory of music—has now been established.

The correct delineation of musical modality is the crucial problem in presenting the particulars of my theory; all questions of meaning must be referred back to that delineation. As always, acceptable terminology is hard to arrive at; we must have serviceable words that do not carry too heavy a freight of associations and which can be relied upon to point out what is indubitably there, in its musical (and nonverbal) suchness. (I have taken the calculated risk of retaining *symbol*, but I have also taken pains to define it for my purposes.) The particular theory must, of course, be consonant with the more general one. If we examine those comprehensive hypotheses once more, it should be feasible to draw the distinctly musical corollaries.

The "objective image," musically speaking, I have already referred to as the aural image; Copland calls it the *sonorous image,* a good description. As music, it retains the quality of objectivity; it is, actually or potentially, "there," inviting contemplation. Again, we are stretching a familiar concept. The act of musical contemplation is made possible, first of all, by attentive listening. The musical composition has form, as a visual image has, but not in the same way; the modality of the form is auditory. The form, moreover, is not instantly apprehended in its entirety; it can be realized only as its configurations move through time. The aspect of the static configurations on a musical score, whereby the conductor, for example, takes in the page at a glance and hears the music, is another thing altogether. That hearing, though actually inaudible, is an imaginative projection based upon past knowledge and experience; and no matter how rapidly the conductor hears in this manner, the passage of time is of the essence. Similarly, E. M. Forster's example of hearing a piece of music *in toto* after it has been played is a remembering—however condensed it may be—of what has already been heard. We all remember and hear melodies in this way. But time is consumed in the remembering; and unless the music is heard, whether internally or externally, it is the experience that is remembered, not the music itself.

The modality of music being auditory, its raw
material is sound; the organization of that sound in
terms of pitch and rhythm constitutes its ideal motion—
or, to use a term which I prefer, its *virtual motion* in
time. But, although actual time is consumed, musical
time is also virtual. Here is a paradox, that music is in
essence nontemporal. The distinction is this: music is
virtual motion in virtual time; its modality provides an
analogue to actual movement in actual time; but they
are not the same. Yes, you say, but it takes time to hear
music. True; but it takes time to contemplate any work
of art. The source of confusion here is the force of the
analogy itself which impresses itself upon the listener;
for the experience of any motion is accompanied by a
sense of passage. At the end of a musical performance
one already speaks of it in the past tense, while a painting, a presentational symbol, appears still to be there,
in the present. One looks at the "space" of a painting—
whether it is representational or not is irrelevant—and
one has no difficulty distinguishing that space, as artistic
form, from the space outside: that is to say, from actual
space. Yet the painting itself is also in actual space; but
that fact, though a necessary condition for perception,
is not the source of our interest. A musical performance
similarly is in time, but no person in command of his
faculties has the slightest interest in a piece of music
because it takes ten minutes, or whatever number of
minutes it takes for performance. One becomes aware
of actual time, as a matter of fact, to the extent that he
is bored with the performance. Virtual time, like the
virtual space of the painter, is set apart; this relative

isolation and this relative autonomy are the conditions of its objectivity, its *raison d'être* as *image,* as musical symbol.

The *intimacy* of musical experience, which invades the body of the listener, is a great source of confusion to the discursive understanding which so easily misinterprets the emotive signals. Music is an objective symbol, but it is felt personally: the alleged capacity of the art to stir emotions is widely looked upon as the source of its power and as its chief significance for man. But the feelings really exacerbated—discounting those occasions when a fortuitous piece of music and the supposedly corresponding extramusical associations conspire to excitement—are those that reflect one's musical predilections: what one likes, what one does not like. These feelings run high, and these are under the direction of that part of the mind which determines choice— the reason. It presumably is also human reason which regulates religious and political preferences. In those very provinces—not excluding science—which demand its highest capacities and which may be the fields of its greatest glory, the discursive reason is most challenged by the forces of the irrational, most subject to the confusions of ambivalence, most frustrated. Men are commonly emotional about music but not, in a state of health, directly stirred to any sort of action by it. Music, like all art, like religion, touches upon the unknown: nonverbal modalities, symbolic forms, appear; they resist labelling and classification; they cannot, it seems, be understood. And this situation the discursive reason, that engine of our strongest emotions, cannot tolerate.

Listening disinterestedly—that musical species of contemplation—presupposes a measure of detachment. (Need I add that this is not the same thing as listening without interest?) The relevance of music to life is not fundamentally a utilitarian one. We have recognized the indispensable quality of distance in the objective image, the symbol itself. Musical apprehension requires a corresponding distance in the perceiver at the very instant he is permeated by the music. He is, in a sense, immersed in the symbol; but if he is to "grasp its essence" he must be wide awake, keenly aware. If the demands of the music are great, he should listen at the peak of his attention. Hindemith's *Ludus Tonalis* is hardly calculated to induce a swoon; but if the listener is moved to react in that way, the dialogue—for that participant, at any rate—will end at once.

The fixing of one's attention upon what is happening musically, automatically suspends other conscious activities of the mind. To the extent, then, that one is following the music, his emotional concentration will be a musical one; it may be an intensely emotional involvement, but it will be devoted to *that* ideal purpose. This, I think, is the reason Gurney thought it expedient to postulate a distinctive musical faculty.

At this point I can best defend that element of *transcendence* which I believe to be integral to symbolic expression. Again, let me say that it need not be a supernatural transcendence. It is the function of the symbolic analogue to give a more meaningful configuration to the vagaries of experience: disparate elements become ordered. Such order probably is within human reach only through the modalities of art: the forms are there to be looked at, heard, examined—they are virtual. Transcendence is implicit in the very concept of the virtual: for although the virtual image may, and does (inevitably), reflect certain aspects of the here and now, its design is not to serve the immediate only. It is not so perishable. The experiences of art are repeatable; and if the symbol is strong enough, the repetitions will not exhaust it. A luminosity might be said to inhere in the symbol; or if we are transcendentalists with a capital "T," a numenosity.

To say that music is nonutilitarian is not to say that it is unnecessary to human discourse. On the contrary: it is the meaning, the import—the invitation to transcendence—that makes great music more valuable to man than any artifact. Transcendence is a human necessity; and it is not, after all, such a lofty word. Alcohol and drugs are means to some kind of transcendence by which one may attempt to change the world as presently perceived into something different—a world more glamorous, quickened, more responsive to oneself, more bearable. Transcendence may be downward, not only in the phenomenon of "herd intoxication" but as the result of a highly conscious effort toward a desired end. *Pecca Fortiter!*

There are, of course, artistic cul-de-sacs: one can rattle prepared gourds, if he chooses, until Gabriel blows his horn. It is possible to imagine elaborate musical settings for the Black Mass. But the destructiveness of art when its influences are negative is usually of a relatively innocuous and tedious kind.

The musical symbol is an intelligible structure of sound, apprehended through actual hearing in its own modality of virtual time and motion.

A definition any less general than this would entail qualifications appropriate only to specific examples—and these surely are without end. What is needed is a symbolic criterion of the widest possible applicability; and this I have given—a definition as relevant to Balinese temple music as to a Schubert quartet. If the musical structure is intelligible, it is unnecessary to add that it is a unity of form and content. The structure of sound provides for all rhythmic, melodic, and harmonic possibilities, as well as for any exactions of timbre and dynamic coloring a given musical idea may demand.

The definition, if valid, may be expected to provide an instrument of analysis which will pass pragmatic tests and facilitate insight into what may initially be, for a given listener, the strangest and most inaccessible examples of the musical symbol. Its generality alone will make it useful for dealing with the most disparate, particular compositions. Its primary theoretical function lies in setting the boundaries of the distinctly musical experience so that the common blurring of distinctions between music and the extramusical—that source of so many other confusions—may be avoided from the outset. The definition serves as the point of departure for my particular theory of music, and its adequacy as a fundamental hypothesis will determine the adequacy of the theory.

Before testing can be undertaken, however, there are elements in the definition itself that need further clarification: I mean the references to the virtual. If the concept of virtual time is a source of confusion to the intellect, that of virtual motion is no less so. I have spoken of the intimate physical experience of music; yet the fact of psychic distance is nonetheless a condition of musical apprehension. The perception of change in music is integral to that modality—a modality of sound in motion. The sensation of motion, in this case an auditory one with its concomitant correspondence to motion in general, gives a consciousness of change. Intuited physically as well as psychically the sensation of change, of passage, is strong: it is a dynamic analogue to the actual, and exhibiting that quality I hypothesized for the symbol, it embodies at the same time that it suggests: therefore a "dynamis" is captured. The sense of distance, of objectivity, is not so pronounced as with other modalities which can be seen, even touched; the separation of virtual and actual is more subtle in music than in the other arts. The musical modality, like all art, signifies that which is general; but the experience of music is intimate.

It seems likely that in all artistic contemplation there is a shifting between virtual and actual: the mind, chameleon-like, is now here, now there. Associations alone do not account for the shifts, though they play a part. The point I wish to make is that such shifting between the virtual and the actual is particularly easy while listening to music: from the standpoint of physical motion alone, the analogue to life is so very close. The protean modality of sound in motion accommodates itself with comparable ease to an alliance with other artistic modalities, as in song and dance; the merging of modalities consequently has become an unconscious automatism of the mind. Again, let me say this is not a normative problem; the merging may be desirable and productive, as indeed it has often proved to be. What is remarkable is that the discursive reason has so far displayed very little capacity to distinguish these modalities. Such discrimination, then, must be developed in order to satisfy what is, artistically speaking, a moral imperative.

In modern physics, motion and time coalesce in the light-year. Space-time is another concept in terms of which the frequencies of certain physical manifestations can be comprehended. However, in the world of human experience, space, time, and motion are easily distinguishable facets of actuality. What we call time is a measuring of motion, of passage, but we do not ordinarily think of it in that way. For ordinary purposes one goes somewhere in a certain length of time (how long it takes to get there depending upon speed of movement) and traverses space en route. It is a familiar three-dimensional world that we move about in. The musical analogue to that world is relevant to functional human limits: tempo is fast or slow; there are ritardandos and accelerandos; there are the minor shocks of accents and the stronger ones of sforzandos; there are, within the limits of a given rhythmic pace, the alternations of steadiness and caprice and often, as in jazz, the frenzied pulsations of subtle metrical subdivisions—all this, and more, rhythm alone can do; I have not touched upon melody in its myriad monodic, polyphonic, and harmonic ramifications. But remaining with the rhythmic analogue that music provides to actuality, it is permissible to say that the compass of possibilities is manageable in human terms. A performer with an active metabolism and perhaps high blood pressure as well usually exhibits a quicker sense of tempo than a more sluggish colleague: the judgments of "too fast," "too slow," with which every musician is familiar are then invoked. But the rhythmic manifestations, whatever we may think of them, are still within the range of recognizability. What the electronic revolution will finally mean in terms of musical comprehensibility cannot be foreseen; certain outer limits of human tolerance appear to have been reached already, though this may prove to be a premature judgment if evolution proceeds from now on at an unprecedented rate—or in a different direction.

Music, alone of the arts, does not mirror all three dimensions of the actual world; music idealizes motion and time, but not space. It has no corporeality. One understands, of course, what is happening acoustically; sound waves occur in space. But even when he understands this discursively, the listener does not experience music through that concept; music does not, in its quality *qua* sound, put him in mind of space. The contours of a melody, on the other hand, may suggest spatial concepts: it is common to think of "up" or "down" in connection with more or less intense frequencies of pitch. But this is analogical and we make the comparison for descriptive purposes; it has little to do with the quality of musical understanding. Music cannot present virtual space to us in the way the plastic arts can.

This bypassing of space, this functional immediacy (and sometimes, inescapability) of music, is doubtless a factor in its special power of suggestibility. It is also a source of heightened mystery; for the analogue to life, insofar as that analogue is consciously experienced, is felt rather than visualized. Darkness is as suitable for listening to music as light, and many persons prefer it. Maritain, it will be remembered, speaks of that magic that music, more than any other art, exhibits.

But mystery, too, if we acknowledge it—and on this point my theory is neutral, though an element of transcendence is assumed—is at least humanly admissible; there is precedence for it; and if the evidence not only of art but of myths and dreams is relevant, mystery is probably not only admissible but necessary as well. The symbol that is too explicit is wanting in power, just as in ordinary discourse the definitive and final solution to a problem of vital concern brings dissatisfaction; one longs once again for the uncertainty of yet unrealized possibilities. Real life is never settled, nor is great art.

In music we start with sound and its organization. Physics can break music down into smaller constituents and examine them from an acoustical vantage point. But just as the light-year is beyond the functional grasp of the human world, so do the vibratory rates of individual tones fail to signify per se anything corresponding to the configurations of that world: only their combination in units of meaning—or symbols—relates them to human experience. Research in physics has taken the human mind to far frontiers of speculation and discovery. The bounds of what has heretofore been considered the distinctly human world may be stretched more and more; any significant changes in that world will be mirrored, as always, in its art. Perhaps the discontinuities of quantum mechanics are already being reflected in the experimental music of today.

I am not suggesting a setting of musical limits. I am suggesting a functional theory of music that is testable in the laboratory of the human enviroment as most of us know it: a theory relevant to that very large patrimony of musical literature to which we have common access, not excluding the compositions of our own time. If we can cope with the problem of musical meaning on this large scale, I think we need not fear that we will fail to recognize the intelligibility of any valid symbol that may confront us.

CHAPTER TWELVE

MUSICAL TIME: THE DYNAMIC VIRTUAL

* * * THE WHOLE EDIFICE OF THOUGHT BELONGS to the empirical world. What is insufficiently remarked upon is that all concepts of the eternal, the timeless, the transcendent, are human constructs. It is easy to forget this, to forget, for example, that Plato's world of eternal objects is a human inference; it may be there— but we can know it only from this side. If our world is but a pale reflection of the real, we must nevertheless, as human beings, create that real world through the imagination. A sufficiently powerful projection of the imagination has the effect of revelation.

As percipients, as recipients, of art we dwell in at least two human worlds: the empirical and its annex, the conceptual. The *virtual* refers to that domain of the

Portions of this chapter were presented at the 1966 meeting of the American Society for Aesthetics, in Santa Fe, New Mexico.

conceptual world wherein the human imagination cre-
ates *ideal forms:* it is a plastic realm of possibilities
which interpenetrates, and is interpenetrated by, the
empirical world at every point. The virtual is that
particular department of the conceptual world in which
elaborations of formal awareness—*symbols*—subsist. The
gradations of both the virtual and the empirical are
many, and they are subject only to the bounds of consciousness. We are justified in applying the term *organic* to the virtual because it must be looked upon as
a property of human mentality. Virtual patterns are
dynamic, so long as they continue to influence us.

Musical performance takes place in empirical
time: it may be said that we have an impingement of
the virtual upon the actual. A performance of any kind
of music has a presentational immediacy and in that
aspect is concrete, not abstract; we listen to it in the
here and now. But musical idea is dependent for its
strength upon conceptual power: upon its virtuality.

There are degrees of virtuality, of abstraction
in the sense of the virtual. We might characterize the
musical symbol, on its *virtual side,* as an "organized
ready," a vital potential, a formal entity, which may be
brought again and again into actuality. The strongest
musical idea is that which I would describe as strongest
in virtuality: it is the most abstracted from the ephemeral circumstances or demands of the empirical world
and therefore most independent, in essence, of physical
time.

On this basis, a highly provisional hierarchy
can be set up: four distinct "orders of abstraction,"

with music of the fourth order possessing the highest degree of virtuality. My categories are tentative, but I believe the existence of a hierarchy of musical abstractions is a valid inference which can be supported at once by evidence. According to the canons I am suggesting, music of fourth-order abstraction would fulfill most satisfactorily the concept of an art work as an *organism*, having the capacity to endure, but having also the flexibility of an organism: remaining recognizable even though its contours may be somewhat fluid.

Extramusical considerations must be excluded as irrelevant; hence either absolute (so-called) or program music may be of fourth-order abstraction. The musical value is the determinant. It may be thought (and rightly) that much programmatic music is of a lower order of abstraction than fourth; this is because of the dependence of so much programmatic music on extramusical devices or, especially, referents which support the structure and in some instances give it the only viability it possesses.

Examples of either classical or Romantic music may qualify as abstractions of the fourth order. The hierarchy is fundamentally one of musical value; in each category, too, a gradation from superior to inferior is recognizable. A particular fourth-order example, moreover, may exhibit less viability in its own sphere than a vigorous and highly successful musical symbol of the second order—owing perhaps to some deformity or partial failure in realization. A single composer, of course, may contribute works to several of the classifications. Tentatively, let us observe characteristics of the proposed four orders.

In music of the fourth order of abstraction there is a dominance of idea. Coloristic devices are never central to the concept and there is, in general, little reliance upon them. Although the idea and its intended means of projection are in most instances indissolubly bound together (as in the symphonies of Brahms), even the medium in some works may be changed without serious loss. Thus in the *Well-tempered Clavier* the musical ideas survive performance on the modern piano quite well. Bach himself was given to making transcriptions of his own and others' works. Bach's lack of accommodation to particular instrumental or vocal requirements is rediscovered by every generation of students; players and singers are expected to perform the same kinds of melodic configurations. This accounts in part for the great difficulty in the execution of some passages: they are possible, but they do not compromise with the medium. No better example of fourth-order abstraction could be offered than the *Art of Fugue.* It should be observed that works of this classification—music of idea—make considerable demands upon the listener. Portions of the late Beethoven quartets—to say nothing of those of Schoenberg and Bartók, or the "Five Pieces" of Webern—carry fourth-order abstraction to a pinnacle of concentration and austerity.

 Music of the third order of abstraction is strong in idea but represents a more balanced fusion of conceptual and material forces: it is an earthier symbol, as the Richard Strauss "orchestral poems"; Debussy's *La Mer;* the symphonies of Dvořák, Tschaikowsky, and Rachmaninoff; Bartók's *Concerto for Orchestra;* and the works of Ernest Bloch give testimony. Early Stravinsky, like early Schoenberg, occupies an intermediate position between the third and second orders: the addiction to idea was already established in each, but the "unfleshing" of their music was a gradual process; the final works of both are unmistakably of fourth order.

The second order of abstraction accommodates works in which auditory color or extramusical idea is a structural determinant. Because of its utility to extramusical associations, color tends to be rich and varied in works of this order. The sensuous component of the symbol is dominant, although musical idea is also present. The Wagnerian music drama very probably represents the upper reaches of this order. Somewhat lower in the scale would be such amalgams as Berlioz's *Harold in Italy;* still lower, Rimsky-Korsakov's *Scheherezade;* next, Ravel's *Bolero;* and finally, Moussorgsky's *Night on Bald Mountain* and Saint-Saëns's *Danse Macabre.* Of nonprogrammatic works, the Chopin piano pieces (notably the Ballade in G Minor) would rank high in this category; and occupying various levels of the classification would be very nearly all instrumental virtuoso works such as the rhapsodies of Liszt and the caprices of Paganini.

In the first order of abstraction, music is dependent largely upon the heterogeneous and chance elements of the material world: the random is explicitly acknowledged, but not stabilized; for the random elements will change in successive performances. Musical idea is weak or nearly absent, although a general organization—a kind of conceptual fence—may be a limiting factor. There is an emphasis upon sound textures.

Much of the music of John Cage belongs in this classification and examples occur also in the compositions of David Tudor, Lou Harrison, and Karlheinz Stockhausen. The world is exploited for its infinite store of sounds and the auditory sensations they may produce.

It should be pointed out that electronic music, as a genre, may contribute compositions to any of the four categories I have named. But first-order works, whether electronic or not, never achieve recognizability as symbols, since they have no firm identity and are not repeatable. They do not, in the vernacular of information theory, exhibit the character of a stochastic process: no system of probabilities is discernible. This situation corresponds to what Leonard Meyer describes as "undesirable uncertainty."

Music of the first order of abstraction is weakest in virtuality. Emphasis is upon actual sensation, derived in many instances from the happily (or otherwise) fortuitous combinations of whatever sound producing agents may be available. Significantly, *cantabile* and *legato* passages are not in evidence. "Continuity concerns what is potential," says Whitehead, "whereas actuality is incurably atomic."[1] The composer of a first-order piece may issue a directive that its elements are to consume a given amount of clock time, or he may enjoin a fixed period of silence. These are examples of the "conceptual fences" of which I have spoken: a means of enclosing chaos, but not of ordering it. No avenue to the virtual is provided.

---

[1] Alfred North Whitehead, *Process and Reality* (New York: [Torchbook] Harper & Brothers, 1960), p. 95.

There is an interaction on all levels between musical and physical time, but the greatest musical autonomy will be found among compositions that belong to a high level of abstraction: here musical time approaches most closely to a nontemporal essence. Music of the fourth order is, by and large, most difficult of access but is most productive of further revelations; it is most universal.

It is demonstrable that music which has the widest immediate appeal combines familiar melodic and harmonic idioms (in our culture, predominantly homophonic ones) with exploitation of sensuous tone color. Music of this description can belong, as we have seen, to a second or third order of abstraction. Curiously, the relative absence of idea, observable in music of the first order, is as great an impediment to immediate comprehension as the dominance of idea, notwithstanding the preoccupation of first-order music with sensuous experience. A very intense organization of musical elements, at one limit, and the autonomy of discrete particulars, at the other, are both beyond the common spectrum.

Improvisation, which is very nearly a lost art, belongs in a classification of its own: a musical improvisation does not aspire to the identity and repeatability of fully realized composition. (Recording an improvisation—a procedure very likely to affect the course of the music making unless the performer is unaware of the machinery—does not invalidate this fact, although the recording may be played as often as desired.) Skillful improvisation, however, is indicative of strong conceptual power and belongs to a high order of abstraction. It is not an exploitation of random, unrelated, and accidental elements.

Music is relevant to the multiple worlds of human experience. It is literally in and out of time. Whatever its order of abstraction, it can never have the stillness of a Chinese jar, because we can conceive it only as moving. We use up physical time even as we imagine the course of a melody. We can have it both ways. The authentic music is actual and potential: it takes place in and out of time.

It is possible to imagine the empirical world as derivative. But in fact we have no choice but to start with the empirical and speculate on the virtual. Yet we cannot live without such speculation. The composer envisions performance for his work, to be realized in time, but to transcend it. If he has the genius to produce a masterpiece, no single performance will exhaust it. No one questions the existence of Brahms's Fourth Symphony—with or without performance—nor does an inadequate performance invalidate the work or nullify its reality. Just where, then, does it abide?

The virtual has no "where," except in thought; nor has it a fixed "when." The unperformed Beethoven symphony is latent: any recognizable reading will give quickness, immediacy, urgency to its fire—but with no diminution of that original burning. The viable work of art is established conceptually: but it demands occasions.

I have heard the statement, following the first hearing of a piece of music: "It was a pleasant experience and I'd like to repeat it." The listener does not say when he wants it repeated, nor where; this is hardly the point. He wants the pattern again. Surely he is not seeking a particular ordering of his own experience, though the music may in part accomplish this; his desire is disinterested: the music is an object of intensive listening. Nor is he intrigued because the music, by some canons, "means itself." The music is an object of *his* attention. It is an exploration in awareness that he seeks: an exercise of his consciousness—for delight.

I have spoken of the necessity of the virtual. To the extent that he has a conceptual ideal, the performer measures his efforts against his ideal performance—something corresponding to the composer's commanding form. The strength of the conception, if it is a powerful one, will often carry a performance which is unsatisfactory from the purely technical point of view. The critic—that dangerous, vulnerable, and highly equivocal listener—must measure the dynamic concepts of composer and performer against his own and do justice, if he can, to all.

The musical symbol bridges the empirical and virtual; it belongs to the now, and if not to the everlasting also, perhaps—if it is a work of a high order of abstraction—to the eternal within the now. A musician, it appears to me, must be—if only unconsciously—something of a spiritual existentialist by nature. If he is, more than musician, an artist, he is no stranger to paradox, though he may be ignorant of the term. A great artist—a friend and teacher of mine—who, I am confident, knew nothing of Buddhism, was nevertheless the Western prototype of a Zen master; in the most cogent directions for *tempo rubato* I have ever heard, he said, "Hold back; but go ahead."

The dynamic rendering of the virtual is a commentary on one level of the familiar world: the patterns of the empirical, the symbolic analogue of the organic. Even this stylization, this giving of form, is an enlargement of the immediate data:

> At the still point of the turning world. Neither
>   flesh nor fleshless;
> Neither from nor towards; at the still point,
>   there the dance is,
> But neither arrest nor movement.[2]

The musical symbol is transcendent on more than one level; it gives an account—even as utility music—of vagaries of the here and now and perhaps endows such recognizable data with heightened significance. But in the complexities of developed art it delineates to the very limits of human awareness the nuances of ambivalence; the simultaneous push-pull of conflicting forces; and, above all, the incorrigibility of idea.

[2] T. S. Eliot, "Burnt Norton," *Four Quartets* (New York: Harcourt, Brace and Co., 1943), p. 5.

* * *
BIBLIOGRAPHY

ALLEN, WARREN DWIGHT. *Philosophies of Music History.*
New York: Dover Publications, Inc., 1962.
ARISTOTLE. *Politics.* Translated by BENJAMIN JOWETT. New
York: Modern Library, 1943.
AUROBINDO, SRI. *The Life Divine.* New York: E. P. Dutton
& Co., Inc., 1951.
BARRETT, WILLIAM. *Irrational Man.* New York: Double-
day & Co., 1958; Anchor Books Edition, 1962.
BEARDSLEY, MONROE C. *Aesthetics.* New York: Harcourt,
Brace & World, Inc., 1958.
BENNET, E. A. *C. G. Jung.* New York: E. P. Dutton & Co.,
Inc., 1962.
BERGSON, HENRI. *An Introduction to Metaphysics.* Trans-
lated by T. E. HULME. New York: Liberal Arts Press,
1949.
———. *Creative Evolution.* Translated by ARTHUR MITCH-
ELL. New York: Modern Library, 1944.
———. *The Creative Mind.* Translated by MABELLE L.
ANDISON. New York: Philosophical Library, 1946.

BERGSON, HENRI. *The Two Sources of Morality and Religion.* Translated by R. ASHLEY AUDRA AND CLOUDESLEY BRERETON. New York: (Anchor) Doubleday & Co., 1956.
———. *Time and Free Will.* Translated by F. L. POGSON. New York: (Torchbook) Harper & Brothers, 1960.
BERTOCCI, ANGELO P. *From Symbolism to Baudelaire.* Carbondale: Southern Illinois University Press, 1964.
BRITAIN, HALBERT H. *The Philosophy of Music.* New York: Longmans, Green and Co., 1911.
BROWN, CALVIN S. *Music and Literature.* Athens, Georgia: The University of Georgia Press, 1948.
CARLYLE, THOMAS. *Sartor Resartus.* Chicago: Hooper, Clarke & Co. (n.d.).
CARRITT, E. F. "Aesthetics," *Encyclopaedia Britannica,* Vol. 1. London: Encyclopaedia Britannica, Inc., 1956.
CARY, JOYCE. *Art and Reality.* New York: Harper and Brothers, 1958; Anchor Books Edition, 1961.
CASSIRER, ERNST. *An Essay on Man.* New Haven: Yale University Press, 1944. Anchor Books Edition (n.d.).
CHAVEZ, CARLOS. *Musical Thought.* Cambridge: Harvard University Press, 1961.
———. *Toward a New Music.* New York: W. W. Norton, 1937.
COHEN, MORRIS R. *A Preface to Logic.* New York: Henry Holt & Co., 1944.
COLERIDGE, SAMUEL TAYLOR. *Selected Poetry and Prose,* ed. ELISABETH SCHNEIDER. New York: Rinehart & Co., 1956.
COOKE, DERYCK. *The Language of Music.* London: Oxford University Press, 1959.
COOMARASWAMY, ANANDA K. *Christian and Oriental Philosophy of Art.* New York: Dover Publications Inc., 1956.
COPLAND, AARON. *Music and Imagination.* Cambridge: Harvard University Press, 1952; Mentor Press, 1959.
CROCE, BENEDETTO. *Aesthetic.* Translated by DOUGLAS AINSLIE. London: Macmillan and Co., 1922.

DEBUSSY, CLAUDE. *Monsieur Croche: The Dilettante Hater.*
Translated by B. N. LANGDON DAVIES. New York: Lear
Publishers, 1948.

DEWEY, JOHN. *Art as Experience.* New York: (Capricorn)
G. P. Putnam's Sons, 1958.

EDMAN, IRWIN. *Arts and the Man.* New York: W. W. Norton, 1928; Mentor Press, 1949.

ELIOT, T. S. *Four Quartets.* New York: Harcourt, Brace
and Co., 1943.

FERGUSON, DONALD N. *A History of Musical Thought.* New
York: Appleton-Century-Crofts, 1948.

————. *Music as Metaphor.* Minneapolis: University of
Minnesota Press, 1960.

FREEMAN, KATHLEEN. *Ancilla to the Pre-Socratic Philosophers.* Cambridge: Harvard University Press, 1957.

FRENCH, RICHARD F. (ed.). *Music and Criticism: A Symposium.* Cambridge: Harvard University Press, 1948.

FROMM, ERICH. *Escape From Freedom.* New York: Rinehart & Co., 1941.

————. *The Forgotten Language.* New York: Grove Press,
1951.

GHISELIN, DREWSTER. *The Creative Process.* Berkeley and
Los Angeles: The University of California Press, 1952;
Mentor Press, 1955.

GIDE, ANDRÉ. *Reflections on Literature and Morality,* ed.
JUSTIN O'BRIEN. Various translators. New York:
(Greenwich) Meridian Books, 1959.

GURNEY, EDMUND. *The Power of Sound.* London: Smith,
Elder, & Co., 1880; New York: Basic Books Publ. Co.,
Inc., 1967.

HANSLICK, EDUARD. *The Beautiful in Music.* Translated by
GUSTAV COHEN. New York: Liberal Arts Press, 1957.

HAYAKAWA, S. I. *Language in Thought and Action.* New
York: Harcourt, Brace and Co., 1949.

HINDEMITH, PAUL. *A Composer's World.* Cambridge:
Harvard University Press, 1952; Anchor Books Edition,
1961.

312   BIBLIOGRAPHY

HOSPERS, JOHN. *Meaning and Truth in the Arts.* Chapel
Hill: University of North Carolina Press, 1946; Ham-
den, Conn.: Archon Books, 1964.
HOYLE, FRED. *The Nature of the Universe.* New York:
Mentor Press, 1955.
HUXLEY, ALDOUS. *Collected Essays.* New York: Harper &
Brothers, 1958.
————. *Point Counterpoint.* New York: Harper & Broth-
ers, 1947.
JAMES, WILLIAM. *The Varieties of Religious Experience.*
New York: Modern Library, 1929.
JASPERS, KARL. *Truth and Symbol* (from *Von der Wahrweit.*
Munich: R. Piper & Co., 1947). Translated by JEAN
T. WILDE, WILLIAM KLUBACK AND WILLIAM KIMMEL.
New Haven: College and University Press (n.d.).
JUNG, C. J. *Collected Papers on Analytical Psychology.*
Translated by CONSTANCE E. LONG. London: Baillière,
Tindall and Cox, 1920.
————. *Psyche and Symbol,* ed. VIOLET S. DE LASZLO. Trans-
lated by CARY BAYNES AND F. C. R. HULL. New York:
(Anchor) Doubleday & Co., 1958.
KAUFMANN, WALTER (ed.). *Existentialism from Dostoevsky
to Sartre.* New York: Meridian Books, 1956.
KÖHLER, WOLFGANG. *Gestalt Psychology.* New York: H.
Liveright, 1929; Mentor Press, 1959.
KRUTCH, JOSEPH WOOD. *Experience and Art.* New York:
Crowell-Collier, 1962.
LÁNG, PAUL HENRY. *Music in Western Civilization.* New
York: W. W. Norton & Co., 1941.
LANGER, SUSANNE K. "Abstraction in Art," *The Journal of
Aesthetics and Art Criticism,* XXII, No. 4 (Summer,
1964), 379–92.
————. *Feeling and Form.* New York: Charles Scribner's
Sons, 1953.
————. *Philosophical Sketches.* Baltimore: The Johns
Hopkins Press, 1962; New York: Mentor Press, 1964.
————. *Philosophy in a New Key.* Cambridge: Harvard
University Press, 1942; New York: Mentor Press, 1948.

————. *Problems of Art*. New York: Charles Scribner's Sons, 1957.

LEHMANN, A. G. *The Symbolist Aesthetic in France 1885–1895*. Oxford: Basil Blackwell, 1950.

LEICHTENTRITT, HUGO. *Music, History, and Ideas*. Cambridge: Harvard University Press, 1946.

LESSING, G. E. *Laocoön*. Translated by ELLEN FROTHINGHAM. New York: Noonday Press, 1957.

LIN YUTANG (ed.). *The Wisdom of Confucius*. Translated by LIN YUTANG. New York: Modern Library, 1938; London: Michael Joseph, 1958.

LORD, CATHERINE. "Organic Unity Reconsidered," *The Journal of Aesthetics and Art Criticism*, XXII, No. 3 (Spring, 1964), 263–68.

LUNDIN, ROBERT W. *An Objective Psychology of Music*. New York: Ronald Press Co., 1953.

MARITAIN, JACQUES. *Creative Intuition in Art and Poetry*. New York: Pantheon Books, Inc., 1953; Meridian Books, 1955.

MEYER, LEONARD B. *Emotion and Meaning in Music*. Chicago: The University of Chicago Press, 1956; Phoenix Books, 1961.

————. "Meaning in Music and Information Theory," *The Journal of Aesthetics and Art Criticism*, XV, No. 4 (June, 1957), 412–24.

————. "Some Remarks on Value and Greatness in Music," *The Journal of Aesthetics and Art Criticism*, XVII, No. 4 (June, 1959), 486–500.

MORGENSTERN, SAM (ed.). *Composers on Music*. New York: Pantheon Books, Inc., 1956; Bonanza Edition (n.d.).

MUNRO, THOMAS. *The Arts and Their Interrelations*. New York: Liberal Arts Press, 1949.

NIETZSCHE, FRIEDRICH. "The Birth of Tragedy from the Spirit of Music" in *The Philosophy of Nietzsche*. Translated by CLIFTON P. FADIMAN. New York: Modern Library, 1954.

ORTEGA Y GASSET, JOSÉ. *The Dehumanization of Art*. New York: (Anchor) Doubleday & Co., 1956.

PARKER, DEWITT. *The Analysis of Art.* New Haven: Yale University Press, 1926.

PATER, WALTER. *The Renaissance.* New York: Mentor Press, 1959.

PERRY, RALPH BARTON (ed.). *The Thought and Character of William James.* New York: George Braziller, 1954.

PLATO. *Laches.* Translated by BENJAMIN JOWETT. New York: Modern Library (n.d.).

————. *Republic.* Translated by BENJAMIN JOWETT. New York: Modern Library (n.d.).

The Collected Dialogues of Plato, ed. EDITH HAMILTON AND HUNTINGTON CAIRNS. New York: Pantheon Books, Inc., 1963.

POLE, WILLIAM. *The Philosophy of Music.* Boston: Houghton, Osgood, and Co., 1879.

PORTNOY, JULIUS. *The Philosopher and Music.* New York: Humanities Press, 1954.

PROUST, MARCEL. *The Past Recaptured.* Translated by FREDERICK A. BLOSSOM. New York: Modern Library, 1932.

RADER, MELVIN (ed.). *A Modern Book of Esthetics.* New York: Henry Holt & Co., 1953.

READ, HERBERT. *The Forms of Things Unknown.* New York: Horizon Press, 1960.

————. *The Meaning of Art.* London: Faber & Faber, 1931. Pelican Books, 1949.

RUSSELL, BERTRAND. *A History of Western Philosophy.* New York: Simon and Schuster, 1945.

SACHS, CURT. *The Commonwealth of Art.* New York: W. W. Norton, 1946.

SANTAYANA, GEORGE. *The Sense of Beauty.* New York: Crowell-Collier, 1961.

SAYERS, DOROTHY. *The Mind of the Maker.* New York: Harcourt, Brace and Co., 1941.

SCHILPP, PAUL A. (ed.). *The Philosophy of Alfred North Whitehead.* New York: Tudor Publishing Co., 1951.

SCHOEN, MAX. *The Psychology of Music.* New York: Ronald Press Co., 1940.

SCHOENBERG, ARNOLD. *Style and Idea.* New York: Philosophical Library, 1950.

SCHOPENHAUER, ARTHUR. *The World as Will and Idea.* Translated by R. B. HALDANE AND J. KEMP. Garden City, N.Y.: (Dolphin) Doubleday & Co., 1961.

SCHUMANN, ROBERT. *On Music and Musicians,* ed. KONRAD WOLFF. Translated by PAUL ROSENFELD. New York: Pantheon Books, 1946.

SEASHORE, CARL E. *In Search of Beauty in Music.* New York: Ronald Press Co., 1947.

SEEGER, CHARLES. "On the Moods of a Music-Logic," *Journal of the American Musicological Society,* XIII (1960), 224–61.

SENIOR, JOHN. *The Way Down and Out: The Occult in Symbolist Literature.* Ithaca, N.Y.: Cornell University Press, 1959.

SESSIONS, ROGER. *The Musical Experience of Composer, Performer, Listener.* Princeton: Princeton University Press, 1950; Atheneum Publishers, 1962.

SNELL, BRUNO. *The Discovery of the Mind: The Greek Origins of European Thought.* Translated by T. G. ROSENMEYER. Cambridge: Harvard University Press, 1953.

STACE, W. T. *Time and Eternity.* Princeton: Princeton University Press, 1952.

STRAVINSKY, IGOR. *An Autobiography.* New York: M. & J. Steur, 1958.

———. *Poetics of Music.* Cambridge: Harvard University Press, 1947; New York: Vintage Books, 1956.

STRUNK, OLIVER. *Source Readings in Music History.* New York: W. W. Norton, 1950.

SYMONS, ARTHUR. *The Symbolist Movement in Literature.* New York: E. P. Dutton & Co., Inc., 1958.

TAGORE, RABINDRANATH. *Reminiscences.* London: Macmillan & Co., 1945.

TOVEY, DONALD F. *The Main Stream of Music and Other Essays.* New York: Oxford University Press, 1949.

316   BIBLIOGRAPHY

TWAIN, MARK. *Wit and Wisecracks.* Mount Vernon, N.Y.: Peter Pauper Press, 1961.

WEINBERG, HARRY L. *Levels of Knowing and Existence: Studies in General Semantics.* New York: Harper & Brothers, 1959.

WEITZ, MORRIS. *Philosophy of the Arts.* Cambridge: Harvard University Press, 1950.

———. *Problems in Aesthetics.* New York: The Macmillan Co., 1959.

WELLEK, RENÉ, AND WARREN, AUSTIN. *Theory of Literature.* New York: Harcourt, Brace and Co., 1956.

WHITEHEAD, ALFRED NORTH. *Process and Reality.* New York: (Torchbook) Harper & Brothers, 1960.

———. *Symbolism.* New York: (Capricorn) G. P. Putnam's Sons, 1959.

WHYTE, LANCELOT LAW. *The Next Development in Man.* New York: Mentor Press, 1961.

WORDSWORTH, WILLIAM. *The Prelude and Other Works,* ed. CARLOS BAKER. New York: Rinehart & Co., 1957.

Index

317

320   INDEX

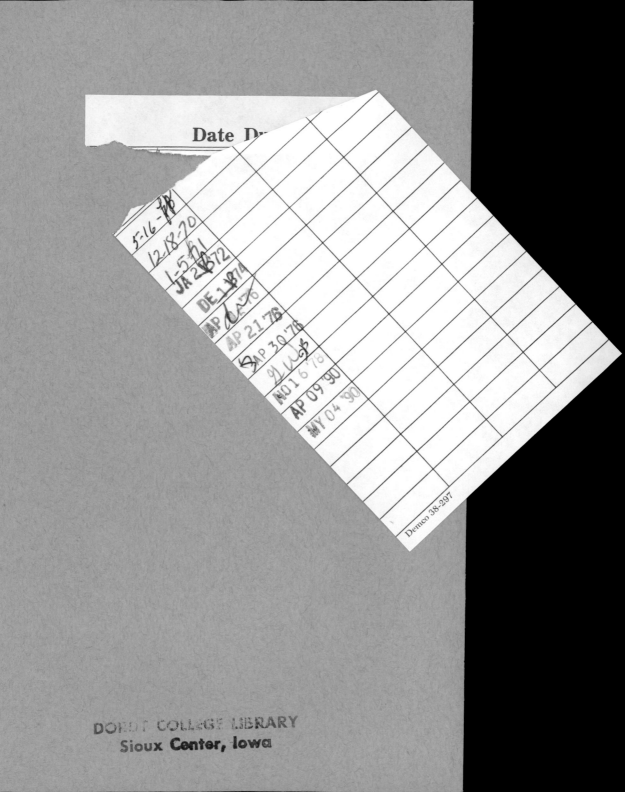

Date Du

5-16-70
12-18-70
1-5-71
JA 2 3 '72
DE 1 '74
AP '76
AP 21 '76
AP 30 '76
NO 16 '78
AP 09 '90
MY 04 '90

Demco 38-297